THE
LITERATURE
OF SPAIN AND LATIN AMERICA

THE BRITANNICA GUIDE TO WORLD LITERATURE

THE LITERATURE
OF SPAIN AND LATIN AMERICA

EDITED BY J.E. LUEBERING, MANAGER AND
SENIOR EDITOR, LITERATURE

Britannica®
Educational Publishing

IN ASSOCIATION WITH

ROSEN
EDUCATIONAL SERVICES

Published in 2011 by Britannica Educational Publishing
(a trademark of Encyclopædia Britannica, Inc.)
in association with Rosen Educational Services, LLC
29 East 21st Street, New York, NY 10010.

First Edition

Britannica Educational Publishing
Michael I. Levy: Executive Editor
J.E. Luebering: Senior Manager
Marilyn L. Barton: Senior Coordinator, Production Control
Steven Bosco: Director, Editorial Technologies
Lisa S. Braucher: Senior Producer and Data Editor
Yvette Charboneau: Senior Copy Editor
Kathy Nakamura: Manager, Media Acquisition
J.E. Luebering: Manager and Senior Editor, Literature

Rosen Educational Services
Jeanne Nagle: Senior Editor
Nelson Sá: Art Director
Cindy Reiman: Photo Director
Nicole Russo: Designer
Matthew Cauli: Cover Designer
Rebecca Carranza: Introduction

Library of Congress Cataloging-in-Publication Data

The literature of Spain and Latin America / edited by J.E. Luebering.—1st ed.
  p. cm.—(The Britannica guide to world literature)
"In association with Britannica Educational Publishing, Rosen Educational Services."
Includes bibliographical references and index.
ISBN 978-1-61530-105-8 (lib. bdg.)
1. Spanish literature—History and criticism. 2. Spanish American literature—History and
criticism. I. Luebering, J. E.
PQ6033.L58 2010
860.9—dc22

2009045098
Manufactured in the United States of America

On the cover: A panoply of talented authors throughout the ages—from Spain's Cervantes
(background) to Chilean American best-seller Isabelle Allende (foreground)—have
contributed to the rich heritage of Spanish and Latin American literature. *Caroline Schiff/
Getty Images (Allende); Hulton Archive/Getty Images (Cervantes)*

Pp. 20 (map), 297, 299, 307, 317 © www.istockphoto.com / Linda & Colin McKie; pp. 20
(books), 21, 54, 95, 109, 171, 223, 296 © www.istockphoto.com

CONTENTS

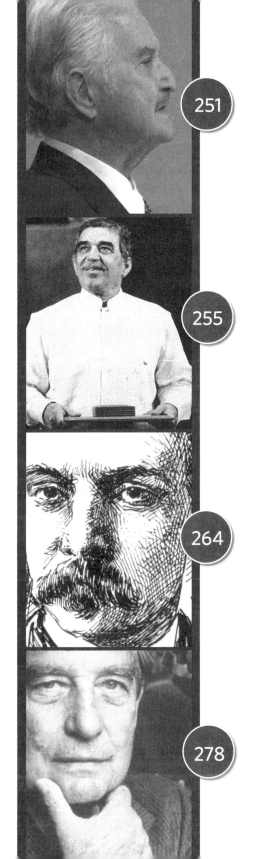

251

255

264

278

INTRODUCTION

Within these pages are tales of enchantment, romance, adventure, war, death, time travel, horror, fantasy and more. Such are the foundations of the rich literary heritage of Spain and Spanish-speaking Latin America. This volume opens doors to the literature of Spain, Mexico, Central America, and the Spanish-speaking countries of the Caribbean and South America. Readers will come to a deeper understanding of the events and cultural differences that have shaped these nations' texts, the lives of their writers, and the overall impact the literature of Spain and Latin American have had—and continue to have—on readers around the world.

Although the earliest written texts in Spanish, created during the 10th century, were explanations of Latin texts from monasteries, the first true literature was in the form of short songs that evolved from poems composed in Hebrew and, in particular, Arabic. These songs were written in Mozarabic, a dialect of Spanish used during the Arab occupation of the Iberian Peninsula, which began in the early 8th century, developed from Latin but written using the Arabic alphabet. The Arabic language would have considerable influence on the literature of Spain.

By the mid-13th century, Christian rulers had reclaimed much of Spain by way of the Reconquista, a series of wars that stretched over many years and resulted in the recapture of the Iberian Peninsula. At about this time, Castilian, a dialect of Spanish, became the dominant language within the history of Spanish literature. The first important Castilian work is *Song of El Cid*, an epic poem that narrates the adventures of El Cid, a heroic warrior of the Reconquista.

The ancient palace and fortress Alhambra, located in the Andalusian city of Grenada. Andalusia, in the southernmost portion of Spain, is considered the cradle of many early Castilian-language texts. CE © www.istockphoto.com /Dr. Heinz Linke

The introduction of the printing press to Spain during the 15th century brought about huge changes in the availability of literature. No longer was it necessary for books to be hand-copied in monasteries. Reading was no longer a privilege only the clergy and aristocracy were afforded, and literature was no longer dominated by religious works.

Certain elements of the prose, poetry, and drama written in Spain and Latin America make the most sense when framed within historical, social, and regional contexts. For instance, without knowing the political and social climate of Spain in the late 16th and early 17th centuries, readers cannot fully grasp the courage and brilliance of Miguel de Cervantes in his clever and subversive novel *Don Quixote*, a novel that mixes humour with the historical realities of Spain at the time of its writing. This timeless satire of chivalric romance and ideals is arguably the most famous novel ever written in Spanish, and one of the most important books of all time in any language.

Don Quixote was written during the Golden Age of Spanish literature, known as the Siglo de Oro. This was a fertile period in which the Spanish language evolved and its literary forms matured. The novel became less idealistic and more realistic. *Lazarillo de Tormes*, published in the 1550s and considered by some to be the first "modern" Spanish novel, introduced the picaresque genre, which is often used as a form of social criticism. The features of picaresque are use of the first-person narrative to recount the adventures of a protagonist who is poor and of low social standing, and cynical in attitude. This genre has remained popular to this day.

Mystic, or devotional, writings such as those by St. Teresa of Ávila and St. John of the Cross had a strong influence on the development of the Spanish language. These writers were reformers within the Roman Catholic Church who inspired religious devotion based on desire rather than obligation. Early Spanish drama also had roots in the church, but by the 16th and 17th centuries plays designed to reflect contemporary, secular mores were being written and performed for the general public. Spanish theatre of this period achieved its highest form with Lope de Vega, whose *New Art of Writing Plays at This Time* set the standard for Spanish playwrights for years to come. The poetry of the later part of the Siglo de Oro, characterized by its elaborate forms, was refined in this period in an effort to elevate the genre. This fruitful period effectively ended with the death of playwright Pedro Calderón de la Barca in 1681. *Life Is a Dream* stands out among his many plays. It reveals a fierce beauty delineated by refined dramatic structure and philosophical depth.

The Siglo de Oro was not a "golden" time for writers in the northeast section of Spain known as Catalonia. Catalan literature had flourished earlier, sparked by writers such as Ramon Llull, a 13th-century scribe who enriched the language greatly by coining many new words and expressions. Yet from the 16th century to the 18th century, writing in Catalan was relegated almost exclusively to the lyrics of common folk ballads. The Renaixensa saw great changes in the Catalan language and literature. This was followed by the Modernisme period, with its naturalistic approach to character and theme in a primarily rural setting, and Noucentisme, which was an attempt to create a distinctly Catalan style with a decidedly urban bent.

During the Spanish Civil War (1936–39) and Generalissimo Francisco Franco's subsequent regime, however, developments such as these came to a halt. Many writers throughout Spain were forced into exile. Members of the Catalonian media were persecuted for writing in

Catalan. Publishing in the language continued but at a greatly diminished level, at least until restrictions were eased in the 1960s.

Spanish literature underwent a series of transformations as well. During the 18th century, Neoclassical principles, which decreed an adherence to notions of order and harmony, influenced prose, poetry, and theatre, and sparked disagreements among writers about the purpose of literature. In the first half of the 19th century, Spanish Romanticism represented an about-face; liberty and individual freedom became foremost concerns. This was followed by a period of realism, in which the novel, which was often focused on minute description of everyday life, became the predominant genre. The Generation of 1898 was a movement consisting of writers who, driven by Spain's loss in the Spanish-American War, decried what they perceived as the weakening of Spain. This sentiment led to a period of national self-examination in literature. Later, poets of the Generation of 1927 ingested a dizzying range of wider European movements. Poets such as Federico García Lorca exerted a lasting influence on Spanish literature.

In the later half of the 20th century, Castilian writers, among them Ana María Matute and Antonio Buero Vallejo, began to represent the social realities of the time. Parallel works by Spanish writers living abroad told of their memories and longing for Spain. Prominent among these was the Nobel Prize-winning poet Juan Ramón Jimenez, who wrote about his country's intellectual reconstruction after civil war. The death of Franco in 1975 and the transition from a dictatorship to a more democratic form of government in Spain led to an even more fertile, creative surge in culture and literature. A multitude of genres came to the fore, including memoirs, detective novels, and historical fiction.

At about this time, Latin American literature was receiving an unprecedented level of worldwide recognition. While there are many geographic, historical, political, and ethnic differences that make the literature of each Latin American country stand out on its own, there are just as many commonalities and historical, political, cultural, and artistic phenomena that cut across national boundaries. One hallmark of much of the writing that has emerged from Latin America is the inextricable tie between nature and humankind.

Latin American literature can be traced back as far as the 15th century, as explorers kept logs of their travels and colonists described the distinct landscapes and indigenous cultures they encountered. Those highly developed cultures had vibrant oral traditions, often recorded by colonists, which ranged from hymns to forms of theatre. Printing in the Spanish colonies was at first controlled by the colonial governments and was largely limited to writings on religion and law. The preferred genre of the early colonial period was heroic poetry.

After the colonies became independent from Spain in the first decades of the 19th century, the novel achieved wide popularity. *María*, a tale of doomed love published in 1867 by Colombian writer Jorge Isaacs, is among the most widely read works of Latin American Romantic literature. The local detail in this and other novels of the period links them to *costumbrismo,* a trend within Spanish literature in which the special ways and habits of a particular country or region are a primary focus.

As the 19th century progressed, realism seeped more deeply into authors' writing—a trend that was closely associated with a sense of nationalism and the emerging identities of the new Latin American nations. In the early years of the 20th century, the regionalist novel, also called the *novella de la tierra* or *novella criollista,* appeared, featuring distinct regional landscapes and folkways. Regionalist novels include Venezuelan writer Rómulo Gallegos's *Doña Bárbara*, about a villain and her renegade daughter, and *Don Segundo Sombra* by Argentine Ricardo Güiraldes, about a wise gaucho traveling throughout the countryside.

The first half of the 20th century also brought the emergence of magical realism; which is arguably Latin America's best-known literary export. Cuba's Alejo Carpentier was the first to use the term, which refers to works that feature a combination of fantasy elements and masterfully handled narrative time to suggest contradictory events happening simultaneously. Among the most prominent of writers who made use of magical realism were the Argentine Jorge Luis Borges and the Columbian Gabriel García Márquez.

Unprecedented economic growth in the region during the 1960s gave way to an explosion of literary riches referred to as the "boom" period. Novelists García Márquez, Mario Vargas Llosa of Peru, Carlos Fuentes of Mexico, and many other "boom" novelists applied what they had found in the writings of James Joyce, Marcel Proust, Virginia Woolf, Joseph Conrad, and William Faulkner to Latin American literary traditions. The result changed Latin American narrative fiction dramatically. Specifically, García Márquez and Fuentes took great liberties with space and time in their novels to allow contradictory points of view, intrigue, and mystery to be drawn from ambiguities in the text.

More Latin American writers gained fame in the wake of the "boom" novelists. Argentine poet Jorge Luis Borges became known as the master of the short story. Mexican Juan Rulfo's *Pedro Páramo*, published in 1955, became a landmark Latin American novel because of its social criticism and the mix of otherworldliness and realism.

Women writers have been present throughout the history of Latin American literature. Sor Juana Inés de la Cruz, a 17th-century nun, is among the region's most iconic. In 1945, Gabriela Mistral became the first Latin American to win the Nobel Prize for Literature. During the "post-boom" period, many more women writers found their voices. Chilean-born Isabel Allende is among the prominent today, with fellow Chilean Diamela Eltit, Rosario Ferré of Puerto Rico, and Cuban Daina Chaviano also finding audiences.

New generations of Latin American poets have explored the themes of solitude, love, revolution, and torture. Among them are Pablo Neruda of Chile and Octavio Paz of Mexico. Both poets are among the numerous writers in the Spanish language to have been awarded the highest prize in world literature, the coveted Nobel. Such themes persist in the contemporary literature of Spain and Latin America, which today encompasses all forms and genres, from realistic novels to experimental theatre, to detective stories and thrillers. These texts both extend and exemplify the regions' rich literary traditions.

CHAPTER 1

SPANISH LITERATURE

A lthough literature in the vernacular was not written until the medieval period, Spain had previously made significant literary contributions. Lucan, Martial, Quintilian, and Prudentius, as well as Seneca the Younger and Seneca the Elder, are among writers in Latin who lived in, or were born in, Spain before the modern Romance languages emerged. Women were also writing in Spain during the Roman period: Serena, believed to have been a poet; Pola Argentaria, the wife of Lucan, whom she is thought to have assisted in writing his *Pharsalia*; and the poet and Stoic philosopher Teofila. Later, the writings of Spanish Muslims and Jews formed important branches of Arabic literature and Hebrew literature. (The literature of the former Spanish colonies in the Americas is treated separately in chapters on Latin American literature.)

The body of literary works produced in Spain fall into three major language divisions: Castilian, Catalan, and Galician.

CASTILIAN LITERATURE THROUGH THE 18TH CENTURY

Castilian (Spanish: Castellano) is a dialect of the Spanish language that is the basis of modern standard Spanish. Originally the local dialect of Cantabria in north central

Spain, Castilian spread to Castile and became the language of the court of the kingdoms of Castile and Leon in the 12th century. After the merger of the kingdoms of Castile, Leon, and Aragon in the late 15th century, it became the standard language of all Spain and, in the following centuries, the language also of Spanish America.

There are differences in accent and, to a lesser extent, vocabulary in Castilian as it is spoken in various regions of the country. The most significant difference is in the pronunciation of *c* before *i* or *e*. In northern Castile, where the language is said to be spoken in its purest form, this is pronounced as an English *th*; in southern and western Spain it is pronounced as an English *s*. The prominence of people from these latter regions in the colonization of Latin America led to their pronunciation becoming the standard in American Spanish.

Works written in Castilian represent the bulk of the body of the writings known as Spanish literature. The earliest such literature was a product of the rich cultural milieu that existed during the medieval period on the Iberian Peninsula. There the Arabic language, from which many words in Castilian are derived, played a particularly important role in the literature's early history.

THE ORIGINS OF VERNACULAR WRITING

By 711, when the Muslim invasion of the Iberian Peninsula began, Latin spoken there had begun its transformation into Romance. Tenth-century glosses to Latin texts in manuscripts belonging to the monasteries of San Millán de la Cogolla and Silos, in north-central Spain, contain traces of a vernacular already substantially developed. The earliest texts in Mozarabic (the Romance dialect of

Spaniards living under the Muslims) were recovered from Hebrew and from Arabic *muwashshahs* (poems in strophic form, with subjects such as panegyrics on love). The last strophe (group of verses that form a distinct unit) of the muwashshaḥ was the *markaze*, or theme stanza, popularly called the *kharjah* and transcribed in Spanish as *jarcha*. These *jarchas* provide evidence of a popular poetry begun perhaps as early as the 10th century, and they are related to traditional Spanish lyric types (e.g., the *villancico*, "carol") of the later Middle Ages and Renaissance. The *jarcha* was generally a woman's love song, and the motif, in Romance, was a cry of passion on which the whole poem was based, providing a clear thematic relationship to Galician-Portuguese cantigas of the late 12th through mid-14th centuries. Women poets in the region of Andalusia writing in Arabic during the 11th and 12th centuries include al-Abbadiyya and Ḥafṣa bint al-Hājj al-Rukuniyya; the best known were Wallada la Omeya, Butayna bint 'Abbād, and Umm al-Kiram bint Sumadih, all of royal blood.

THE RISE OF HEROIC POETRY

The earliest surviving monument of Spanish literature, and one of its most distinctive masterpieces, is the *Cantar de mío Cid* ("Song of My Cid"; also called *Poema de mío Cid*), an epic poem of the mid-12th century for which the only existing manuscript is an imperfect copy from 1307. *Cantar de mío Cid* tells of the fall from and restoration to royal favour of a Castilian noble, Rodrigo Díaz de Vivar, known as the Cid or El Cid; (derived from the Arabic title *sidi*, "lord"). Because of the poem's setting, personages, topographical detail, and realistic tone and treatment and because the poet wrote soon after the Cid's death, this poem has been accepted as historically authentic, a

The Cid orders the execution of Valencia's king following his conquest of the region. Military victories such as this one elevated the Cid to national hero status and inspired the poetry and legends written about his life. Three Lions/Hulton Archive/Getty Images

conclusion extended to the Castilian epic generally. The second and third sections of *Cantar de mío Cid*, however, appear to be imaginative, and the mere six lines accorded the Cid's conquest of Valencia, taking it from the Muslims, show that the poet's approach is subjective. Nevertheless, the Cid's adventures lived on in epic, chronicle, ballad, and drama, reputedly embodying Castilian character.

Folk epics, known as *cantares de gesta* ("songs of deeds") and recited by jongleurs, celebrated heroic exploits such as the Cid's. Medieval historiographers often incorporated prose versions of these *cantares* in their chronicles, Latin and vernacular; it was by this process that the fanciful *Cantar de Rodrigo* ("Song of Rodrigo"), chronicling the Cid's early manhood with elements of the later legend, was preserved. Fragments of the *Cantar de Roncesvalles* ("Song of Roncesvalles") and *Poema de Fernán González* ("Poem of Fernán González") rework earlier epics. Vernacular chroniclers mention many other heroic minstrel narratives, now lost, but, as a result of the incorporation of these narratives into chronicles, themes and textual passages can be reconstructed. Heroic narratives partially recovered include *Los siete infantes de Lara* ("The Seven Princes of Lara"), *El cerco de Zamora* ("The Siege of Zamora"), *Bernardo del Carpio*, and other themes from Castile's feudal history, subject matter that echoes remote Visigothic origins rather than French epics.

THE BEGINNINGS OF PROSE

A major influence on prose was exercised by Arabic. Eastern learning entered Christian Spain with the capture (1085) of Toledo from the Muslims, and the city became a centre of translation from languages of Asia and the Middle East. An anonymous translation from Arabic (1251)

Learned Narrative Poetry

The *mester de clerecía* ("craft of the clergy") was a new poetic mode, indebted to France and the monasteries and presupposing literate readers. It adapted the French alexandrine in the "fourfold way"—i.e., 14-syllable lines used in four-line monorhyme stanzas—and treated religious, didactic, or pseudo-historical matter. During the 13th century, Gonzalo de Berceo, Spain's earliest poet known by name, wrote rhymed vernacular chronicles of saints' lives, the miracles of the Virgin, and other devotional themes with ingenuous candour, accumulating picturesque and affectionately observed popular detail.

of the beast fable *Kalīlah wa Dimnah* exemplifies early storytelling in Spanish. A romance of the Seven Sages, the *Sendebar*, was translated likewise through Arabic, with other collections of Eastern stories.

By the mid-12th century, the Christians had recovered Córdoba, Valencia, and Sevilla. A propitious intellectual atmosphere fomented the founding of universities, and under Alfonso X of Castile and Leon (reigned 1252–84) vernacular literature achieved prestige. Alfonso, in whose chancery Castilian replaced Latin, mandated translations and compilations aimed at fusing all knowledge—as taken from the Classical, Muslim, Hebrew, and Christian traditions—in the vernacular. These works, some under his personal editorship, include the great legal code *Las Siete Partidas* ("The Seven Divisions"), containing invaluable information on daily life, and compilations from Arabic sources on astronomy, the magical properties of gems, and games, especially chess.

The *Crónica general*, a history of Spain, and the *General estoria*, an attempted universal history from the Creation onward, were foundational works of Spanish historiography. The *Crónica general*, overseen by Alfonso to 711 CE and completed by his son Sancho IV, was Spain's most influential medieval work. Alfonso, sometimes called the father of Castilian prose, was also a major poet, and he compiled early Spain's greatest collection of medieval poetry and music, the *Cantigas de Santa María* ("Songs to St. Mary"), in Galician.

THE 14TH CENTURY

Following the period of translation and compilation came brilliant original creations, represented in prose by Alfonso's nephew Juan Manuel and in poetry by Juan Ruiz (also called Archpriest of Hita). Juan Manuel's eclectic *Libro de los enxiemplos del conde Lucanor et de Patronio* ("The Book of Count Lucanor and Patronio")—which consists of 51 moral tales variously didactic, amusing, and practical—drew partly on Arabic and popular Spanish sources. It was Spain's first collection of prose fiction rendered in the vernacular. Juan Manuel's seven surviving books treat such subjects as hunting, chivalry, heraldry, genealogy, education, and Christianity. The frame story that links Count Lucanor's tales anticipates novelistic structure: The young count repeatedly seeks advice from his tutor Patronio, who responds with exemplary tales.

Chivalric romances of the Arthurian or Breton cycle, which had been circulating in translation, partially inspired Spain's first romance of chivalry and first novel, *El caballero Cifar* (c. 1305; "The Knight Cifar"), based on St. Eustace, the Roman general miraculously converted to Christianity. *Amadís de Gaula*—the oldest known version of which, dating from 1508, was written in Spanish by Garci Rodríguez (or Ordóñez) de Montalvo, although it may have begun circulation in the early 14th century—is another chivalric romance related to Arthurian sources. It enthralled the popular imagination through the 16th century with its sentimental idealism, lyrical atmosphere, and supernatural adventure.

Juan Ruiz, an intensely alert, individual early poet, composed the *Libro de buen amor* (1330, expanded 1343; "Book of Good Love"), which combined disparate elements, including Ovid, Aesop, the Roman Catholic liturgy, and the 12th-century Latin *Pamphilus de amore*, an anonymous elegiac comedy. The result mingled eroticism with devotion and invited readers to interpret often-equivocal teachings. Ruiz's Trotaconventos became Spanish literature's first great fictional character. Ruiz handled alexandrine metre with new vigour and plasticity, interspersing religious, pastoral-farcical, amorous, and satirical lyrics of great metrical variety.

More-exotic elements appeared in the *Proverbios morales* (c. 1355; "Moral Proverbs") of Santob de Carrión de los Condes and an Aragonese version of the biblical story of Joseph, which was based on the Qur ān and written in Arabic characters. Drawing on the Hebrew Bible (the Christian Old Testament), the Talmud, and the Hebrew poet and philosopher Ibn Gabirol, Santob's *Proverbios introduced* Hebrew poetry's grave sententiousness and aphoristic concision.

Pedro López de Ayala dominated poetry and prose during the later 1300s with his *Rimado de palacio* ("Poem of Palace Life"), the last major relic of the "fourfold-way" verse form, and with family chronicles of 14th-century Castilian monarchs Peter, Henry II, John I, and Henry III, which stimulated production of personal, contemporary history. An early humanist, Ayala translated and imitated Livy, Boccaccio, Boethius, St. Gregory, and St. Isidore.

A subgenre vigorously cultivated was the misogynistic treatise warning against women's wiles. Rooted in works that condemned Eve for the Fall of Man, they include such works as *Disciplina clericalis* ("The Scholar's Guide"), written in the late 11th or early 12th century by Pedro Alfonso (Petrus Alfonsi); *El Corbacho*, also known as *El Arcipreste de Talavera* (*c.* 1438; "Little Sermons on Sin"), by Alfonso Martínez de Toledo; and *Repetición de amores* (*c.* 1497; "Repetitious Loves"; Eng. trans. *An Anti-feminist Treatise of Fifteenth Century Spain)* by Luis Ramírez de Lucena. Numerous examples from medieval Spanish literature and folklore echoed the same themes, among them Juan Manuel's *Count Lucanor* and Juan Ruiz's *Book of Good Love.*

THE 15TH CENTURY

The early 15th century witnessed a renewal of poetry under Italian influence. During the reign of King John II, the anarchy of feudalism's death throes contrasted with the cultivation of polite letters, which signified good birth and breeding. The *Cancionero de Baena* ("Songbook of Baena"), compiled for the king by the poet Juan Alfonso de Baena, anthologized 583 poems (mostly courtly lyrics) by 55 poets from the highest nobles to the humblest versifiers. The collection showed not merely the decadence of Galician-Portuguese troubadours but also the stirrings of more-intellectual poetry incorporating symbolism, allegory, and Classical allusions in the treatment of moral, philosophical, and political themes. Other significant verse collections include the *Cancionero de Estúñiga* (*c.* 1460–63) and the important *Cancionero general* (1511) of Hernando del Castillo. Among the latter's 128 named poets is Florencia Pinar, one of the first Castilian women poets to be identified by name. Francisco Imperial, a Genoese who settled in Sevilla and a leader among new

29

poets, drew on Dante, attempting to transplant the Italian hendecasyllable (11-syllable line) to Spanish poetry.

The poet, scholar, soldier, and statesman marqués de Santillana collected masterpieces of foreign literatures and stimulated translation. His *Proemio e carta al condestable de Portugal* (1449; "Preface and Letter to the Constable of Portugal"), which initiated literary history and criticism in Spanish, reflected his readings in contemporary foreign languages and translated classics. Santillana's sonnets in the "Italian style" launched the formal enrichment of Spanish poetry. He is still acknowledged as a precursor of the Renaissance, though his sonnets and long poems, which reflect his Italian-influenced training, are often neglected in favour of his charming rustic songs of native inspiration. Juan de Mena's *El laberinto de fortuna* (1444; "The Labyrinth of Fortune"), a vast allegorical poem dramatizing history past, present, and future that is a more conscious attempt to rival Dante, suffers from pedantry and over-Latinization of syntax and vocabulary.

An outstanding anonymous 15th-century poem, the *Danza de la muerte* ("Dance of Death"), exemplifies a theme then popular with poets, painters, and composers across western Europe. Written with greater satiric force than other works that treated the dance of death theme, it introduced characters (e.g., a rabbi) not found in its predecessors and presented a cross section of society via conversations between Death and his protesting victims. Although not intended for dramatic presentation, it formed the basis for later dramas.

THE RENAISSANCE AND THE SIGLO DE ORO

The unification of Spain in 1479 and the establishment of its overseas empire, which began with Christopher

Columbus's first voyage to the New World (1492–93), contributed to the emergence of the Renaissance in Spain, as did the introduction of printing to the country (1474) and the cultural influence of Italy. The early Spanish humanists included the first grammarians and lexicographers of any Romance tongue. Juan Luis Vives, the brothers Juan and Alfonso de Valdés, and others were followers of Erasmus, whose writings circulated in translation from 1536 onward and whose influence appears in the Counter-Reformation figure of St. Ignatius of Loyola, who founded the Society of Jesus (Jesuits), and in the later religious writer and poet Luis de León.

Nor did Spain lack women humanists. Some exceptional women renowned for their erudition taught in universities, including Francisca de Nebrija and Lucía Medrano. Beatriz Galindo ("La Latina") taught Latin to Queen Isabella I. Luisa Sigea de Velasco—a humanist, scholar, and writer of poetry, dialogues, and letters in Spanish and in Latin—taught at the Portuguese court.

Connecting the Middle Ages and the Renaissance is the masterful *Comedia de Calixto y Melibea* (1499), a novel of 16 "acts" in dialogue form published anonymously but attributed to Fernando de Rojas. The dominant character, the procuress Celestina, is depicted with unsurpassed realism and gives the work the title by which it is commonly known, *La Celestina*. The analysis of passion and the dramatic conflict that lust unleashes attain great psychological intensity in this early masterpiece of Spanish prose, sometimes considered Spain's first realistic novel.

These figures and works of the early Renaissance prepared the way for the Siglo de Oro ("Golden Age"), a period often dated from the publication in 1554 of *Lazarillo de Tormes*, the first picaresque novel, to the death in 1681 of dramatist and poet Pedro Calderón. Comparable to the Elizabethan era in England, albeit longer, Spain's Siglo de

Oro spanned both the Renaissance and Baroque periods and produced not only drama and poetry that match Shakespeare's in stature but also Miguel de Cervantes's celebrated novel *Don Quixote*.

Castilian Renaissance Poetry

Surviving for centuries in the oral tradition, Spanish ballads (*romances*) link medieval heroic epic to modern poetry and drama. The earliest datable *romances*—from the mid-15th century, although the *romance* form itself has been traced to the 11th century—treated frontier incidents or lyrical themes. Anonymous *romances* on medieval heroic themes, commemorating history as it happened, formed everyman's sourcebook on national history and character; they were anthologized in the Antwerp *Cancionero de romances* ("Ballad Songbook") and the *Silva de varios romances* ("Miscellany of Various Ballads"), both published about 1550 and repeatedly thereafter. The *romance* form (octosyllabic, alternate lines having a single assonance throughout) was quickly adopted by cultured poets and also became the medium of choice for popular narrative verse.

The Catalan Juan Boscán Almogáver revived attempts to Italianize Spanish poetry by reintroducing Italian metres; he preceded Garcilaso de la Vega, with whom the cultured lyric was reborn. Garcilaso added intense personal notes and characteristic Renaissance themes to a masterful poetic technique derived from medieval and Classical poets. His short poems, elegies, and sonnets shaped the development of Spain's lyric poetry throughout the Siglo de Oro.

Fray Luis de León, adopting some of Garcilaso's verse techniques, typified the "Salamanca school," which emphasized content rather than form. Poet and critic

Fernando de Herrera headed a contrasting school in Sevilla, which was derived equally from Garcilaso but was concerned with subtly refined sentiment; Herrera's remarkable verse vibrantly expressed topical heroic themes. The popularity of the short native metres was reinforced by traditional ballad collections (*romanceros*) and by the evolving drama.

Models for epic poetry were the works of Italian poets Ludovico Ariosto and Torquato Tasso, but the themes and heroes of Spanish epics celebrated overseas conquest or defense of the empire and the faith. Alonso de Ercilla y Zúñiga achieved epic distinction with *La Araucana* (published 1569–90), chronicling native resistance to Spain's conquest of Chile. A similar attempt at epic, Lope de Vega's *Dragontea* (1598), retells Sir Francis Drake's last voyage and death.

EARLY DRAMA

Spanish drama originated in the church. The *Auto de los reyes magos* ("Play of the Three Wise Kings"), dated from the second half of the 12th century, is an incomplete play of the Epiphany cycle. It is medieval Spanish drama's only extant text. The play's realistic characterization of the Magi and of Herod and his advisers and its polymetric form foreshadowed aspects of later dramatic development in Spain.

A reference in King Alfonso X's legal code suggested the existence of some popular secular drama in the 13th century, but no texts have survived. These *juegos* (short satiric entertainments given by traveling players) antedated the plays that constitute one of Spain's main contributions to dramatic genres: the *pasos*, *entremeses*, and *sainetes*, all short, typically humorous works originally used as interludes.

Juan del Encina helped emancipate the drama from ecclesiastical ties by giving performances for noble patrons. His *Cancionero* (1496; "Songbook") contains pastoral-religious dramatic dialogues in rustic dialect, but he soon turned to secular themes and vivid farce. His conception of drama evolved during his long stay in Italy, with native medievalism transforming into Renaissance experimentation. The work of Encina's Portuguese disciple Gil Vicente, a court poet at Lisbon who wrote in both Castilian and Portuguese, showed a significantly improved naturalness of dialogue, acuteness of observation, and sense of situation.

Drama's transition from court to marketplace and the creation of a broader public were largely accomplished by Lope de Rueda, who toured Spain with his modest troupe performing a repertoire of his own composition. His four prose comedies have been called clumsy, but his 10 *pasos* showed his dramatic merits. He fathered Spain's one-act play, perhaps the country's most vital and popular dramatic form.

The first dramatist to realize the ballads' theatrical possibilities was Juan de la Cueva. His comedies and tragedies derived largely from Classical antiquity, but in *Los siete infantes de Lara* ("The Seven Princes of Lara"), *El reto de Zamora* ("The Challenge of Zamora"), and *La libertad de España por Bernardo del Carpio* ("The Liberation of Spain by Bernardo del Carpio"), all published in 1588, he revived heroic legends familiar in *romances* and helped to found a national drama.

HISTORICAL WRITING

Prose before the Counter-Reformation produced some notable dialogues, especially Alfonso de Valdés's *Diálogo de Mercurio y Carón* (1528; "Dialogue Between Mercury and

Historian and missionary Bartolomé de Las Casas championed social justice for the native peoples of the Americas under Spanish colonial rule. Mansell/ Time & Life Pictures/Getty Images

Charon"). His brother Juan de Valdés's *Diálogo de la lengua* ("Dialogue About the Language") attained great critical prestige. The themes of history and patriotism flourished as Spain's power increased; among the finest achievements from this epoch was Juan de Mariana's own translation into Spanish (1601) of his Latin history of Spain, which marked the vernacular's triumph for all literary purposes.

Major landmarks in historical writing emanated from the New World, transmuting vital experience into literature with unaccustomed vividness. Christopher Columbus's letters and accounts of his voyages, the letters and accounts to King Charles V by Hernán Cortés, and similar narratives by more humble conquistadores opened new horizons to readers. Attempting to capture exotic landscapes in words, they enlarged the language's resources. The most engaging of such writings was the *Historia verdadera de la conquista de la Nueva España* (1632; *True History of the Conquest of New Spain*) by the explorer Bernal Díaz del Castillo. Friar Bartolomé de Las Casas, sometimes called the "Apostle of the Indies," wrote *Brevísima relación de la destrucción de las Indias* (*A Short Account of the Destruction of the Indies, or The Tears of the Indians*) in 1542, criticizing Spanish colonial policy and abuse of the native population. His work helped to give rise among Spain's enemies to the infamous *Leyenda Negra* ("Black Legend").

THE NOVEL

Popular taste in the novel was dominated for a century by progeny of the medieval courtly romance *Amadís de Gaula*. These chivalric romances perpetuated certain medieval ideals, but they also represented pure escapism, eventually provoking such literary reactions as the pastoral novel and the picaresque novel. The former, imported from Italy, oozed nostalgia for an Arcadian golden age. Its shepherds were courtiers and poets who, like the knights-errant of chivalric romance, turned their backs on reality. Jorge de Montemayor's *Diana* (1559?) initiated Spain's pastoral vogue, which was later cultivated by such major writers as Cervantes (*La Galatea*, 1585) and Lope de Vega (*La Arcadia*, 1598).

Another reaction appeared in the picaresque novel, a genre initiated with the anonymous *Lazarillo de Tormes* (1554). This native Spanish genre, widely imitated elsewhere, featured as its protagonist a *pícaro* ("rogue"), essentially an antihero, living by his wits and concerned only with staying alive. Passing from master to master, he depicted life from underneath. Significant for guiding fiction to direct observation of life, the picaresque formula has long been imitated, up to such 20th-century writers as Pío Baroja, Juan Antonio de Zunzunegui, and Camilo José Cela.

Miguel de Cervantes, the preeminent figure in Spanish literature, produced in *Don Quixote* (part 1, 1605; part 2, 1615) the prototype of the modern novel. Nominally satirizing the moribund chivalric romance, Cervantes presented "reality" on two levels: the "poetic truth" of Don Quixote and the "historic truth" of his squire, Sancho Panza. Where Don Quixote saw and attacked an advancing army, Sancho saw only a herd of sheep; what Sancho perceived as windmills were menacing giants to the questing knight-errant. The constant interaction of these rarely compatible attitudes revealed the novel's potential for philosophical commentary on existence. The dynamic interplay and evolution of the two characters established psychological realism and abandoned prior fiction's static characterizations. In the *Novelas ejemplares* (1613; "Exemplary Tales"), Cervantes claimed to be the first to write novelas (short stories in the Italian manner) in Spanish, differentiating between narratives that interest for their action and those whose merit lies in the mode of telling.

María de Zayas y Sotomayor, Spain's first woman novelist, was among the few women writers of the period who did not belong to a religious order. She too published Italian-inspired short stories, in the collections *Novelas amorosas y ejemplares* (1637; Eng. trans. *The Enchantments of Love: Amorous and Exemplary Novels*) and *Desengaños amorosos* (1647; "Disillusion in Love"). Both employ framing structures in which, like Giovanni Boccaccio's *Decameron*, men and women gather to tell stories; many

Don Quixote, right, and Sancho Panza in a scene from Miguel de Cervantes's Don Quixote. Hulton Archive/Getty Images

characters from the first collection appear in the second, including the protagonist, Lisis. The stories of *Novelas amorosas* are told during the nights, those of *Desengaños* during the days; most concern the "battle of the sexes," featuring innocent victims and evildoers of both sexes, but plots turn upon men's seduction, treachery, abuse, and even torture of defenseless women.

MYSTICAL WRITINGS

The flowering of Spanish mysticism coincided with the Counter-Reformation, although antecedents appear, particularly in the expatriate Spanish Jew León Hebreo, whose *Dialoghi di amore* (1535; "The Dialogues of Love"), written in Italian, profoundly influenced 16th-century and later Spanish thought. The mystics' literary importance derives from attempts to transcend language's limitations, liberating previously untapped resources of expression. The writings of St. Teresa of Ávila, notably her autobiography and letters, reveal a great novelist in embryo. In his prose as in his poetry, Fray Luis de León showed

Writings By and About Women

Among the feminine voices that defended women's interests during the Renaissance and Siglo de Oro were Sor Teresa de Cartagena in the 15th century and Luisa de Padilla, Isabel de Liaño, and Sor María de Santa Isabel in the early 16th century. They were champions of women's rights to education and free choice in matrimony. Traditionalist reactions during the Counter-Reformation included treatises on the training of women, such as Fray Alonso de Herrera's *Espejo de la perfecta casada* (c. 1637, "Mirror of the Perfect Wife").

passionate devotion, sincerity, and profound feeling for nature in a style of singular purity. He also wrote a conservative tract on educating women, *La perfecta casada* (1583; *The Perfect Wife*), glossing Proverbs 31. St. John of the Cross achieved preeminence through poems of exalted style expressing the experience of mystic union.

LATER DRAMA

The drama achieved its true splendour in the genius of Lope de Vega (in full Lope Félix de Vega Carpio). Its manifesto was Vega's own treatise, *Arte nuevo de hacer comedias en este tiempo* (1609; "New Art of Writing Plays at This Time"), which rejected Neoclassical "rules," opting to blend comedy and tragedy with metrical variety, and made public opinion the arbiter of good taste. The new *comedia* ("drama") advocated respect for the crown, church, and human personality. The last was symbolized in the theme that Vega considered best of all: the *pundonor* ("point of honour"), grounded in a gender code that made women the repository of family honour, which could be tarnished or lost by the woman's slightest indiscretion. Vega's drama was concerned less with character than with action and intrigue, seldom approaching the essence of tragedy. What this great Spanish playwright did possess was a remarkable sense of stagecraft and the ability to make the most intricate plot gripping.

Vega, who claimed authorship of more than 1,800 *comedias*, towered over his contemporaries. With his unerring sense of what could move an audience, he exploited evocations of Spain's greatness, making its drama "national" in the truest sense. Two main categories of his work are the native historical drama and the *comedia capa y espada* ("cloak-and-sword") of contemporary manners. Vega ransacked the literary past for heroic themes, chosen to illustrate aspects of the national character or of social solidarity. The cloak-and-sword play, which dominated drama after Vega, was pure entertainment, exploiting disguise, falling in and out of love, and false alarms about honour. In it affairs of the lady and her gallant are often parodied through the actions of the servants. The cloak-and-sword play delighted by the dexterity of its intricate plotting, its sparkling dialogue, and the entangled relationships depicted between the sexes.

The greatest of Vega's immediate successors, Tirso de Molina (pseudonym of Fray Gabriel Téllez), first dramatized the Don Juan legend in his *Burlador de Sevilla* (1630; "The Trickster of Sevilla"). *La prudencia en la mujer* (1634; "Prudence in Woman") figured among Spain's greatest historical dramas, as did *El condenado por desconfiado* (1635; *The Doubter Damned*) among theological plays. Tirso's cloak-and-sword plays excelled in liveliness.

Mexican-born Juan Ruiz de Alarcón struck a distinctive note. His 20 plays were sober, studied, and imbued with serious moral purpose, and his *Verdad sospechosa* (1634; "The Truth Suspected") inspired the great French dramatist Pierre Corneille's *Menteur* (1643). Corneille's famous *Le Cid* (1637) similarly drew upon the conflict between love and honour presented in *Las mocedades del Cid* (1599?; "The Youthful Exploits of the Cid") by Guillén de Castro y Bellvís.

Although their names were suppressed and their works left largely unperformed for centuries, several women dramatists of the Siglo de Oro left extant plays. Ángela de Acevedo, a lady-in-waiting to Elizabeth (Isabel de Borbón), wife of King Philip IV, left three extant plays of unknown dates: *El muerto disimulado* ("The Pretending Dead Man"), *La Margarita del Tajo que dió nombre a Santarem* ("Margarita of Tajo Who Named Santarem"), and *Dicha y desdicha del juego y devoción de la Virgen* ("Bliss and Misfortune in

Gaming and Devotion to the Virgin"). Ana Caro Mallén de Soto, friend of the novelist María de Zayas, wrote *El Conde Partinuplés* ("Count Partinuples") and *Valor, agravio y mujer* ("Valour, Dishonour, and Woman"), both probably during the 1640s. Feliciana Enríquez de Guzmán, thought to have flourished about 1565 but whose identity is disputed, wrote *Tragicomedia de los jardines y campos Sabeos* ("Tragicomedy of the Sabaean Gardens and Fields"). In the middle of the 17th century María de Zayas wrote *Traición en la amistad* ("Betrayal in Friendship"). Sor Marcela de San Félix was an illegitimate daughter of Lope de Vega. Born Marcela del Carpio, she entered a convent at age 16 and wrote, directed, and acted in six one-act allegorical plays, the *Coloquios espirituales* ("Spiritual Colloquies"). She also penned short dramatic panegyrics, romances, and other books. Common denominators in these women's works are religious themes, honour, friendship, love, and misfortune.

CULTERANISMO AND *CONCEPTISMO*

In poetry and prose the early 17th century in Spain was marked by the rise and spread of two interrelated stylistic movements, often considered typical of the Baroque. Authors shared an elitist desire to communicate only with the initiated, so that writings in both styles present considerable interpretive difficulties. *Culteranismo*, the ornate, roundabout, high-flown style of which Luis de Góngora y Argote was archpriest, attempted to ennoble the language by re-Latinizing it. Poets writing in this style created hermetic vocabulary and used stilted syntax and word order, with expression garbed (and disguised) in Classical myth, allusion, and complicated metaphor, all of which rendered their work sometimes incomprehensible.

Góngora's major poetic achievement, *Soledades* (1613; "Solitudes") invited many untalented imitations of his uniquely elaborate style, which came to be known as Gongorism (*gongorismo*). The other stylistic movement, *conceptismo*, played on ideas as *culteranismo* did on language. Aiming at the semblance of profundity, *conceptista* style was concise, aphoristic, and epigrammatic and thus belonged primarily to prose, especially satire. Concerned with stripping appearances from reality, it had as its best outlet the essay. Francisco Gómez de Quevedo y Villegas, the greatest satirist of his time and a master of language, was, in *Sueños* (1627; "Dreams"), an outstanding exponent of conceptismo; similar traits appear in his picaresque satire *La vida del buscón llamado don Pablos* (1626; "The Life of the Trickster Called Don Pablos"; Eng. trans. *The Scavenger and The Swindler*).

Baltasar Gracián reduced *conceptista* refinement to an exact code in *Agudeza y arte de ingenio* (1642, 2nd ed. 1648; "Subtlety and the Art of Genius"). He also tried to codify in a series of treatises the art of living. Gracián's thought in his allegorical novel *El criticón* (1651, 1653, 1657; *The Critick*) reflected a pessimistic vision of life as "daily dying."

THE PLAYS OF CALDERÓN

Pedro Calderón de la Barca adapted Lope de Vega's formula for producing tightly structured dramas, wherein formal artistry and poetic texture combine with thematic profundity and unified dramatic purpose. One of the world's outstanding dramatists, Calderón wrote plays that were effective in both the public playhouses and Madrid's newly built court theatre of Buen Retiro, whose elaborate stage technology allowed him to excel in mythological drama (*La estatua de Prometeo* [1669; "The Statue of Prometheus"]).

Calderón contributed to an emerging musical comedy form, the zarzuela (*El jardín de Falerina* [1648; "The Garden of Falerina"]), and cultivated many subgenres; his numerous secular plays encompassed both comedy and tragedy. His best comedies provide subtle critiques of urban mores, combining laughter with tragic foreboding (*La dama duende* [1629; *The Phantom Lady*]). His tragedies probe the human predicament, exploring personal and collective guilt (*Las tres justicias en una* [*c.* 1637; "Three Judgments at a Blow"]), the bathos of limited vision and lack of communication (*El pintor de su deshonra* [*c.* 1645; "The Painter of His Own Dishonour"]), the destructiveness of certain social codes (*El médico de su honra* [1635; "The Surgeon of His Honour"]), and the conflict between the constructive nature of reason and the destructive violence of self-centred passion (*La hija del aire* [1653; "The Daughter of the Air"]). His best-known plays, appropriately classified as high drama, include *El alcalde de Zalamea* (*c.* 1640; *The*

A 2004 performance of Pedro Calderón's La hija del aire *("The Daughter of the Air"), coproduced by the Teatro Español of Madrid and the Teatro General San Martín of Buenos Aires.* Quim Llenas/Hulton Archive/Getty Images

Mayor of Zalamea), which rejects social honour's tyranny, preferring the inner nature of true human worth and dignity. Philosophical problems of determinism and free will dominate *La vida es sueño* (1635; "Life Is a Dream"), a masterpiece that explores escaping from life's confusion to awareness of reality and self-knowledge.

Calderón's overtly religious plays range from Jesuit drama emphasizing conversion (*El mágico prodigioso* [1637; "The Wonder-Working Magician"]) and heroic saintliness (*El príncipe constante* [1629; "The Constant Prince"]) to his *autos sacramentales*, liturgical plays employing formal abstractions and symbols to expound the Fall of Man and Christian redemption, in which he brought to perfection the medieval tradition of the morality play. These liturgical plays range in their artistry from the immediate metaphorical appeal of *El gran teatro del mundo* (*c.* 1635; *The Great Theatre of the World*) to the increasingly elaborate

Pedro Calderón de la Barca

(b. Jan. 17, 1600, Madrid, Spain—d. May 25, 1681, Madrid)

Pedro Calderón de la Barca was a dramatist and poet who succeeded Lope de Vega as the greatest Spanish playwright of the Golden Age.

Calderón's father, a fairly well-to-do government official who died in 1615, was a man of harsh and dictatorial temper. Strained family relations apparently had a profound effect on the youthful Calderón, for several of his plays show a preoccupation with the psychological and moral effects of unnatural family life, presenting anarchical behaviour directly traced to the abuse of paternal authority.

Destined for the church, Calderón matriculated at the University of Alcalá in 1614 but transferred a year later to Salamanca, where he continued his studies in arts, law, and probably theology until 1619 or 1620. Abandoning an ecclesiastical career, he entered the service of the constable of Castile and in 1623 began to write plays for the court, rapidly becoming the leading member of the small group of dramatic poets whom King Philip IV gathered around him. In 1636 the king made him a Knight of the Military Order of St. James. Calderón's popularity was not confined to the court, for these early plays were also acclaimed in the public theatres. On the death of Lope de Vega (1635) Calderón became the master of the Spanish stage.

On the outbreak of the Catalan rebellion, he enlisted in 1640 in a cavalry company of knights of the military orders and served with distinction until 1642, when he was invalided out of the army. In 1645 he entered the service of the Duke de Alba, probably as secretary. A few years later an illegitimate son was born to him. Nothing is known about the mother, and the idea that sorrow at her death led him to return to his first vocation, the priesthood, is pure surmise. He was ordained in 1651 and announced that he would write no more for the stage. This intention he kept as regards the public theatres, but at the king's command he continued to write regularly for the court theatre. He also wrote each year the two Corpus Christi plays for Madrid.

Appointed a prebendary of Toledo Cathedral, he took up residence in 1653. The fine meditative religious poem *Psalle et sile* ("Sing Psalms and Keep Silent") is of this period. Receiving permission to hold his prebend without residence, he returned to Madrid in 1657 and was appointed honorary chaplain to the king in 1663.

Aesthetic Milieu and Achievement

The court patronage that Calderón enjoyed constitutes the most important single influence in the development of his art. The court drama grew out of the popular drama, and at first there was no distinction in themes and style between the two. The construction, however, of a special theatre in the new palace, the Buen Retiro, completed in 1633, made possible spectacular productions beyond the resources of the public stage. The court plays became a distinctive Baroque genre, combining drama with dancing, music, and the visual arts and departing from contemporary life into the world of classical mythology and ancient history.

Thus Calderón, as court dramatist, became associated with the rise of opera in Spain. In 1648 he wrote *El jardín de Falerina* ("The Garden of Falerina"), the first of his zarzuelas, plays in two acts with alternating spoken and sung dialogue. In 1660 he wrote his first opera, the one-act *La púrpura de la rosa* ("The Purple of the Rose"), with all of the dialogue set to music. This was followed by *Celos, aun del aire matan* (1660; "Jealousy Even of the Air Can Kill"), an opera in three acts with music by Juan Hidalgo. As in the Italian tradition, the music was subordinate to the poetry, and all of Calderón's musical plays are poetic dramas in their own right.

Calderón's drama must be placed within the context of the court theatre, with its conscious development of an unrealistic and stylized art form. For two centuries after his death, his pre-eminence remained unchallenged, but the realistic canons of criticism that came to the fore toward the end of the 19th century produced a reaction in favour of the more "lifelike" drama of Lope de Vega. Calderón appeared mannered and conventional: the structure of his plots artificially contrived, his characters stiff and unconvincing, his verse often affected and rhetorical. Although he used technical devices and stylistic mannerisms that by constant repetition became conventional, Calderón remained sufficiently detached to make his characters, on occasion, poke fun at his own conventions. This detachment indicates a conception of art as a formal medium that employs its artistic devices so as to compress and abstract the externals of human life, the better to express its essentials.

In this direction Calderón developed the dramatic form and conventions established by Lope de Vega, based on primacy of action over characterization, with unity in the theme rather than in the plot. He created a tightly knit structure of his own, while leaving intact the formal framework of Vega's drama. From the start he manifested his technical skill by utilizing the characters and incidents of his plots in the development of a dominant idea. As his art matured his plots became more complex and the action more constricted and compact. The creation of complex dramatic patterns in which the artistic effect arises from perception of the totality of the design through the inseparability of the parts is Calderón's greatest achievement as a craftsman. *El pintor de su deshonra* (*c.* 1645; *The Painter of His Own Dishonor*) and *La cisma de Ingalaterra* (*c.* 1627; "The Schism of England") are masterly examples of this technique, in which poetic imagery, characters, and action are subtly interconnected by dominant symbols that elucidate the significance of the theme. Although rhetorical devices typical of the Spanish Baroque style remained a feature of his diction, his verse developed away from excessive ornamentation toward a taut style compressed and controlled by a penetrating mind.

patterns of his later productions, such as *La nave del mercader* [1674; "The Merchant's Ship").

After Calderón's death, Spanish drama languished for 100 years. *Culteranismo* and *conceptismo*, although symptoms rather than causes of decline, contributed to stifling imaginative literature, and, by the close of the 17th century, all production characterizing the Siglo de Oro had essentially ceased.

THE 18TH CENTURY

During the early 18th century, men of letters began again to study abroad, which led them to discover how far Spain had diverged from the intellectual course of western Europe. New inquiries into Spain's national heritage also led scholars to unearth forgotten medieval literature. Such activities served as a prologue to an era in which writers looked back to Spain's literary past while engaging in vigorous debate over Neoclassicism, which became of central concern to writers, particularly dramatists, during the second half of the century.

New Critical Approaches

In 1700, Charles II, the last monarch of the Habsburg dynasty, died without an heir, thereby provoking the War of the Spanish Succession (1701–14), a European conflict over control of Spain. The resultant establishment of the Bourbon dynasty initiated French domination of Spain's political and cultural life. Following patterns of the Enlightenment in England and France, numerous academies were created, such as the Real Academia de la Lengua Española (1713, now the Real Academia Española [Royal Spanish Academy]), founded to guard linguistic integrity. Gregorio Mayáns y Siscar produced the first biographical study of Cervantes in 1737, and church historian Enrique Flórez, embarking in 1754 on a vast historical enterprise, *España sagrada*, resurrected the cultural backgrounds of medieval Christian Spain. Literary landmarks included the first publication of the 12th-century epic *Poema de mío Cid*, the works of Gonzalo de Berceo, and Juan Ruiz's *Libro de buen amor*.

Debates concerning values of the old and the new raged during the century's middle decades, compelling both sides to initiate new critical approaches to literature. Leaders—including Ignacio de Luzán Claramunt, whose work on poetics launched the great Neoclassical polemic in Spain, and Benito Jerónimo Feijóo y Montenegro, a Benedictine monk who assailed error, prejudice, and superstition wherever he found them—contributed significantly to Spain's intellectual emancipation. Fray Martín Sarmiento (Benedictine name of Pedro José García Balboa), a scholar and friend of Feijóo, treated subjects from religion and philosophy to science and child rearing. Much of his work remains unpublished. Feijóo's monumental *Theatro crítico universal* (1726–39; "Universal Critical Theatre"), a compendium of knowledge, exemplifies the interests and achievements of the encyclopaedists. Another major encyclopaedic talent, Gaspar Melchor de Jovellanos, produced streams of reports, essays, memoirs, and studies on agriculture, the economy, political organization, law, industry, natural science, and literature, as well as ways to improve them, in addition to writing Neoclassical drama and poetry.

Pedro de Montengón y Paret introduced narrative genres then popular in France—philosophical and pedagogical novels in the style of Jean-Jacques Rousseau—with such works as *Eusebio* (1786–88), a four-volume novel set in America that exalted the religion of nature. Montengón also published *El Antenor* (1778) and *El Rodrigo, romance épico* (1793; "Roderick, Epic Ballad"). *Fray Gerundio* (1758) by José Francisco de Isla, satirizing exaggerated pulpit oratory, reincorporated aspects of the picaresque novel. This genre was also echoed in works of Diego de Torres Villarroel, whose *Vida, ascendencia, nacimiento, crianza y aventuras* (1743–58; "Life, Ancestry, Birth, Upbringing, and Adventures"), whether a novel or an autobiography, remains among the century's most readable narratives. Torres Villarroel experimented with all literary genres, and his collected works, published 1794–99, are fertile sources for studying 18th-century character, aesthetics, and literary style. Josefa Amar y Borbón defended women's admission to learned academies, asserting their equal intelligence in *Discurso en defensa del talento de las mujeres y de su aptitud para el gobierno y otros cargos en que se emplean los hombres* (1786; "Discourse in Defense of the Talent of Women and Their Aptitude for Government and Other Positions in Which Men Are Employed"). Amar published on many topics, most frequently women's right to education.

About 1775, Diego González led the Salamanca poetry revival group seeking inspiration in Fray Luis de León.

Two decades later a group at Sevilla turned to Fernando de Herrera. Juan Meléndez Valdés, a disciple of English philosopher John Locke and English poet Edward Young, best exemplified the new influences on poetry during this period. Employing Classical and Renaissance models, these reformers rejected Baroque excess, restoring poetry's clarity and harmony. Tomás de Iriarte, who was a Neoclassical poet, dramatist, theoretician, and translator, produced successful comedies (e.g., *El señorito mimado* [1787; "The Pampered Youth"] and *La señorita malcriada* [1788; "The Ill-Bred Miss"]) as well as the satire *Los literatos en cuaresma* (1772; "Writers in Lent"), which attacked Neoclassicism's foes. His fame rests on *Fábulas literarias* (1782; "Literary Fables"), a collection of fables and Neoclassical precepts rendered in verse. The fabulist, literary critic, and poet Félix María Samaniego published an enduringly popular collection, *Fábulas en verso* (1781; "Fables in Verse"), which, with Iriarte's fables, is among Neoclassicism's most enjoyable, best-loved poetic productions.

In drama, the second half of the century witnessed disputes concerning the Neoclassical "rules," chiefly the unities of place, time, and action. *La Raquel* (1778), a Neoclassical tragedy by Vicente García de la Huerta, showed the capabilities of the reformist school. Ramón de la Cruz, representing the Spanish "nationalist" dramatists against the *afrancesados* (imitators of French models), resurrected the earlier *pasos* and longer *entremeses* of Lope de Rueda, Cervantes, and Luis Quiñones de Benavente. Satires of the Madrid scene, Cruz's one-act sketches neither transgressed the unities nor offended the purist; they delighted the public, bringing drama back to observation of life and society. Leandro Fernández de Moratín applied the lesson to full-length plays, producing effective comedies imbued with deep social seriousness. His dialogue in

La comedia nueva (1792; "The New Comedy") and *El sí de las niñas* (1806; *The Maiden's Consent*) ranks with the 18th century's best prose.

The work of the dramatist, poet, essayist, and short-fiction writer José de Cadalso y Vázquez (pseudonym Dalmiro) moves between Neoclassic aesthetics and Romantic cosmic despair. Scion of a distinguished noble family, he chose a military career and died in 1782, at age 41, during Spain's unsuccessful attempt to recover Gibraltar from Great Britain. Banished from Madrid to Aragón in 1768 on suspicion of being the author of a sharp satire, he wrote the poems later collected in *Ocios de mi juventud* (1773; "Pastimes of My Youth"). In 1770 he returned to Madrid, where his close friendships with Moratín and leading actresses prompted his heroic tragedy *Don Sancho García* (1771) as well as *Solaya; o, los circasianos* ("Solaya; or, The Circassians") and *La Numantina* ("The Girl from Numancia").

Cadalso's most important works are two satires—*Los eruditos a la violeta* (published 1772; "Wise Men Without Learning") and the brilliant *Cartas marruecas* (written *c.* 1774, published 1793; "Moroccan Letters"), inspired by the epistolary fictions of Oliver Goldsmith and Montesquieu— and the enigmatic *Noches lúgubres* (written *c.* 1774, published 1798; "Mournful Nights"), a Gothic and Byronic work that anticipates Romanticism.

WOMEN WRITERS

Several women writers emerged during the Enlightenment and were active from 1770 onward in the male-dominated Spanish theatre. They wrote Neoclassic drama: *comedias lacrimosas* (tearful plays), *zarzuelas* (musical comedies), *sainetes*, Romantic tragedies, and *costumbrista* comedies. While some women wrote for small private audiences in convents and literary salons, others wrote for the public stage. Margarita Hickey and María Rosa Gálvez were both quite successful, with the former producing translations of Jean Racine and Voltaire and the latter composing some 13 original plays from opera and light comedy to high tragedy. Gálvez's Moratín-style comedy *Los figurones literarios* (1804; "The Literary Nobodies") ridicules pedantry. Her tragedy *Florinda* (1804) attempts to vindicate the woman blamed for Spain's loss to the Muslims, and her biblical drama *Amnón* (1804) recounts the biblical rape of Tamar by her brother Amnon. Neoclassical poet Manuel José Quintana praised Gálvez's odes and elegies, and considered her the best woman writer of her time.

Some women exerted influence during the Enlightenment through their salons. That of Josefa de Zúñiga y Castro, countess of Lemos, called the Academia del Buen Gusto (Academy of Good Taste), was famous, as were those of the duchess of Alba and the countess-duchess of Benavente. The number of periodicals for women increased dramatically, and *La Pensadora Gaditana* (1763–64), the first Spanish newspaper for women, was published by Beatriz Cienfuegos (believed by some to have been a man's pseudonym). But the death of King Charles III in 1788 and the horror spread by the French Revolution brought an abrupt halt to Spain's incursion into the Age of Reason.

CHAPTER 2

CASTILIAN LITERATURE IN THE 19TH AND 20TH CENTURIES

Early 19th-century Spanish literature suffered as a result of the Napoleonic Wars and their economic repercussions. Spain experienced soaring inflation, and manpower across the peninsula was at a low ebb as a result of emigration and military service. Spain's agriculture was crippled, its cottage industries dwindled and nearly disappeared, and industrialization lagged behind that of other western European countries. These problems were further aggravated by the loss of its American colonies. Ferdinand VII's anachronistic attempts to restore the absolutist monarchy drove many liberals into exile in England and France, both countries then under the sway of Romanticism.

THE ROMANTIC MOVEMENT

Traditional scholarship has viewed Spanish Romanticism as imported by liberals returning after Ferdinand VII's death in 1833, the year frequently deemed the beginning of Spanish Romanticism. Some, however, recognize Cadalso and several lesser cultivators of Gothic fiction as 18th-century Spanish antecedents. Debates that prepared the way for Romanticism flourished from 1814 onward; in Cádiz, in discussions of literary values initiated by Johann Niklaus Böhl von Faber, in Barcelona with the founding of the literary periodical *El europeo* ("The European") in 1823, and in Madrid with Agustín Durán's essay on Siglo de Oro drama (1828) and his *Colección de romances antiguos* (1828–32; "Collection of Ancient Ballads").

Romanticism in Spain was, in many respects, a return to its earlier classics, a continuation of the rediscovery initiated by 18th-century scholars. Important formal traits of Spanish Romantic drama—mingling genres, rejecting the unities, diversifying metrics—had characterized Lope de Vega and his contemporaries, whose themes reappeared in Romantic garb. Some have therefore argued that the native flowering of Spanish Romanticism was not a tardy import. Its principles were instead already present in Spain, but their full expression was delayed by the reactionary, tyrannical monarchy's persecution of members of a movement that was, at its beginning, liberal and democratic. Production of Romantic dramas was also postponed until after Ferdinand's death.

Spanish Romanticism, typically understood as having two branches, had no single leader. José de Espronceda y Delgado and his works epitomize the "Byronic," revolutionary, metaphysical vein of Spanish Romanticism, and his *Estudiante de Salamanca* (in two parts, 1836 and 1837; "Student of Salamanca"), *Canciones* (1840; "Songs"), and *El diablo mundo* (unfinished, published 1840; "The Devilish World") were among the period's most celebrated subjective lyrics. The enormously successful drama *Don Álvaro o la fuerza del sino* (1835; "Don Alvaro; or, The Force of Destiny") by Ángel de Saavedra, duque de Rivas, and the preface, by the critic Antonio Alcalá Galiano, to Saavedra's narrative poem *El moro expósito* (1834; "The Foundling Moor") embody the Christian and monarchical aesthetics and ideology of the second, more traditional branch of Spanish Romanticism, whose quintessential representative is José Zorrilla y Moral, author of the period's most enduring drama, *Don Juan Tenorio* (1844). Prolific, facile, and declamatory, Zorrilla produced huge numbers of plays, lyric and narrative verse collections, and enormously popular rewrites of Siglo de Oro plays and legends; he was treated as a national hero.

One major Romantic theme concerned liberty and individual freedom. The late Romantic poet Gustavo Adolfo Bécquer, in *Rimas* (published posthumously in 1871; "Rhymes"), expressed his own tortured emotions, suffering, and solitude but also celebrated love, poetry, and intimacy while experimenting with free verse. *Rimas* influenced more 20th-century Spanish poets than any other 19th-century work.

A number of notable women writers emerged under Romanticism. Carolina Coronado's early fame rested on a collection of poetry, *Poesías*, first published in 1843. Her poems sounded many feminist notes, although she in later life became conservative. In 1850 she published two short novels, *Adoración and Paquita. La Sigea* (1854), the first of three historical novels, recreated the experience of the Renaissance humanist Luisa Sigea de Velasco; *Jarilla and La rueda de desgracia* ("The Wheel of Misfortune") appeared in 1873.

Poet, dramatist, and prose writer Gertrudis Gómez de Avellaneda was born in Cuba but spent most of her adult life in Spain. She was the author of a pioneering abolitionist novel, *Sab* (1841), as well as novels on Mexico's Aztec past and a protofeminist novel (*Dos mujeres* [1842; "Two Women"]). She also wrote 16 full-length original plays, four of which were major successes. Rosalía de Castro is known primarily for her poetry and novels in Galician, but her last collection of poems, *En las orillas del*

Sar (1884; "Beside the River Sar"), written in Castilian, brought her a wider audience.

While poetry and theatre claimed the major honours, Spanish Romanticism also produced many novels. The best, *El Señor de Bembibre* (1844) by Enrique Gil y Carrasco, reflects Gil's carefully researched history of the Templars in Spain. Other important novels are Mariano José de Larra's *El doncel de Don Enrique el doliente* (1834; "The Page of King Enrique the Invalid") and Espronceda's *Sancho Saldaña* (1834).

Costumbrismo

Costumbrismo began before Romanticism, contributing to both Romanticism and the later realism movement through realistic prose. The *cuadro de costumbres* and *artículo de costumbres*—short literary sketches on customs, manners, or character—were two types of *costumbrista* writing, typically published in the popular press or included as an element of longer literary works such as novels. The *cuadro* was inclined to description for its own sake, whereas the *artículo* was more critical and satirical.

Cartas de un pobrecito holgazán (1820; "Letters from a Poor Idler") by Sebastián de Miñano points the way, but the most important *costumbrista* titles were by Mariano José de Larra, an outstanding prose writer and the best critical mind of his age, who dissected society pitilessly in *Artículos* (1835–37). Ramón de Mesonero Romanos, in *Escenas matritenses* (1836–42; "Scenes of Madrid"), humorously portrayed contemporary life, and Serafín Estébanez Calderón depicted the manners, folklore, and history of *Andalusia in Escenas andaluzas* (1847; "Andalusian Sketches"). Such writings, realistically observing everyday life and regional elements, bridged the transition to realism.

REVIVAL OF THE SPANISH NOVEL

For two centuries the novel, Spain's greatest contribution to literature, had languished. Early revival novels are of interest more for their powers of observation and description (a continuation of *costumbrismo*) than for their imaginative or narrative quality. Fernán Caballero (pseudonym of Cecilia Böhl de Faber) essayed techniques of observation new to the novel in *La gaviota* (1849; *The Seagull*). The regional novel's flowering began with *El sombrero de tres picos* (1874; "The Three-Cornered Hat"), a sparkling tale of peasant malice by Pedro Antonio de Alarcón. Andalusian regionalism prevailed in many of Juan Valera's novels, but his remarkable psychological insights in *Pepita Jiménez* (1874) and *Doña Luz* (1879) made him the father of Spain's psychological novel. He was a prolific writer, his works ranging from poetry and newspaper articles to critical essays and memoirs. Regionalist José María de Pereda produced minute re-creations of nature, which was depicted as an abiding reality that dwarfed individuals. His most celebrated novels, *Sotileza* (1884; "Subtlety") and *Peñas arriba* (1895; "Up the Mountains"), support a rigid class structure and traditional values of religion, family, and country life.

Emilia, condesa (countess) de Pardo Bazán, attempted to combine the aesthetics of naturalism with traditional Roman Catholic values in her novels of Galicia, *Los pazos de Ulloa* (1886; "The Son of a Bondwoman") and *La madre naturaleza* (1887; "Mother Nature"), sparking considerable controversy. Her 19 major novels also represent mainstream Spanish realism, experiments with Symbolism, and spiritualism. She figures among Spain's major short-story writers with some 800 stories.

Armando Palacio Valdés was the novelist of Asturias, his native province, while Jacinto Octavio Picón was more cosmopolitan; both experimented with naturalism. The reputed author of more than 100 works, María del Pilar Sinués y Navarro made women her primary subjects, treating marriage, motherhood, domestic life, and women's education. Ana García de la Torre (Ana García del Espinar), a more progressive contemporary, treated problems of class, gender, and the proletariat, writing especially on the "working girl" and portraying utopian workers' socialist movements.

Benito Pérez Galdós, Spain's most significant novelist after Cervantes, perfected the Spanish realistic novel and created a new type of historical novel, imaginatively reproducing many turbulent chapters of Spain's 19th-century history. His *Episodios nacionales* (1873–79 and 1898–1912; "National Episodes") comprise 46 volumes and cover the 70 years from the Napoleonic Wars to Spain's short-lived First Republic. Galdós's enduring fame rests, however, on what have come to be known as the *Novelas españolas contemporáneas* ("contemporary Spanish novels"), especially his portrayals of Madrid's bureaucracy and its middle class and *pueblo* (working class). Included among these many novels is his masterpiece, *Fortunata y Jacinta* (1886–87), a paradigm of Spanish realism. This massive four-volume work presents the whole of Madrid's social spectrum via the families, loves, and acquaintances of the two women in the life of a wealthy but weak bourgeois: Fortunata, his mistress and the mother of his son, and Jacinta, his wife. The novel has been seen as an allegory of the sterility of the upper classes, but its complexity transcends facile summary.

Galdós's later works represent naturalism or reflect turn-of-the-century spiritualism. He was a liberal crusader whose criticism of the Roman Catholic Church's interventions in civic matters, of caciquism (*caciquismo*, or political bossism), and of reactionary power-grabs made him many enemies. He also wrote more than 20 successful and often controversial plays. Some have argued that his political enemies conspired to deny him the Nobel Prize, but today he ranks with such world-class realists as the English novelist Charles Dickens and the French novelist Honoré de Balzac.

In the late 1880s—a time of nascent industrialism, a growing proletariat, and an influx of international labour organizers—other naturalistic novelists followed, notably Vicente Blasco Ibáñez. A crusader, adventurer, and short story writer, he achieved enormous international success with novels widely translated and adapted for the screen and became Spain's best-known novelist in the first third of the 20th century, though he was seldom well received at home. Contemporaneous with the Generation of 1898 but belonging aesthetically to the 19th century, Blasco Ibáñez wrote regional novels of Valencia, crusaded for socialism, and treated contemporary social problems from an anarchist perspective in such novels as *La bodega* (1905; "The Wine Vault"; Eng. trans. *The Fruit of the Vine*) and *La horda* (1905; *The Mob*). He won international renown with *Los cuatro jinetes del apocalipsis* (1916; "The Four Horsemen of the Apocalypse"), on World War I, and *Mare nostrum* (1918; "Our Sea"), on German submarine warfare in the Mediterranean.

Leopoldo Alas (byname Clarín), like Valera a well-respected critic and author of volumes of influential articles, has long been considered a naturalist, but his works exhibit none of the sordidness and social determinism typical of that movement. Rich in detail, his writings abound in irony and satire as they expose the evils of Spanish Restoration society, most notably in *La Regenta* (1884–85; "The Regent's Wife"), which is today considered Spain's most significant novel of the 19th century. Alas's

Statue in Oviedo, Spain, of Ana Ozores, the title character in Leopoldo Alas's novel La Regenta *("The Regent's Wife"), whose fictional setting was inspired by Oviedo.* © age fotostock/SuperStock

masterful short stories rank with the best in Spanish and world literature.

POST-ROMANTIC DRAMA AND POETRY

Realistic drama in Spain produced few masterpieces but established a bourgeois comedy of manners further developed in the 20th century. Manuel Tamayo y Baus achieved fame with *Un drama nuevo* (1867; "A New Drama"), whose characters, members of William Shakespeare's acting company, include Shakespeare himself. Adelardo López de Ayala pilloried bourgeois vices in *El tejado de vidrio* (1857; "The Glass Roof") and *Consuelo* (1870). The more than 60 plays of José Echegaray y Eizaguirre include both enormously popular melodramas lacking verisimilitude of character, motivation, and situation and serious bourgeois dramas of social problems. In 1904 he shared the Nobel Prize for Literature with the Provençal poet Frédéric Mistral. Joaquín Dicenta utilized class conflict and social injustice as themes, dramatizing working-class conditions in *Juan José* (performed 1895).

In poetry, realistic trends produced little of note. Ramón de Campoamor y Campoosorio wrote *Doloras* (1845; "Sufferings"), *Pequeños poemas* (1871; "Little Poems"), and *Humoradas* (1886; "Pleasant Jokes"), works that attempted to establish a poetry of ideas. The poet, playwright, and politician Gaspar Núñez de Arce published *Gritos del combate* (1875; "Combat Cries"), patriotic declamatory exhortations defending democracy. He used a realistic approach to treat contemporary moral, religious, and political conflicts in his works, although his work also shows Romantic and medieval themes.

THE MODERN PERIOD: NOVELS AND ESSAYS

For some two decades before 1900, political and social unrest grew in Spain, conditions that inspired Ángel Ganivet's influential *Idearium español* (1897; *Spain, an Interpretation*), which analyzed Spanish character. The Spanish empire, founded in 1492, ended with defeat in the Spanish-American War of 1898, which prompted Spanish intellectuals to diagnose their country's ills and to seek ways to jolt the nation out of what they perceived to be its abulia (lack of will). The novel acquired new seriousness, and critical, psychological, and philosophical essays gained unprecedented importance. Novelists and essayists constituted what Azorín (pseudonym of José Martínez Ruiz) named the Generation of 1898, today considered an "Age of Silver," second only to Spain's Siglo de Oro (Golden Age).

Miguel de Unamuno studied national problems perceptively in *En torno al casticismo* (1895), a collection of essays whose title—which means, roughly, "Concerning Spanishness"—reflects its analysis of the "essence" of Spanish national identity. In *Vida de Don Quijote y ancho* (1905; *The Life of Don Quixote and Sancho*) Unamuno explored the same subject by way of an examination of Cervantes's fictional characters. He despairingly questioned immortality in his most important work, *Del sentimiento trágico de la vida* (1913; *The Tragic Sense of Life in Men and Peoples*). A provocative, somewhat unsystematic thinker, Unamuno aimed at sowing spiritual disquiet. The novel became his medium for exploring personality, as in *Niebla* (1914; *Mist*), *Abel Sánchez* (1917), and *Tres novelas ejemplares y un prólogo* (1920; "Three Cautionary Tales and a Prologue"), with his final spiritual position—Kierkegaardian existentialism—revealed in *San Manuel Bueno, mártir* (1933; "San Manuel Bueno, Martyr"). Unamuno was an influential journalist and an unsuccessful but powerful dramatist who also ranks among Spain's greatest 20th-century poets.

In novels such as *Don Juan* (1922) and *Doña Inés* (1925), Azorín created retrospective, introspective, and nearly motionless narratives that shared many of the qualities of works by his contemporary Marcel Proust. Azorín's essays—in *El alma castellana* (1900; "The Castilian Soul"), *La ruta de Don Quijote* (1905; "Don Quixote's Route"), *Castilla* (1912), and numerous additional volume—reinterpreted and sought to eternalize earlier literary values and visions of rural Spain. An artistic critic and sensitive miniaturist, he excelled in precision and ekphrasis (description of a visual work of art). Philosopher José Ortega y Gasset developed themes from criticism and psychology

(*Meditaciones del Quijote* [1914; "Meditations on Quixote"]) to national problems (*España invertebrada* [1921; "Invertebrate Spain"]) and international concerns (*El tema de nuestro tiempo* [1923; "The Modern Theme"], *La rebelión de las masas* [1929; "The Revolt of the Masses"]). He and Unamuno were Spain's intellectual leaders during the first half of the 20th century.

Novelist Pío Baroja repudiated tradition, religion, and most forms of social organization and government, initially advocating something approaching anarchism but later turning more conservative. A neonaturalist, he saw the world as a cruel place, and many of his works— including the trilogies *La raza* (1908–11; "The Race") and *La lucha por la vida* (1903–04; "The Struggle for Life") and the two-part *Agonías de nuestro tiempo* (1926; "Agonies of Our Time")—portray squalid, subhuman conditions, prostitutes and criminals, and ignorance and disease. His most-read work is *El árbol de la ciencia* (1911; *The Treeof Knowledge*), which tells the story of the education of the protagonist, a medical student. The novel depicts the shortcomings of those teaching medicine, the callousness of many doctors treating Spanish society's most vulnerable, and the abject

Azorín *(pseudonym of José Martínez Ruiz), detail of an oil painting by Joaquín Sorolla y Bastida, 1917; in the collection of the Hispanic Society of America.* Courtesy of the Hispanic Society of America

poverty and filth in the village where the protagonist first practices. Baroja also wrote adventure novels that glorified the "man of action," a type that recurs throughout his novels. In his later works he experimented with Impressionism and Surrealism.

Sometimes omitted from the Generation of 1898, given his Modernist beginnings, Ramón María del Valle-Inclán—a poet, journalist, essayist, short-story writer, and profoundly influential dramatist and novelist—suffered critical neglect following his death in 1936 when the Francisco Franco regime prohibited studies of Republican writers. The three stages of his literary evolution exhibit radical aesthetic change, beginning with exquisite, sometimes decadent, erotic *Modernista* tales, as in his four *Sonatas* (1902–05; Eng. trans. *The Pleasant Memoirs of the Marquis de Bradomin: Four Sonatas*). Each represents a season (of the year and of human life) corresponding to the youth, plenitude, maturity, and old age of the narrator, a decadent Don Juan. Intertextual allusions, nostalgia for an idealized past, aristocratic posing, melancholy, underlying parody, and humour abound. The trilogy *Comedias bárbaras* (1907, 1908, 1923), set in an anachronistic, semifeudal Galicia and linked by a single protagonist, is in dialogue form, which gives these novels the feel of impossibly long cinematographic dramas. This series initiated Valle's aesthetic movement away from *Modernismo's* quest for beauty, which continued with his violent trilogy (1908–09) on the 19th-century Carlist wars.

Valle's third artistic stage, characterized by his invention of the esperpento style, is expressionistic, involving deliberate distortion and calculated inversion of heroic models and values. "Esperpentic" visions appear in the novels *Tirano Banderas* (1926; Eng. trans. *The Tyrant*), *La corte de los milagros* (1927; "The Court of Miracles"), and *Viva mi dueño* (1928; "Long Live My Lord"), the last two belonging to another trilogy, *El ruedo ibérico* ("The Iberian Cycle"). Valle's works usually treat his native Galicia. *Tirano Banderas*, satirizing desultory revolutions and set in a fictional Latin American country, is sometimes considered his masterpiece.

Generation of 1898

A group of novelists, poets, essayists, and thinkers known as the Generation of 1898 were active in Spain at the time of the Spanish-American War (1898). They were responsible for reinvigorating Spanish letters and for restoring Spain to a position of intellectual and literary prominence that it had not held for centuries.

The shock of Spain's defeat in the war, which left it stripped of the last vestiges of its empire and its international prestige, provided an impetus for many writers and thinkers to embark on a period of self-searching and an analysis of Spain's problems and its destiny.

The term Generation of 1898 (Spanish: Generación del 1898) was used loosely at the turn of the century but was elaborated by the literary critic Azorín in critical essays that appeared in various periodicals and were collected in his *Clásicos y modernos* (1913). It was soon generally applied to the writers who concerned themselves with Spain's heritage and its position in the modern world. Never an organized movement or school, the Generation of 1898 worked in diverse fields and styles and rarely agreed on approaches or solutions to Spain's problems, but all had in common a desire to shake the Spanish people out of what they saw as apathy and to restore a sense of national pride.

Joaquín Costa, Ángel Ganivet, and Miguel de Unamuno are generally considered precursors of the Generation of 1898, but many literary historians consider Ganivet and, usually, Unamuno as members of the group proper. Other outstanding figures are

Azorín himself, the philosopher and critic José Ortega y Gasset, the novelists Pío Baroja, Vicente Blasco Ibáñez, and Ramón María del Valle-Inclán, and the poets Antonio Machado y Ruiz and Manuel Machado y Ruiz. In their revitalization of Spanish letters, they brought a new seriousness of purpose to the Spanish novel and elevated the essay—critical, psychological, philosophical—to a position of literary importance. At the same time, they brought to Spain an awareness of foreign trends in literature and thought that enabled the Spanish people to reassess their own values in the context of the modern world, thus awakening a national consciousness that paved the way for Spanish cultural development in the 20th century.

POETRY

Rubén Darío, Latin America's greatest poet, took Modernismo to Spain in 1892. Modernismo rejected 19th-century bourgeois materialism and instead sought specifically aesthetic values. Darío greatly enriched the musical resources of Spanish verse with the daring use of new rhythms and metres, creating an introspective, cosmopolitan, and aesthetically beautiful poetry.

Antonio Machado, one of the 20th century's greatest poets, explored memory through recurrent symbols of multiple meanings, the dimly drawn boundaries of dream and reality, and time past and present. A consummate creator of introspective Modernist poems in *Soledades* (1903, augmented 1907; "Solitudes"), Machado abandoned the cult of beauty in *Campos de Castilla* (1912, augmented 1917; "Fields of Castile"), producing powerful visions of the Spanish condition and the character of the Spanish people that became a guiding precedent for postwar "social" poets. In his anguished grappling with Spain's

Spanish poet and Nobel laureate Juan Ramón Jiménez. Quim Llenas/ Hulton Archive/Getty Images

problems—a characteristic of the Generation of 1898—Machado correctly foresaw the coming Civil War.

Juan Ramón Jiménez, recipient of the Nobel Prize for Literature in 1956, practiced the aesthetics of Modernismo during his first two decades. Anguished by transient reality, Jiménez next sought salvation in an absorbing, manic dedication to poetry stripped of adornment—what he called poesía desnuda ("naked poetry")—as in *Eternidades* (1918; "Eternities") and *Piedra y cielo* (1919; "Stone and Sky"). Seeking Platonic absolutes in his final years, he produced measured, exact poetry that increasingly exulted in mystical discoveries of transcendence within the immanence of self and physical reality. Jiménez's voluminous output—*Rimas* (1902; "Rhymes"); *Sonetos espirituales* (1914–15) (1917; "Spiritual Sonnets [1914–15]"); *Diario de un poeta recién casado* (1917; "Diary of a Poet Recently Married"); *Animal de fondo* (1947; "Animal of the Depth")—springs from his lifelong pursuit of poetry and its modes of expression. Sofía Pérez Casanova de Lutoslawski, a successful early Modernist poet, spent her married life outside Spain. A pioneering feminist and social worker, she was also a prolific novelist, a translator, and an author of short stories, essays, and children's books. She became a foreign correspondent during World War I and the Russian Revolution of 1917.

DRAMA

Contemporaneous with the Generation of 1898 but ideologically and aesthetically distinct was Jacinto Benavente y Martínez. A prolific playwright noted for his craftsmanship and wit, he profoundly altered Spanish theatrical practice and fare. Excelling in the comedy of manners with sparkling dialogue and satiric touches, Benavente never alienated his devoted upper-class public. *Los intereses*

Jacinto Benavente y Martínez. Encyclopædia Britannica, Inc.

creados (1907; *The Bonds of Interest*), echoing the 16th-century commedia dell'arte, is his most enduring work. He won the Nobel Prize for Literature in 1922.

The poetic, nostalgic drama of Eduardo Marquina revived lyric theatre, together with the so-called *género chico* (light dramatic or operatic one-act playlets). Serafín and Joaquín Alvarez Quintero appropriated the latter's popular *costumbrista* setting for comedy, while Carlos Arniches developed it in satirical pieces (often compared with the 18th-century sainete) and Pedro Muñoz Seca used it in popular farces. More-intellectual theatrical experiments by Unamuno attempted the drama of ideas. Azorín renewed comedy, introducing lessons from vaudeville, and produced experimental Surrealist works.

Although undervalued during his lifetime because his radically innovative, shocking works went mostly unproduced, Valle-Inclán is today considered Spain's most significant dramatist since Calderón. This brilliant, original playwright attempted, often futilely, to overcome Spanish theatre's bourgeois complacency and artistic mediocrity. His dramas inveighed against hypocrisy and corrupt values with mordant irony. *Luces de Bohemia* (1920; *Bohemian Lights*) illustrates his theory and practice of esperpento, an aesthetic formula he also used in his fiction to depict reality through a deliberately exaggerated mimesis of its grotesqueness. His work sometimes recalls that of Luis Buñuel, Salvador Dalí, or Pablo Picasso. Jacinto Grau, another would-be reformer, attempted tragedy in *El Conde Alarcos* (1917), adding dignity to his pessimistic view of an absurd reality in *El señor de Pigmalión* (1921).

Generally overlooked is María de la O Lejárraga, who collaborated with her husband, Gregorio Martínez Sierra, and wrote most of the essays, poems, short stories, novels, and newspaper articles they published jointly, plus the more than 50 plays on which their fame rests. She continued writing his plays even after he abandoned her for another woman. Their best-known plays include *Canción de cuna* (1911; *Cradle Song*) and *El reino de Dios* (1916; *The Kingdom of God*), which feature strong, resourceful, maternal women who represent an idealization of motherhood, a typical feature of their plays. Brothers Manuel and Antonio Machado collaborated on several lyric plays during the 1920s and early 1930s.

THE GENERATION OF 1927

The name Generation of 1927 identifies poets that emerged about 1927, the 300-year anniversary of the death of Baroque poet Luis de Góngora y Argote, to whom these

71

Novecentismo

The term *novecentistas* applies to a generation of writers that fall between the Generation of 1898 and the vanguardist Generation of 1927. The *novecentistas*—sometimes also called the Generation of 1914—were more classical and less revolutionary than their predecessors. They sought to renew intellectual and aesthetic standards while reaffirming Classical values. Ortega y Gasset exerted influence over the novel as a genre with *La deshuman-ización del arte* (1925; *The Dehumanization of Art*), which analyzed contemporary "depersonalized" (i.e., nonrepresentational) art. Ramón Pérez de Ayala made the novel a polished art form and a forum for philosophical discussion. *Belarmino y Apolonio* (1921) examines the age-old debate between faith and reason, utilizing symbolic characters and multiple narrative viewpoints, while *Tigre Juan* (1926; *Tiger Juan*) dissects traditional Spanish concepts of honour and matrimony.

Gabriel Miró's polished descriptive prose slowed and nearly displaced the novelistic action. Like Pérez de Ayala, he dealt repeatedly with ecclesiastical intrusions into civil life and satirized the lack of sexual education in Spanish culture. Benjamín Jarnés and others attempted to apply vanguardist and experimental techniques to the novel, emphasizing minimal action, alienated characters, the psychological probing of memory, and experiments with internal monologue. Vanguardism's paradigmatic exponent, Ramón Gómez de la Serna, was the author of some 100 novels, biographies, dramas, collections of articles and short stories, books on art, and works of humour.

Among women writers, Carmen de Burgos Seguí (pseudonym Colombine) wrote hundreds of articles, more than 50 short stories, some dozen long novels and numerous short ones, many practical books for women, and socially oriented treatises on subjects such as divorce. An active suffragist and opponent of the death penalty, she treated feminist themes (*La malcasada* ["The Unhappily Married Woman"], *En la sima* [1915; "On Top"], *La rampa* [1917; "The Ramp"]) as well as spiritualism, the occult, and the supernatural (*El retorno* ["The Reappearance"], *Los espiri-tuados* [1923; "The Possessed"]).

Concepción (Concha) Espina, often considered the first Spanish woman writer to earn her living exclusively from her writings, enjoyed tremendous popularity and was twice nominated for the Nobel Prize. Her novels, with their detailed descriptions, most nearly approach the regional novel as epitomized by Pereda; their melodrama and moralizing also show Espina's independence from novecentismo's influence. *El metal de los muertos* (1920; *The Metal of the Dead*), a work of social-protest fiction, was among her most successful works, as were *La esfinge maragata* (1914; *Mariflor*) and *Altar mayor* (1926; "High Altar").

poets paid homage and which sparked a brief flash of neo-Gongorism. These outstanding poets—among them Rafael Alberti, Vicente Aleixandre, Dámaso Alonso, Luis Cernuda, Gerardo Diego, Federico García Lorca, Jorge Guillén, and Pedro Salinas—drew upon the past (ballads, traditional songs, early metrical structure, and Góngora's poetry), but they also incorporated vanguardism (Surrealism, Futurism, Ultraism), producing intensely personal poetry. Images and metaphors—frequently illogical, hermetic, or irrational—became central to poetic creation. Most of these poets experimented with free verse or exotic forms drawn from the Japanese, Arabic, and Afro-Caribbean literary traditions. By the end of the Spanish Civil War, in 1939, many writers of the Generation of 1927 were dead or in exile.

Lorca, a consummate artist, musician, dramatist, and poet, captured the stark emotions and powerful effects that characterize traditional song and ballad forms. In *Romancero gitano* (1928; *The Gypsy Ballads*), he blended popular styles with sophisticated mythic and symbolic elements evoking mysterious, ambivalent visions of nature. Symbols and metaphors turn hermetic in *Poeta en Nueva York* (1940; *Poet in New York*), a Surrealist reflection of urban inhumanity and disorientation written during his visit to the United States in 1929–30. Salinas sought pure poetry through clearly focused poems and a heightened sensitivity to language. In *La voz a ti debida* (1934; "The Voice Inspired by You"; Eng. trans. *Truth of Two and Other Poems*), profoundly personal love experiences inspire subtle observations on the solidity of external reality and the fleeting world of subjective perception. Guillén's lifelong poetic effort, *Cántico* (*Cántico: A Selection*), first published in 1928 and repeatedly enlarged in successive editions, constitutes a disciplined hymn to the joys of everyday reality. Later works (*Clamor* [1957–63] and *Homenaje* [1967; "Homage"]) displayed keener awareness of suffering and disorder.

Aleixandre, influenced by Surrealism, dabbled in the subconscious and created his own personal myths. In *La destrucción o el amor* (1935; *Destruction or Love*), he evoked human despair and cosmic violence. With his postwar "social" poetry, Aleixandre moved beyond pure poetry, broadening his focus without abandoning a cosmic vision (*Mundo a solas* [1950; "World Alone"], *Historia del corazón* [1954; "History of the Heart"], *En un vasto dominio* [1962; "In a Vast Dominion"]). He received the Nobel Prize for Literature in 1977.

Like Lorca, Alberti initially incorporated popular forms and folk elements. The playful poetry of *Marinero en tierra* (1925; "Landlocked Sailor") yielded to stylistic complexities in *Cal y canto* (1927; "Quicklime and Song") and to the sombre, introspective mood of *Sobre los ángeles* (1929; *Concerning the Angels*), a Surrealist collection reflecting personal crisis. Alberti joined the Communist Party in the 1930s, and during the Civil War and his subsequent exile in Argentina, he wrote poetry of political commitment; later he resumed personal, intimate themes. Cernuda's poetry, as suggested by the title of his collected works *La realidad y el deseo* (first published 1936; "Reality and Desire"), contemplates the gulf between harsh reality and ideal personal aspirations. The tension, melancholy, and sense of alienation resulting from the unbridgeable gap between these realms pervade Cernuda's work.

This generation of Spanish poetry also includes Emilio Prados and Manuel Altolaguirre. Miguel Hernández, a younger poet of the Civil War, bridged the gap between the Generation of 1927 and the post–Civil War poets.

WOMEN POETS

Several significant women poets belong chronologically to the Generation of 1927, including Rosa Chacel, a major essayist, poet, and novelist. Her polished, intellectual verse appeared in *A la orilla de un pozo* (1936; *At the Edge of a Well*), a collection of neo-Gongoristic sonnets, and in *Versos prohibidos* (1978; "Prohibited Verse"), a mixture of unrhymed pieces that resemble in their metre blank verse and alexandrines and in their form epistles, sonnets, and odes. Frequent themes are philosophical inspiration, faith, religiosity, separation, menace (echoing the Civil War), friendships, and her wanderings.

Concha Méndez published four major poetry collections before the Civil War drove her into exile. Drawing upon traditional popular forms and the oral tradition, Méndez's prewar poetry—such as that in *Vida a vida* (1932; "Life to Life")—exudes optimism and vitality, recalling the neopopular airs of Lorca and Alberti. Her exile poetry expresses pessimism, loss, violence, horror, anguish, uncertainty, and pain (e.g., *Lluvias enlazadas* [1939;

"Interlaced Rains"]). Her last book was *Vida; o, río* (1979; "Life; or, The River").

Marina Romero Serrano spent three decades in exile in the United States teaching Spanish and writing poetry, critical works, and children's books. *Nostalgia de mañana* (1943; "Nostalgia for Tomorrow") reflects her generation's predilection for traditional metrics; her other works represent pure poetry and avoid the confessional and autobiographical mode. Her most personal collection, *Honda raíz* (1989; "Deep Roots"), treats lost love remembered, moving from joy to loss and infinite longing.

Ernestina de Champourcin published four volumes of exuberant, personal, intellectual poetry before going into exile (1936–72) with her husband, José Domenchina, a minor poet of the Generation of 1927. *Presencia a oscuras* (1952; "Presence in Darkness") reacted to the marginality she felt while in exile and commenced a spiritual quest intensified by Domenchina's death in 1959. *El nombre que me diste* (1960; "The Name You Gave Me"), *Cartas cerradas* (1968; "Sealed Letters"), and *Poemas del ser y estar* (1972; "Poems of Being and State"), collected with poetry written 1972–91, appeared as *Poesía a través del tiempo* (1991; "Poetry Across Time"). Characterizing her mature writing are religious preoccupations and mystic language. Champourcin ranks with the truly significant poets of her generation. Lesser figures include Pilar de Valderrama and Josefina de la Torre.

Carmen Conde Abellán, a socialist and Republican supporter, suffered postwar "internal exile" in Spain while her husband was a political prisoner. She was contemporaneous with and involved in Surrealism, Ultraism, and prewar experimentation with prose poems, but she is rarely included with the Generation of 1927. Her preoccupation with issues of social justice—especially education of the poor—is often taken as a pretext for this exclusion, even though survivors of that generation remaining in Spain also produced "social" poetry. A novelist, memorialist, biographer, anthologist, critic, archivist, and author of juvenile fiction, Conde published nearly 100 titles, including nine novels and several plays. She became the first woman elected to the Royal Spanish Academy (1978) and was the most honoured woman of her generation. Conde assiduously cultivated poetry's universal themes: love, suffering, nature, dreams, memory, solitude, death, estrangement, religious questing, and grief. Her most important works include *Ansia de la gracia* (1945; "Longing for Grace") and *Mujer sin Edén* (1947; *Woman Without Eden*). The latter implicitly equated the fall of the Spanish Republican government with the Fall of Man, also using Cain and Abel motifs to symbolize the country's Civil War.

Slightly younger, María Concepción Zardoya González, who wrote under the name Concha Zardoya, published 25 poetry collections between 1946 and 1987. She was born in Chile of Spanish parents and lived in Spain in the 1930s, and later spent three decades in the United States before returning in 1977 to Spain, where she remained until her death. Rich in personal experience and spiritual intimacy, her poetry ranks among the best women's lyrics in 20th-century Spain, recording a personal history of war and loss, exile and nostalgia, pain, solitude, and existential doubt.

REFORM OF THE DRAMA

Federico García Lorca towered above his contemporaries with intense poetic dramas that depict elemental passions and characters symbolizing humanity's tragic impotence against fate. His dramatic poetry was modern yet traditional, personal yet universal. The tragic trilogy *Bodas de sangre* (1933; *Blood Wedding*), *Yerma* (1934), and *La casa de Bernarda Alba* (1936; The *House of Bernarda Alba*) depicted extremes of passion involving the traditional Spanish theme of honour and its violent effects on women.

Alberti's contribution to dramatic reform imaginatively adapted classical forms of Spanish drama. In *El hombre deshabitado* (1931; "The Uninhabited Man"), a modern allegorical play in the manner of Calderón's *autos sacramentales*, he created poetic, fatalistic myths out of realistic themes and folk motifs. The renovation of the drama attempted by Azorín, Valle-Inclán, Grau, and others of the Generation of 1898 and continued by the Generation of 1927 (especially Lorca and Alberti) had little effect on the commercial theatre, their efforts ending abruptly with the outbreak of the Civil War.

THE SPANISH CIVIL WAR AND BEYOND

The Spanish Civil War (1936–39), a military revolt against the Republican government of Spain supported by conservative elements within the country, erupted after an initial military coup failed to win control of the entire country. The war was fought with great ferocity on both sides. The Nationalists, as the rebels were called, received aid from Fascist Italy and Nazi Germany. The Republicans received aid from the Soviet Union, as well as from International Brigades, composed of volunteers from Europe and the United States.

The war mobilized many artists and intellectuals to take up arms. Among the most notable artistic responses to the war were the novels *Man's Hope* (1938) by André Malraux, *Homage to Catalonia* (1938) by George Orwell, *The Adventures of a Young Man* (1939) by John Dos Passos, and *For Whom the Bell Tolls* (1940) by Ernest Hemingway, as well as Pablo Picasso's painting *Guernica* (1937) and

Despite the repressive policies of Generalissimo Francisco Franco (pictured) and the deterioration of cultural life during the Spanish Civil War, a new body of literature reacting to the sociopolitical turmoil eventually emerged. Mansell/Time & Life Pictures/Getty Images

Robert Capa's photograph *Death of a Loyalist Soldier, Spain* (1936).

EFFECT ON THE NOVEL

The Civil War drove into political exile some promising novelists whose narrative art matured abroad. Max Aub analyzed the civil conflict in the artistically and thematically impressive cycle of novels *El laberinto mágico* (1943–68; "The Magic Labyrinth"). Ramón José Sender, whose pre–Civil War novels had been realistic and overtly sociopolitical, developed an interest in the mysterious and irrational. While *Crónica del alba* (1942–66; "Chronicle of the Dawn"), a series of novels, dwelt realistically on the Civil War, the magical, myth-dominated worlds of

Epitalamio del prieto Trinidad (1942; *Dark Wedding*) and *Las criaturas saturnianas* (1968; "Saturnine Beings") reflected more universal concerns. Prolific, tendentious, opinionated, and arbitrary, Sender produced some 70 novels of unequal quality, the most esteemed being *Mosén Millán* (1953; later published as *Réquiem por un campesino español*; Eng. trans. *Requiem for a Spanish Peasant*). After more than three decades in exile, Sender returned to Spain to a hero's welcome from younger compatriots.

The diplomat, legal scholar, and critic Francisco Ayala showed a youthful vanguardism early in his career; in later short stories (the collections *Los usurpadores* [1949; "*Usurpers*"] and *La cabeza del cordero* [1949; "The Lamb's Head"]) and novels (*Muertes de perro* [1958; *Death as a Way of Life*, 1964] and its sequel *El fondo del vaso* [1962; "In the Bottom of the Glass"]), he cultivated themes that allowed him to obliquely re-create aspects of the Civil War as well as to address more-universal social concerns. These works offer devastating appraisals of the Spanish political scene from multiple perspectives and with complex narrative techniques. Considered by some to be the best prose writer of his era in the Spanish language, Ayala has published many volumes of essays on philosophy, pedagogy, sociology, and political theory.

The Civil War decimated Spanish intellectuals, artists, and writers, and the country's culture went into decline, uninterrupted by a brief spate of *triunfalismo* ("triumphalism") that lasted through the 1940s, when the victorious Falange, the Spanish Fascist party, engaged in propagandistic self-glorification. *Triunfalismo's* literary expression produced works that were monothematic and repetitive and that insulted the vanquished, showing them as animals. Psychologically perceptive despite its violence, *La familia de Pascual Duarte* (1942; *The Family of Pascual*

Duarte) of Camilo José Cela popularized a harsh, sordid, unsentimental realism (tempered by expressionistic distortion) known as *tremendismo*. Continuing his literary experimentation, Cela attained greater technical heights in *La colmena* (1951; *The Hive*), portraying divided Madrid society during the harsh winter of 1941–42. By his death, in 2002, Cela—who won the Nobel Prize for Literature in 1989—had published by his own count more than 100 books, including a dozen novels, numerous story collections, travel books, critical essays, poetry, and literary sketches. Joining Cela in reviving Spanish fiction during the 1940s was Carmen Laforet, whose *Nada* (1945, "Nothing"; Eng. trans. *Andrea*), with its bewildered adolescent's perspective of war's aftermath, became an instant best seller.

The sociopolitical trauma of civil conflict with its cultural and economic uncertainty revived outmoded forms of realism. Conservative craftsmen such as Juan Antonio de Zunzunegui and Ignacio Agustí produced conventional realistic novels. José María Gironella scored great popular success with his controversial epic trilogy on the Civil War: *Los cipreses creen en Dios* (1953; *The Cypresses Believe in God*), *Un millón de muertos* (1961; *The Million Dead*), and *Ha estallado la paz* (1966; *Peace After War*).

A second postwar current, "social literature," or "critical realism," arrived with the so-called Mid-century Generation, who were adolescents during the war; it expressed more vigorous, if necessarily covert, opposition to the dictatorship. In such works as *La hoja roja* (1959; "The Red Leaf"), which examines poverty and loneliness among the elderly, and *Las ratas* (1962; "Rats"; Eng. trans. *Smoke on the Ground*), which depicts the miserable existence of uneducated cave dwellers, Miguel Delibes conveyed critical concern for a society whose natural values are under constant threat. Greater technical expertise and thematic originality are evinced in his *Cinco horas con Mario* (1966; "Five Hours with Mario"), a powerful novel wherein domestic conflict represents contending ideologies in the Civil War, and *Parábola del náufrago* (1969; "Parable of the Shipwrecked Man"), which examines the individual's plight in a dehumanized technocracy. A publisher, lawyer, teacher, and journalist, Delibes was the author of more than 50 volumes of novels, memoirs, essays, and travel and hunting books and received the prestigious Cervantes Prize in 1993. *El hereje* (1998; The *Heretic*), perhaps his masterpiece, depicts the abuse of power by the Spanish Inquisition.

Elena Quiroga, a conscientious stylist, experimented with varying forms and themes, employing a dead protagonist in *Algo pasa en la calle* (1954; "Something's Happening in the Street") to examine domestic conflict aggravated by Franco's outlawing of divorce. Quiroga's novels typically portrayed women and children. Her crowning achievement is the novelistic cycle of *Tadea: Tristura* (1960; "Sadness"), *Escribo tu nombre* (1965; "I Write Your Name"), and *Se acabó todo, muchacha triste* ("It's All Over Now, Baby Blue"), begun in the late 1960s but left unfinished at Quiroga's death in 1995. The cycle portrays the difficulties of growing up female under Franco through the character Tadea, the novels' protagonist. In 1983 Quiroga became the second woman elected to the Royal Spanish Academy. Social realism also characterizes the largely testimonial, semiautobiographical novels of Dolores Medio, who frequently depicted working girls, schoolteachers, and aspiring writers as positive feminine role models opposing the dictatorship's discouragement of education for women: *Nosotros los Rivero* (1952; "We Riveros"), *El pez sigue flotando* (1959; "The Fish Stays Afloat"), *Diario de una maestra* (1961; "A Schoolteacher's Diary").

Often deprived of access to 19th-century realist and naturalist models, some post–Civil War writers reinvented these modes. Others more closely followed (usually via translations) the Italian Neorealists or the theories of Hungarian critic György Lukács in his *The Historical Novel* (1955). The Spanish Neorealistic variants with their testimonial thrust subjected aesthetic considerations to their content, exhibiting the pedestrian style, simplistic techniques, and repetitive themes traditionally attributed to engagé (socially committed) literature.

During the 1950s, several competent, committed younger novelists strengthened intellectual dissent. Ana María Matute, among the most honoured novelists of her generation, typically employed lyric and expressionistic style with fictions set in mountainous areas of Old Castile, as in *Los hijos muertos* (1958; *The Lost Children*), which sought to reconcile war-born hatreds by showing irreparable losses on both sides. Her trilogy *Los mercaderes* ("The Merchants")—*Primera memoria* (1959; *School of the Sun*, also published as *The Awakening*), *Los soldados lloran de noche* (1964; *Soldiers Cry by Night*), and *La trampa* (1969; *The Trap*)—divides humanity into heroes (considered idealists and martyrs) and merchants (motivated only by money). Matute's greatest popular success, *Olvidado rey Gudú* (1996; "Forgotten King Gudú"), is an antiwar statement disguised as a neochivalric adventure.

Juan Goytisolo, long an expatriate in France and Morocco, moved from an impassive, cinematographic style in his fiction of the 1950s and early 1960s to New Novel experimentalism in his Mendiola trilogy—*Señas de identidad* (1966; *Marks of Identity*), *Reivindicación del conde don Julián* (1970; *Count Julian*), and *Juan sin tierra* (1975; *Juan the Landless*)—all filled with literary borrowings, shifting narrative perspectives, nonlinear chronology, neo-Baroque complexities of plot, and an emphasis upon language rather than action. His brother Luis Goytisolo, a novelist and short-story writer, dissected the Catalan bourgeoisie and chronicled Barcelona's history from the war through the Franco years. His most significant accomplishment, his tetralogy *Antagonía*, comprises *Recuento* (1973; "Recounting"), *Los verdes de mayo hasta el mar* (1976; "May's Greenery as Far as the Sea"), *La cólera de Aquiles* (1979; "The Rage of Achilles"), and *Teoría del conocimiento* (1981; "Theory of Knowledge"), which reveal him as a consummate practitioner of metafiction, pushing the limits of the self-conscious novel while destroying Francoist myths and creating new, liberating ones.Rafael Sánchez Ferlosio's *El Jarama* (1956; "The Jarama"; Eng. trans. *The One Day of the Week*), masterfully utilizing pseudoscientific impassivity and cinematographic

The work of Juan Goytisolo (centre, seated with Carlos Fuentes, left, and Gabriel García Márquez in 2004) evolved from Neorealism to avant-gardism through his use of structuralist and formalist techniques. © AP Images

techniques, depicts the monotonous existence of urban youth via their aimless conversations and exposes postwar apathy. Other young writers who first emerged in the 1950s were Jesús Fernández Santos, Juan García Hortelano, Jesús López Pacheco, and Daniel Sueiro.

By the 1960s, gray, pedestrian critical realism had run its course. Luis Martín-Santos broke the mold with his epoch-making *Tiempo de silencio* (1962; *Time of Silence*), which revisited the familiar topic of life in post–Civil War Spain via conscious artistry, psychoanalytic perspectives, and narrative techniques—such as stream of consciousness and interior monologue—that echoed James Joyce. Had Martín-Santos not died at age 39, Spanish fiction in the 1970s and 1980s might have reached greater heights.

Ignacio Aldecoa was the most gifted short-story writer of his generation and among the most talented exponents of objectivism with his novels *Gran sol* (1957; "Great Sole") and *Parte de una historia* (1967; "Part of a Story"). Significant innovation appears in Juan Benet Goitia, a novelist, critic, dramatist, and short-story writer whose *Volverás a Región* (1967; "You Will Return to Región") combined density of form, myth and allegory presented in tangled neo-Baroque syntax and lexicon, and scathing sarcasm. These features were typical of the numerous subsequent novels of his Región series. Described in minute topographical detail, Benet's Región is an area that resembles Spain's northern mountains, perhaps León. It is isolated, almost inaccessible, and terribly provincial; critics have seen it as a microcosm of Spain. Preferring British and American paradigms that devoted more attention to style, subjectivity, and psychological narrative than did the dominant trends in Spanish literature of the period, Benet condemned *costumbrismo* and social realism as unimaginative.

Carmen Martín Gaite, a gifted observer of contemporary mores and a methodical observer of gender roles and conflicts, portrayed the constraints upon women in patri-archal societies. Her novels, from *Entre visillos* (1958; *Behind the Curtains*) to *El cuarto de atrás* (1978; *The Back Room*) and *La reina de las nieves* (1994; "Snow Queen"; Eng. trans. *The Farewell Angel*), trace the consequences of social conditions in Franco society on individuals. She also documented these conditions in essays such as *Usos amorosos de la post-guerra española* (1987; *Courtship Customs in Postwar Spain*), which describes the ideological indoctrination to which the Falange subjected girls and young women.

Although he published his first novel in 1943, Gonzalo Torrente Ballester came to prominence only in the 1970s. He moved from Joycean models to realism to fantasy before achieving astounding success with his metaliterary, postmodern romps *La saga/fuga de J.B.* (1972; "J.B.'s Flight and Fugue") and *Fragmentos de apocalipsis* (1977; "Fragments of Apocalypse"). He received the Cervantes Prize in 1985.

Established writers of the Franco era—Cela, Delibes, Matute, Martín Gaite, Torrente, the Goytisolos—contin-ued producing until the new millennium, nearly all evolving and reflecting the impact of postmodernism, with some writing in the New Novel mode. José Jiménez Lozano investigates Inquisitorial repression, recondite religious issues, and esoteric historical themes drawn from a variety of cultures in such novels as *Historia de un otoño* (1971; "History of Autumn") and *El sambenito* (1972; "The Saffron Tunic"). He received the Cervantes Prize in 2002, as had Delibes (1993) and Cela (1995) before him. Francisco Umbral, a prolific journalist, novelist, and essayist often compared to 17th-century satirist Francisco Gómez de Quevedo y Villegas for his style and to 19th-century jour-nalist Mariano José de Larra for his biting critiques of contemporary society, won the Cervantes Prize in 2000.

The Generation of 1968 was recognized in the 1980s as a distinct novelistic group. It includes Esther Tusquets,

Álvaro Pombo, and Javier Tomeo, together with nearly a dozen others who belong to this group chronologically if not by reason of aesthetic or thematic similarities. Tusquets is best known for a trilogy of thematically related but independent novels: *El mismo mar de todos los veranos* (1978; *The Same Sea As Every Summer*), *El amor es un juego solitario* (1979; *Love Is a Solitary Game*), and *Varada tras el último naufragio* (1980; "Beached After the Last Shipwreck"; Eng. trans. *Stranded*), all of which explore the solitude of middle-aged women and their deceptions in love. Pombo, originally known as a poet, turned later to the novel. *El metro de platino iradiado* (1990; "The Metre of Irradiated Platinum") is considered by many his masterpiece. He was elected to the Spanish Academy in 2004. Tomeo is an Aragonese essayist, dramatist, and novelist whose works, with their strange, solitary characters, emphasize that "normal" is but a theoretical concept. His novels include *Amado monstruo* (1985; Dear Monster) and *Napoleón VII* (1999). He is also known for his short stories, anthologized in *Los nuevos inquisidores* (2004; "The New Inquisitors").

THEATRE

Post–Civil War Spain suffered no lack of skillful playwrights to provide politically acceptable entertainment. Edgar Neville, José López Rubio, Víctor Ruiz Iriarte, Miguel Mihura, and Alfonso Paso added variety to the ingenious, parodic farces of Enrique Jardiel Poncela and the soul-searching dramas of Alejandro Casona and Joaquín Calvo Sotelo. The period's most significant dramatist was Antonio Buero Vallejo, a former political prisoner; *Historia de una escalera* (1949; *The Story of a Stairway*), a symbolic social drama, marks the rebirth of Spanish theatre after the war. Subtle and imaginative, Buero used myth, history, and contemporary life as dramatic metaphors to explore and critique society in such works as *En la ardiente oscuridad* (1950; *In the Burning Darkness*), *Un soñador para un pueblo* (1958; "A Dreamer for a People"), and *El concierto de San Ovidio* (1962; *The Concert at Saint Ovide*, 1967). Later works exhibit increased philosophical, political, and metaphysical concerns: *Aventura en lo gris* (1963; "Adventure in Gray"), *El tragaluz* (1967; "The Skylight"), *El sueño de la razón* (1970; *The Sleep of Reason*), and *La fundación* (1974; *The Foundation*). Written in the 1960s, *La doble historia del doctor Valmy* ("The Double Case History of Doctor Valmy") was performed in Spain for the first time in 1976; the play's political content made it too controversial to stage there during Franco's rule.

Alfonso Sastre rejected Buero's formula, preferring more-direct Marxist approaches to social problems, but censors prohibited many of his dramas. A dramatic theorist and existentialist, Sastre in his works presents individuals ensnared in Kafkaesque bureaucratic structures, struggling but failing while the struggle itself endures and advances (as exemplified in *Cuatro dramas de la revolución* [1963; "Four Revolutionary Dramas"]). Sastre's first major production, *Escuadra hacia la muerte* (1953; *Death Squad*), a disturbing Cold War drama, presents soldiers who have been accused of "unpardonable" offenses and condemned to stand guard in a no-man's-land where they await the advance of an unknown enemy and face almost certain death. Other plays demonstrate the socially committed individual's duty to sacrifice personal feeling for the sake of revolution (*El pan de todos* [1957; "*The Bread of All*"], *Guillermo Tell tiene los ojos tristes* [1960; *Sad Are the Eyes of William Tell*]).

Sastre's plays are examples of the social realism practiced by the Grupo Realista (Realist Group) during the 1950s and 1960s. Epitomizing this group's realist style is Lauro Olmo's *La camisa* (1962; *The Shirt*), which depicts unemployed workers too poverty-stricken to seek employment because doing so requires a clean shirt. Like the social novel, social theatre featured generic or collective protagonists, economic injustices, and social-class conflicts, their depictions calculated to suggest Franco's responsibility for the exploitation and suffering of the underprivileged. Carlos Muñiz Higuera's plays convey social protests via expressionist techniques. His *El grillo* (1957; "The Cricket") portrays the plight of an office worker who is perpetually overlooked for promotion, and *El tintero* (1961; "The Inkwell") depicts a humble office worker driven to suicide by a dehumanized bureaucracy. Muñiz Higuera depicts individuals who must adapt to dominant reactionary values or be destroyed; his work recalls Valle-Inclán's *esperpento* manner and German playwright Bertolt Brecht's epic theatre.

Other exponents of social-protest theatre include José Martín Recuerda, whose subject matter is hypocrisy, cruelty, and repression in Andalusian towns and villages, and José María Rodríguez Méndez, a novelist, story writer, essayist, and critic whose dramas expose the plight of common people, especially the youth, portrayed as victims (soldiers recruited to serve as cannon fodder, students forced to compete in sordid and degrading conditions for posts in a dehumanizing system). Long-censored members of the Realist Group were compared to contemporaneous British playwrights and novelists called the Angry Young Men.

The Silenced Group, also called the Underground Theatre (Teatro Subterráneo), includes playwrights repeatedly censored under Franco and avoided thereafter by the theatrical establishment for their radically subversive political allegories questioning the legitimacy of power, capitalism, and other "contemporary fundamentals." Their extravagant farces and mordant satires demythologized Spain and its "glorious" past. This group includes Antonio Martínez Ballesteros, Manuel Martínez Mediero, José Ruibal, Eduardo Quiles, Francisco Nieva, Luis Matilla, and Luis Riaza.

Antonio Gala, a multitalented, original, and commercially successful playwright, debunked historical myths while commenting allegorically on contemporary Spain via expressionistic humour and comedy. Jaime Salom, like Gala, defies ideological classification. His psychological drama of the Spanish Civil War, *La casa de las Chivas* (1968; "House of the Chivas"), holds Madrid box-office records. His later works pose political, social, or religious questions; *La piel del limón* (1976; "Bitter Lemon"), a plea for divorce reform, was among the longest-running plays of the 1970s. Salom is often compared to Buero Vallejo and American playwright Arthur Miller. The most important woman dramatist of the last decades of the 20th century, Ana Diosdado, gained national recognition with *Olvida los tambores* (1970; "Forget the Drums"). Other woman dramatists are Paloma Pedrero, Pilar Enciso, Lidia Falcón, Maribel Lázaro, Carmen Resino, and María Manuela Reina.

Some relaxation of censorship in the 1960s prompted interest in the Theatre of the Absurd, its main exponent in Spain being longtime expatriate Fernando Arrabal, a playwright, novelist, and filmmaker who has drawn some of the raw material for his works from his traumatic childhood. Critics have identified a violent resentment of his conservative, pro-Franco mother and innumerable Freudian complexes in Arrabal's plays, and his childlike characters—both innocent and criminal, tender and sadistic, all existing within a Kafkaesque atmosphere—afford these plays enormous individuality. Using black humour and grotesque and Surrealist elements, Arrabal creates nightmarish works.

Antonio Gala mastered the art of allegory on his way to becoming a successful and well-received playwright. Alberto Paredes/Hulton Archive/ Getty Images

Following Franco's death, several new, younger dramatists gained recognition in the 1980s. Acclaimed by critics
and audiences alike were Fernando Fernán Gómez, Fermín
Cabal, and Luis Alonso de Santos. Replete with intertextual references and cinematographic staging techniques,
these playwrights' works treat contemporary problems
but approach them more playfully than their socially committed predecessors. Other playwrights who emerged in
the closing years of the 20th century include Miguel
Romeo Esteo, Francisco Rojas Zorrilla, Angel García
Pintado, Marcial Suárez, Jerónimo López Mozo, Domingo
Miras, and Alberto Miralles.

POETRY

The Civil War and its traumatic aftermath prompted the
abandonment of pure poetry for simpler approaches.
Formal discipline, devotion to clarity through direct imagery, and a reduced vocabulary were stressed, and the social
and human content increased. Leaders of postwar *poesía
social* (social poetry) are sometimes referred to as a "Basque
triumvirate": Gabriel Celaya, a prewar Surrealist who
became a leading spokesman for the opposition to Franco;
Blas de Otero, an existentialist writing in the vein of
Antonio Machado's *Campos de Castilla*; and Ángela Figuera,
a teacher, writer of children's stories, feminist, and social
activist, best known for poetry celebrating women and
motherhood and denouncing the abuse of women and
children.

"Social" poets shared utilitarian views of their art:
poetry became a tool for changing society, the poet being
merely another worker struggling toward a better future.
These altruistic writers renounced artistic experimentation and aesthetic gratification in favour of propagandistic
goals, sociological themes, and authorial self-effacement.

Some describe poetry's trajectory during this period from "pure" to "social" as a move from yo to nosotros ("I" to "we"), from personal to collective concerns. Aleixandre and Alonso, survivors of the Generation of 1927, wrote poetry in the social vein after the Civil War, as did Jesús López Pachecho and many younger poets.

Yet, notwithstanding the predominance of social poetry during the 1950s and '60s, many important poets—such as Luis Felipe Vivanco and Luis Rosales—did not share its concerns, and social poetry as a movement suffered desertions even before the much-publicized launching of the novísimos in 1970. Some, such as Vicente Gaos and Gloria Fuertes, preferred existential emphases. Others made poetry an epistemological inquiry or method, including Francisco Brines, Jaime Gil de Biedma, and José Ángel Valente.

The "newest" poets (novísimos)—among them Pere Gimferrer, Antonio Colinas, Leopoldo Panero, and Manuel Vázquez Montalbán—rejected social engagement, preferring experimental modes from Surrealism to camp. Their poetry, often neo-Baroque, self-consciously cosmopolitan, and intertextual, was a late 20th-century variant of *culteranismo*; it emphasized museums, foreign films, international travel—anything but contemporary Spain with its problems. Paralleling the New Novel of the 1970s, they cultivated language for its own sake and showcased their individuality and culture, abandoning social poetry's authorial invisibility.

Among poets who gained prominence after Franco are Guillermo Carnero, whose work is characterized by a plethora of cultural references and centred upon the theme of death; Jaime Siles, whose abstract, reflexive poetry belongs to Spain's so-called *poesía de pensamiento* ("poetry of thought"); and Luis Antonio de Villena, an outspoken representative of Spain's gay revolution. Prominent women poets during the closing decades of the 20th century include María Victoria Atencia, known for poetry inspired by domestic situations, for her cultivation of the themes of art, music, and painting, and for her later existentialist contemplations; Pureza Canelo, known especially for her ecological poetry and feminist volumes; Juana Castro; Clara Janés; and Ana Rossetti, noteworthy for her erotic verse.

CHAPTER 3

CATALAN AND GALICIAN LITERATURE

C atalan (Catalan: Català) is a Romance language spoken in eastern and northeastern Spain, chiefly in
Catalonia and Valencia. It is also spoken in the Roussillon
region of France, in Andorra, and in the Balearic Isles. The
official language of the kingdom of Aragon in the 12th
century, Catalan has a literary tradition dating from that
period. The earliest written materials date from the 12th
century. In the late 20th century, as Catalonia achieved
greater autonomy, Catalan revived as the principal language of politics and education, as well as of public life in
general, in Catalonia.

Linguistically, there are two main dialect groups in
modern Catalan: Occidental, subdivided into West
Catalan and Valencian; and Oriental, subdivided into East
Catalan, Balearic, and Roussillonnais and including the
dialect spoken in Alghero, Sardinia, where Catalan was
introduced in the 14th century. (After the end of the
Spanish Civil War, politically motivated disputes as to
whether Valencian and Catalan are distinct languages or
variants of the same language occurred within Spain,
becoming especially bitter in the late 20th century. The
Valencian community fiercely promoted the Valencian
language, while much of Catalonia considered the
Valencian language a dialect of Catalan.) These various
dialects differ only in minor respects (details of

pronunciation, vocabulary, and verb conjugation) and are easily mutually intelligible. The dialectal differences are not usually reflected in the written language.

Catalan is most closely related to the Occitan language of southern France and to Spanish, but it is clearly distinct from both. It differs from Spanish in the following characteristics: a lack of rising diphthongs (such as *ie* and *ue*, as in compare Catalan *be* and Spanish *bien* "well," Catalan *bo* and Spanish *bueno* "good") and an abundance of falling diphthongs (such as *eu, au, ou,* as in compare Catalan *peu* and Spanish *pie* "foot," Catalan *bou* and Spanish *buey* "ox"). Catalan also retains the sounds *j* (pronounced like French *j* or the *z* in English "azure"), *z, tj* (pronounced like English *j*), *tz,* and *x* (pronounced like English *sh*); none of these consonants occur in modern Spanish. Catalan stresses certain verbs on the root rather than on the infinitive ending, as in Spanish (Catalan *VENdre,* Spanish *venDER* "to sell"). Catalan differs from Occitan less than from Spanish but often uses different vowel sounds and diphthongs and also has somewhat different grammatical conventions.

The close relationship between Catalan and Occitan is reflected in the origins of the body of written works known as Catalan literature, which has its roots in medieval Occitan.

MEDIEVAL PERIOD

The earliest Catalan literature can be traced to poetic forms cultivated by the troubadours, who dominated the courts of southern France, northern Spain, and northern Italy from the 11th through the 13th century. The early Catalan troubadours Guillem de Bergadà, Hug de Mataplana, and Guillem de Cervera were genuine Provençal poets. In the 14th century the influence of the

troubadours began to lessen, and Catalan poets turned to
northern France for inspiration. They took over the long
French narratives based on romance themes, such as the
Arthurian cycle, and wrote in octosyllabic rhymed cou-
plets (called *noves rimades* ["rhymed news"]).

In 1393 King John I of Aragon created a poetic academy in Barcelona, where he inaugurated a series of poetry
competitions called *jocs florals* ("floral games"). Prizes
named after flowers were awarded yearly to poems by a

*A statue in Palma de Mallorca, Spain, commemorates Catalan mystic and
poet Ramon Llull (1232/33–1315/16), whose writings contributed significantly
to the development of the Catalan language.* © Travel Library Limited/
SuperStock

kind of learned society called the Consistori del Gai Saber ("Consistory of the Gay Science"), the main aim of which was the preservation of the language and style of trouba-dour poetry. This groundwork would make the 15th century the great period of Catalan poetry. After John's death, in 1395, his successors Martin I and Ferdinand I continued to encourage poetry and helped to emancipate Catalan literary style from foreign influences. As the 15th century advanced, Valencia emerged as a new centre of lit-erary activity.

The influence of the *cants d'amor* ("songs of love") and *cants de mort* ("songs of death") of Ausias March, consid-ered by some the finest poems ever written in Catalan, extended to 16th-century Castile and beyond. Jaume Roig's *Spill o llibre de les dones* (c. 1460; "The Mirror or Book of Women"), a caustic satire of more than 16,000 lines, offers a vivid portrait of contemporary Valencian life. Another Valencian writer, Joan Roiç de Corella, is perhaps the best representative of the Renaissance.

After the union of Aragon with Castile in 1479, which unified Spain and ended Catalonia's independence, the Castilian dialect of the Spanish language predominated throughout Spain, spelling a long eclipse of Catalan litera-ture. Juan Boscán was emblematic of the status of Catalan literature during this period. Catalan by birth—he was born in Barcelona—he wrote solely in Castilian and inau-gurated a new school of poetry in that dialect. By the time his works were published in 1543, a year after his death, Catalan poetry had been all but dormant for 50 years.

Literary prose emerged with the *Homilies d'Organyà* (12th- or 13th-century homilies found in the parish of Organyà in the county of Urgell) but did not flourish until the end of the 13th century. Four great chronicles, together with the works of Ramon Llull, represent the peak of medieval Catalan prose. The anonymous chronicle *Llibre dels feyts del rey en Jacme* ("Book of the Deeds of King James"), compiled after James I's death in 1276 but purportedly autobiographical, is distinguished by its skill of narration and its quality of language.

The same qualities are present in Ramon Muntaner's chronicle, which combines accounts of the Grand Catalan Company's expedition to the Morea in southern Greece, of the failed French invasion of Catalonia, and of King James II's conquest of Sardinia. Bernat Desclot's chronicle deals with the reign of King Peter III; King Peter IV planned and revised the last of the four great chronicles.

Llull's encyclopaedic works, written in Catalan, Arabic, and Latin, cover every branch of medieval knowledge. His exhaustive theological treatise *Llibre de contemplació en Déu* (*c.* 1272; "Book of the Contemplation of God") begins the golden age of Catalan literature; it also provides a wealth of information on 13th-century Catalan society. His *Llibre d'Evast e Blanquerna* (*c.* 1284; "Book of Evast and Blanquerna") is the founding text of Catalan fiction. Known as *Blanquerna*, it is the narrative of the lives of Blanquerna and his parents, Evast and Aloma, whose marriage comes to represent an ideal Christian marriage; successive chapters tell of stages in the life of Blanquerna, who ascends from altar boy to the papacy but then abandons his throne to enter monastic life. The narrative aims at representing all aspects of Christian existence. It includes the *Llibre d'amic e amat* (*The Book of the Lover and the Beloved*), a masterpiece of Christian mysticism. Llull's *Llibre de l'orde de cavalleria* (between 1275 and 1281; *The Book of the Order of Chivalry*) and *Félix* (*c.* 1288) are didactic works in a narrative framework.

Bernat Metge translated Giovanni Boccaccio's story of Griselda from Petrarch's Latin version and, clothing his scholastic learning with poetic imagination, achieved the stylistic masterpiece of early Catalan prose. Metge also wrote *Lo somni* (*c.* 1409; *The Dream of Bernat Metge*) in the tradition of medieval fantasy literature; the narrator converses with mythological characters and with the dead John I, who, from purgatory, exculpates Metge. The chivalric romance *Tirant lo Blanc* (*c.* 1460; Eng. trans. *Tirant lo Blanc*) by Joanot Martorell and Martí Joan de Galba offers a fictional treatment of Catalan exploits in the Middle East. The anonymous *Curial e Güelfa* (late 14th century; Eng. trans. *Curial and Guelfa*) draws on Desclot, the only other Catalan romance to do so.

The beginnings of Catalan drama were represented by a 15th-century mystery play, *Misteri d'Elx* ("Mystery of Elx"), which through the turn of the 21st century was performed annually in Spain at Elche (Elx), near Valencia, on the Feast of the Assumption.

DECLINE: 16TH–18TH CENTURY

With the use of Catalan in decline, the 16th century produced only a single major poet working in Catalan, Pere Serafí, who wrote *Cants d'amor* (1565) in imitation of March. In prose, only scholars—chiefly antiquaries and historians—still wrote in Catalan. The abundantly documented *Crònica universal del principat de Catalunya* ("Universal Chronicle of the Principality of Catalonia"), a history of the Catalan kingdom, was the result of 40 years of research by Jeroni Pujadas, although only the first part (1609) is in Catalan. Thereafter literature in Catalan was limited chiefly to folk songs and ballads, which were first collected in *Romancerillo catalán* (1853; "Little Collection of Catalan Ballads") by Manuel Milà i Fontanals, who played a considerable part in the Catalan revival of the 19th century.

THE RENAIXENÇA

In 1813 appeared the *Gramatica y apología de la llengua catha-lana* ("Grammar and Apology of the Catalan Language") of Josep Pau Ballot; its publication heralded the Renaixença ("Rebirth"), the literary and linguistic renaissance that characterized the Romantic period in Catalonia. Bonaventura Carles Aribau's *La pàtria* (1833; "The Fatherland") and the poems of Joaquim Rubió i Ors and Víctor Balaguer prepared the way for Jacint Verdaguer, a great epic poet (*L'Atlántida* [1877], *Canigó* [1886]) whose creativity served to renew literary Catalan. Verdaguer also wrote lyric and mystic verse. Miquel Costa i Llobera culti-vated classical perfection in poetic form. Joan Maragall, Catalonia's first great modern poet, exerted a powerful influence on later poets.

MODERNISME AND NOUCENTISME

A movement known as Modernisme followed the Renaixença. Like similar movements in Europe and the Americas, Modernisme was preoccupied with naturalistic depictions of society, particularly of the rural world. The best-known examples of *modernista* fiction include *Els sots feréstecs* (1901; "The Wild Glens") by Raimon Casellas, *La punyalada* (1902–03; "The Knifing") by Marià Vayreda, and *Solitud* (1905; "Solitude") by Víctor Català (pseudonym of Caterina Albert).

Modernisme also manifested itself in Catalan drama at the turn of the 20th century. Playwright Àngel Guimerà, who was closely associated with the Renaixença, incorporated some modernista elements into his most famous play, *Terra baixa* (1896; "Lowlands"; Eng. trans. *Marta of the Lowlands*), a story of social defiance and spiritual regeneration. *Els vells* (1903; "The Old Ones") is among the many social dramas of Ignasi Iglésias, who was inspired by the early works of the German playwright Gerhart Hauptmann. Adrià Gual, author of several works of fantasy, did his best work as director of the Teatre Íntim, founded in Barcelona in 1898, where he oversaw the production of a wide range of drama from around the world.

Noucentisme was both a continuation of and a reaction to Modernisme. Whereas Modernisme had been rural in its focus, Noucentisme was urban; whereas Modernisme was internationalist, Noucentisme attempted to create a uniquely Catalan style. The term Noucentisme—derived from the Catalan word *noucents*, "1900s," and meaning, literally, "1900s-ism"—was created by the essayist Eugeni d'Ors i Rovira. He publicized it, starting in 1906, in a series of short essays that were published in the Barcelona daily newspaper *La Veu de Catalunya* ("The Voice of Catalonia") under the title *Glosari* ("Glosses"). Some of d'Ors's books first appeared in this form, as did his novel *La ben plantada* (1911; "The Stately Woman"). Among the poets associated with Noucentisme are Josep Carner and Guerau de Liost (pseudonym of Jaume Bofill i Mates). Joan Salvat-Papasseit and J.V. Foix broke away from Noucentisme to experiment with European avant-garde forms; such experimentation is best exemplified by Foix's *Sol, i de dol* (1947; "Alone, and in Mourning"), a collection of sonnets on futuristic themes.

Unlike Modernisme, Noucentisme was more strongly tied to political and institutional action. Among the institutions that helped to develop and propagate a uniquely Catalan style was the Institut d'Estudis Catalans (Institute of Catalan Studies), which was founded in Barcelona in 1907 and played an integral role in the orthographic regulation of Catalan throughout the 20th century.

Further develop-
ment of Catalan
literature was delayed
by the dictatorship
(1923–30) of Miguel
Primo de Rivera, who
banned the use of any
language other than
Castilian in Spain, and
by the Spanish Civil War
(1936–39). Many Catalan
intellectuals fled abroad,
and those who remained
found the political cli-
mate hardly conducive
to literary activity
Conditions in Catalonia
remained unfavourable to
writers after the war, with
Gen. Francisco Franco
adopting a repressive policy
toward Catalan culture.
Although some Catalan

Spanish general and dictator Miguel Primo de Rivera, 1928. Catalan literature, which suffered from Primo de Rivera's repressive policies, regained momentum during the latter half of the 20th century. Hulton Archive/Getty Images

writers chose to ignore the prevailing realities and cultivated a literature of artistic escape, the most influential
poets of the mid-20th century, Salvador Espriu and Pere
Quart (pseudonym of Joan Oliver i Sallarès), began writing
poetry that dealt with social issues.

AFTER 1950

Catalan literature gained in vitality during the second half
of the 20th century. Josep Pla and Joan Fuster amassed a
considerable readership for their collections of historical

and biographical essays. The best-known of these are the series of profiles Pla, published in several volumes, beginning in 1958, under the title *Homenots* ("Great Men"). Pla's overall project was to portray Catalan culture through its key protagonists: artists, architects, politicians, scientists, and writers.

Mercè Rodoreda was a Catalan novelist who achieved international critical and popular success during the second half of the 20th century. Her *La plaça del diamant* (1962; *The Time of the Doves*, or *The Pigeon Girl*) tells the story of a working-class woman during the time of the Spanish Civil War. Rodoreda had a great influence on later woman novelists, the best-known of whom was Montserrat Roig, whose *L'òpera quotidiana* (1982; "The Everyday Opera"), built around three interlacing love stories, depicts the social diversity of Barcelona. Llorenç Villalonga's *Bearn* (Eng. trans. *The Dolls' Room*), which first appeared in Castilian translation in 1956 and was published in its original Catalan in 1961, tells the story of an enlightened and impoverished petty nobleman from the island of Majorca. An edition published in 1966 and titled *Bearn; o, la sala de les nines* ("Bearn; or, The Dolls' Room") includes an epilogue that had previously been suppressed by Spanish censors. A series of novels by Baltasar Porcel, beginning with *Cavalls cap a la fosca* (1975; *Horses into the Night*), similarly takes a Majorcan family as its focus.

The generation of writers active in the 1970s experimented with and substantially expanded the traditional boundaries of the Catalan novel. Working under the influence of Latin American novelists publishing during the "boom" of the 1960s and 1970s, Catalan writers were especially interested in exploring the relationship between literature and film. They were also inspired by Pere Calders, a Catalan novelist whose *Ronda naval sota la boira* (1966; "Navy Rounds in the Fog"), a playful experiment in metafiction, found less popular success than did his ironic short stories. Terenci Moix was perhaps the most prominent member of this generation. His gruesome and irreverent novel *Món mascle* (1971; "Male World") is a profound analysis of the contradictions within contemporary society.

Among the poets who followed Foix's avant-garde example was Joan Brossa, who gradually turned to concrete poetry, attempted to bridge the gap separating poetry from sculpture, and began to use film as a means of poetic expression. Among his collections of poetry are *Poesia rasa* (1970; "Plain Poetry") and *Poemes de seny i de cabell* (1977; "Poems of Sense and Hair"). Of the other poets who wrote in Catalan during the second half of the 20th century, the most influential was Gabriel Ferrater. His introspective free verse, gathered in *Les dones i els dies* (1968; "Women and Days"), inspired a number of younger contemporaries, including Francesc Parcerisas (*L'edat d'or, i altres poemes* [1983; *The Golden Age, and Other Poems*]) and Narcís Comadira (*Àlbum de família* [1980; "Family Album"]). The witty verse of David Jou shows an approach much more firmly grounded in traditional forms than most Catalan poetry of the period. The poetry of Pere Gimferrer, who shifted between Catalan and Castilian over the course of his career, shows his erudition and his admiration for T.S. Eliot, notably in *L'espai desert* (1977; "Deserted Space"). In his verse can be traced the disappearance of the lyrical "I" that informs most of his predecessors' work.

Catalan theatre began to revive only in the mid-1970s, after the end of Franco's dictatorship. Although Carner, Espriu, and Oliver wrote for the stage prior to that decade, their work could not be performed before the general public. In Espriu's *Primera història d'Esther* (1948, revised 1966; *The Story of Esther*) the characters take the form of puppets introduced by a narrator. As the Catalan theatre started to recover and perform the work of canonical writers such as Espriu, it also promoted younger playwrights, such as Josep Maria Benet i Jornet and Sergi Belbel. In *Desig* (1991; "Desire"), Benet uses metatheatrical techniques to present a philosophical fable. Over the course of Belbel's comedy *Morir* (1995; "Dying") actors exchange roles as they portray characters in events that seem to lead to their death in the first act, although they are shown to have escaped death in the second act. During the last decades of the 20th century, theatrical troupes such as Els Joglars ("The Jongleurs"), Els Comediants ("The Comedians"), and La Cubana ("The Cuban"), as well as the women's group T de Teatre ("T as in Theatre") and the nonverbal theatre group La Fura dels Baus (a nonsensical phrase), gained international recognition.

At the turn of the 21st century, poetry continued to move away from the forms of personal expression that dominated the middle of the 20th century, and theatre turned increasingly exploratory. Fiction also abandoned the introspective tone and themes of previous decades. Quim Monzó's *Vuitanta-sis contes* (1999; "Eighty-six Stories") includes ironic retellings of folk stories that have a postmodern twist. The American *roman noir*, or "black novel," was a genre brought to Catalan literature in the 1950s by Manuel de Pedrolo; 50 years later it had come to be cultivated as a self-conscious literary exercise. Ferran Torrent's works place him among the noir novelists. His *Cambres d'acer inoxidable* (2000; "Stainless Steel Chambers") dissects contemporary Valencia; the city's social divisions are reflected in the novel's multiple narrators.

Other novelists followed a different trend in which they sought to reconsider historical moments that had been previously ignored or suppressed by government censorship or social taboo. Carme Riera's novel *Dins el darrer blau* (1994; *In the Last Blue*), for instance, is an engrossing blend of voices—religious and secular, learned and rustic, male and female, local and foreign, straight-talking and convoluted—that describe the tension between Jews forced to convert (at least superficially) to Roman Catholicism and those who betray them to the Inquisition in 17th-century Majorca.

Catalan literature, among the strongest of the non-national literatures of Europe, continued to flourish in the 21st century. New novelists such as Alfred Bosch, Ada Castells, and Albert Sánchez Piñol saw their works translated into other European languages. Established poets continued to publish and were joined by new voices, such as David Castillo. The Catalan theatrical scene was most lively in Barcelona, and many works, including novels as well as plays and other works written for the stage, were adapted for Catalan television.

GALICIAN LITERATURE

Galician is closely related to Portuguese, and there is no separating the two languages in the three great repositories of medieval verse, the 14th-century *Cancioneiro* ("Songbook") *da Ajuda, Cancioneiro da Vaticana*, and *Colocci-Brancuti*. Indigenous lyric origins were overlaid by Provençal influence, and a dominance of emotion over thought identified Galician with subjective lyricism, so that for over a century Castilian poets made it their medium for lyrics. Of 116 names in the *Cancioneiro da Vaticana*, 75 have been tentatively identified as Galician; none achieved particular individuality. Macías El Enamorado (flourished mid-14th century) was the last Galician troubadour; Galicians thereafter wrote in

Castilian, and, though there were echoes of their tradition, the Renaissance and Castilian political hegemony finally ended Galician literature until the 19th century.

The Romantic movement, like the Peninsular War, revived local feeling and interest in things Galician but not in the language. The *xogos froraes* ("floral games," or poetry congresses; an equivalent of Catalan and Provençal *jocs florals*) of 1861, with the first dictionary (1863) and first grammar (1864) of Galician, marked a change. Francisco Añón y Paz was the first notable poet in the resurrected idiom, his most stirring notes being love of country and of freedom. Rosalía de Castro, the greatest name in Galician literature, identified herself with the spirit and people of the Galician countryside in *Cantares gallegos* (1863; "Galician Songs"); her *Follas novas* (1880; "New Leaves"), introspective to the verge of despair, reflected deep personal sorrows. Eduardo Pondal y Abente, a bard of a dimly sensed heroic past, was concerned with nature and Celtic mythology. Valentín Lamas Carvajal has been remembered as the voice of the peasant.

Prose showed no comparable achievement. Aurelio Ribalta, Manuel Lugrís Freire, and Heraclio Pérez Placer wrote short stories but were overshadowed by novelists of stature—Emilia, condesa de Pardo Bazán, and Rosalía de Castro—who chose to write for a larger public in Castilian.

The 20th century, especially after 1920, produced an abundance of Galician poets who underlined the identification of Galician literature with a markedly poetic regional temperament and language.

CHAPTER 4

MAJOR SPANISH WRITERS

The following writers represent a selection of the most important creators of literature written in Spanish and produced primarily on the Iberian Peninsula. Presented in alphabetical order, they include novelists, dramatists, poets, and nonfiction writers from the Middle Ages to the 21st century.

LEOPOLDO ALAS

(b. April 25, 1852, Zamora, Spain—d. June 13, 1901, Oviedo)

Leopoldo Alas y Ureña, also known by the byname Clarín, was a novelist, journalist, and the most influential literary critic in late 19th-century Spain. His biting and often-bellicose articles, sometimes called *paliques* ("chitchat"), and his advocacy of liberalism, anticlericalism, and literary naturalism not only made him Spain's most feared critical voice but also created many enemies who later obscured his fame.

After studying law in Madrid, he went to the University of Oviedo in 1870, received his degree, and took a position in the university as professor of law and political economy, a post he held until his death. He published thousands of articles in national magazines and newspapers, through which he cultivated drama, poetry, and fiction. These articles were collected in some 30 volumes, which occasionally mixed articles with short stories, as in *Solos de Clarín* (1881; "Solos of Clarín").

His most important novels, *La regenta* (2 vol., 1884–85; "The Regent's Wife"; Eng. trans. *La Regenta*) and *Su único hijo* (1890; *His Only Son*), are among the greatest Spanish novels of the 19th century. Although often called naturalistic novels, neither adheres to naturalism's scientific principles or its characteristic depiction of sordidness and violence. Where naturalism rejects the spiritual and psychological in favour of behaviouristic observation, Alas's novels avoid emphasis on the physiological; they instead sensitively explore the tormented psyches of a soul in disintegration (*La Regenta*) and of a quester who loses his way (*His Only Son*).

In *La Regenta*, Alas mercilessly depicted the provincial society of Vetusta, an imaginary town modeled upon Oviedo, Spain. The novel dissects decadent Restoration society from the perspective of an outsider, Ana Ozores, sometimes called Spain's Madame Bovary. Isolated by her elderly husband's benign neglect and victimized by Spain's narrow-minded, morally conservative, and misogynist society, she undergoes a spiritual and psychological decline that parallels what Alas perceived to be his country's collective ills and degeneration.

In *His Only Son,* the central character, Bonifacio Reyes, is a weak Romantic dreamer married to a spoiled, domineering, and wealthy woman. He escapes their painful marriage by frequenting theatre and opera groups. Dissatisfied with life, he seeks deeper meaning. The novel's ironic title alludes to doubts about whether his only son was fathered by another while he found solace with actresses. A somewhat enigmatic novel, *His Only Son* moves between scathing satire and gentle reverie.

Alas wrote several outstanding short novels, and he is also considered the father of the modern Spanish short story. His intellectual integrity and ethical preoccupations appear in his wide-ranging collections, which include *Pipá* (1886), *Doña Berta, cuervo, superchería* (1892; "Miss Bertha, Crow, Fraud"), *El señor y lo demás son cuentos* (1893; "God and the Rest Is Fairy Tales"), *Cuentos morales* (1896; *The Moral Tales*), and *El gallo de Sócrates* (1901; "The Rooster of Socrates"), all marked by his characteristic humour and sympathy for the poor, the lonely, and the downtrodden.

AZORÍN

(b. June 8/11, 1873, Monóvar, Spain—d. March 2, 1967, Madrid)

Azorín—the pseudonym of José Martínez Ruiz—was a novelist, essayist, and the foremost Spanish literary critic of his day. He was one of a group of writers who were engaged at the turn of the 20th century in a concerted attempt to revitalize Spanish life and letters. Azorín was the first to identify this group as the Generation of 1898—a name that prevails.

Azorín studied law at Valencia, Granada, and Salamanca, but later he went to Madrid to be a journalist, only to find that his outspokenness closed most doors. He then wrote a trilogy of novels, *La voluntad* (1902; "Volition"), *Antonio Azorín* (1903), and *Las confesiones de un pequeño filósofo* (1904; "The Confessions of a Minor Philosopher"), which are actually little more than impressionistic essays written in dialogue. This trilogy operated with unifying force on the Generation of 1898, however. Animated by a deep patriotism, Azorín tirelessly sought through his work to bring to light what he believed was of lasting value in Spanish culture.

His book *El alma castellana* (1900; "The Castilian Soul") and his essay collections *La ruta de Don Quijote* (1905; "The Route of Don Quixote") and *Una hora de*

España 1560–1590 (1924; *An Hour of Spain, 1560–1590*) carefully and subtly reconstruct the spirit of Spanish life, directing the reader's sensibility by the suggestive power of their prose. Azorín's literary criticism, such as *Al margen de los clásicos* (1915; "Marginal Notes to the Classics"), helped to open up new avenues of literary taste and to arouse a new enthusiasm for the Spanish classics at a time when a large portion of Spanish literature was virtually unavailable to the public. The simplicity of Azorín's style attracted innumerable imitators, all of whom failed to achieve his intellectual subtlety, vitality, and poetic rhythm.

Because he was interested in keeping Spain aware of current foreign thinking, Azorín edited the periodical *Revista de Occidente* ("Magazine of the West") from 1923 to 1936. He spent the period of the Spanish Civil War in Paris, writing for the Argentine newspaper *La Nación,* but he returned to Madrid in 1949. After his death a museum including his library was opened at Monóvar.

ANTONIO BUERO VALLEJO

(b. Sept. 29, 1916, Guadalajara, Spain — d. April 29, 2000, Madrid)

The playwright Antonio Buero Vallejo is considered the most important Spanish dramatist of the post–World War II generation.

Buero Vallejo studied art in Madrid and Guadalajara from 1934 to 1936. During the Civil War, he served as a medical orderly in the Spanish Republican Army. After the war, he was condemned to death by the Nationalists, but the sentence was commuted to imprisonment. He was held in prison for more than six years.

During the 1940s and 1950s, a period known as the "years of silence" in Spain because of the repressive nature of Francisco Franco's regime, Buero Vallejo managed to give a voice to the downtrodden. He won national notice in 1949 with his play *Historia de una escalera* (1950; *History of a Stairway*), for which he was awarded the Lope de Vega, an important literary prize. The play portrays the frustrations of apartment house tenants in a slum in Madrid. His one-act play produced in the same year, *Palabras en la arena* ("Words in the Sand"), which had for its theme adultery and the need for mercy, won the Amigos de los Quinteros Prize; many of his subsequent plays also earned Spanish literary awards.

In *En la ardiente oscuridad* (1951; *In the Burning Darkness*), his second full-length play, a home for the blind stands as a metaphor for society. *La tejedora de sueños* (1952; *The Dream Weaver*, 1967) is based on mythology, and *Irene; o, el tesoro* (1954; "Irene; or, The Treasure") on the fantastic. His basic theme is the yearning for human happiness and the obstacles that frustrate its attainment. In *Hoy es fiesta* (1956; *Today's a Holiday*), Buero Vallejo returned to the slums of Madrid for his ironic and realistic material. His realism echoes the style of Arthur Miller. Buero Vallejo's later writing shows the influence of Bertolt Brecht, whose works he translated.

Buero Vallejo's historical plays were carefully researched. They include *Un soñador para un pueblo* (1958; "A Dreamer for the Nation"), which deals with the failure to modernize Spain under Charles III, *Las meninas* (1960; "The Ladies-in-Waiting"), which is about the court painter Velázquez, and *El concierto de San Ovidio* (1962; *The Concert at Saint Ovide*), which is set in Paris during the French Revolution. *El tragaluz* (1967; *The Basement Window*) deals with the Spanish Civil War. Later works include *El sueño de la razón* (1970; *The Sleep of Reason*) and *La doble historia del Doctor Valmy* (1970; "The Double Life of Doctor Valmy").

In 1971 Buero Vallejo was elected to the Spanish Academy.

CAMILO JOSÉ CELA

(b. May 11, 1916, Iria Flavia, Spain—d. Jan. 17, 2002, Madrid)

The Spanish writer Camilo José Cela Trulock, who won the Nobel Prize for Literature in 1989, is perhaps best known for his novel *La familia de Pascual Duarte* (1942; *The Family of Pascual Duarte*) and is considered to have given new life to Spanish literature. His literary production—primarily novels, short narratives, and travel diaries—is characterized by experimentation and innovation in form and content. Cela is also credited by some critics with having established the narrative style known as tremendismo, a tendency to emphasize violence and grotesque imagery.

Cela attended the University of Madrid before and after the Spanish Civil War (1936–39), during which he served with Franco's army. His first novel, *Pascual Duarte*, established his European reputation. Traditional in form, it was both a popular and a critical success. His second novel, *La colmena* (1951; *The Hive*), with its fragmented chronology and large cast of characters, is an innovative and perceptive story of postwar Madrid. It solidified Cela's critical and popular reputation. Another of his better-known avant-garde novels, *San Camilo*, 1936 (1969), is one continuous stream of consciousness. His later novels include *Cristo versus Arizona* (1988; "Christ Versus Arizona") and the Galician trilogy—*Mazurca para dos muertos* (1983; *Mazurka for Two Dead People*), *La cruz de San Andrés* (1994; *St. Andrew's Cross*), and *Madera de boj* (1999; *Boxwood*).

Cela's acute powers of observation and skill in colourful description also are apparent in his travel books, based on his trips through rural Spain and his visits to Latin American countries. The most noted of these are *Viaje a la Alcarría* (1948; *Journey to the Alcarría*), *Del Miño al Bidasoa* (1952; "From the Miño to the Bidasoa"), and *Judíos, moros y cristianos* (1956; "Jews, Moors, and Christians"). He retraced the itinerary of his first travel book for *Nuevo viaje a la Alcarría* (1986). Among his numerous short narratives are *Esas nubes que pasan* (1945; "The Passing Clouds") and the four works included in the collection *El molino de viento, y otras novelas cortas* (1956; "The Windmill and Other Short Fiction"). Cela also wrote essays, poetry, and memoirs and in his later years made frequent television appearances.

In 1955 Cela settled in Majorca, where he founded a well-respected literary review, *Papeles de Son Armadans* (1956–79), and published books in fine editions. He began in 1968 to publish his multivolume *Diccionario secreto*, a compilation of "unprintable" but well-known words and phrases. He became a member of the Spanish Academy in 1957.

MIGUEL DE CERVANTES

(b. Sept. 29?, 1547, Alcalá de Henares, Spain—d. April 22, 1616, Madrid)

The Spanish novelist, playwright, and poet Miguel de Cervantes is best known as the creator of the novel *Don Quixote* (Part I, 1605; Part II, 1615) and the most important and celebrated figure in Spanish literature. *Don Quixote* has been translated, in full or in part, into more than 60 languages. Editions continue to be printed , and critical discussion of the work has proceeded unabated since the 18th century. At the same time, owing to their widespread representation in art, drama, and film, the figures of Don Quixote and Sancho Panza are probably familiar visually to more people than any other imaginary characters in world literature. Cervantes was a great experimenter. He tried his hand in all the major literary genres save the epic. He was a notable short-story writer,

Miguel de Cervantes is arguably the most famous Spanish writer, based largely on his creation of the beloved character Don Quixote. Hulton Archive/Getty Images

and a few of those in his collection of *Novelas exemplares* (1613; Exemplary Stories) attain a level close to that of *Don Quixote*, on a miniature scale.

Miguel de Cervantes Saavedra was born some 20 miles (32 km) from Madrid, probably on September 29 (the day of San Miguel). He was certainly baptized on October 9. He was the fourth of seven children in a family whose origins were of the minor gentry but which had come down in the world. His father was a barber-surgeon who set bones, performed bloodlettings, and attended lesser medical needs. The family moved from town to town, and little is known of Cervantes's early education. The supposition, based on a passage in one of the "Exemplary Stories," that he studied for a time under the Jesuits, though not unlikely, remains conjectural. Unlike most Spanish writers of his time, including some of humble origin, he apparently did not go to a university.

What is certain is that at some stage he became an avid reader of books. The head of a municipal school in Madrid, a man with Erasmist intellectual leanings named Juan López de Hoyos, refers to a Miguel de Cervantes as his "beloved pupil." This was in 1569, when the future author was 21, so—if this was the same Cervantes—he must either have been a pupil-teacher at the school or have studied earlier under López de Hoyos. His first published poem, on the death of Philip II's young queen, Elizabeth of Valois, appeared at this time.

SOLDIER AND SLAVE

That same year he left Spain for Italy. Whether this was because he was the "student" of the same name wanted by the law for involvement in a wounding incident is another mystery; the evidence is contradictory. In any event, in going to Italy, Cervantes was doing what many young Spaniards of the time did to further their careers in one way or another. It seems that for a time he served as chamberlain in the household of Cardinal Giulio Acquaviva in Rome. However, by 1570 he had enlisted as a soldier in a Spanish infantry regiment stationed in Naples, then a possession of the Spanish crown. He was there for about a year before he saw active service.

Relations with the Ottoman Empire under Selim II were reaching a crisis, and the Turks occupied Cyprus in 1570. A confrontation between the Turkish fleet and the naval forces of Venice, the papacy, and Spain was inevitable. In mid-September 1571 Cervantes sailed on board the *Marquesa*, part of the large fleet under the command of Don Juan de Austria that engaged the enemy on October 7 in the Gulf of Lepanto near Corinth. The fierce battle ended in a crushing defeat for the Turks that was ultimately to break their control of the Mediterranean. There are independent accounts of Cervantes's conduct in the action, and they concur in testifying to his personal courage. Though stricken with a fever, he refused to stay below and joined the thick of the fighting. He received two gunshot wounds in the chest, and a third rendered his left hand useless for the rest of his life. He always looked back on his conduct in the battle with pride.

From 1572 to 1575, based mainly in Naples, he continued his soldier's life; he was at Navarino and saw action in Tunis and La Goleta. He must also, when opportunity offered, have been familiarizing himself with Italian literature. Perhaps with a recommendation for promotion to the rank of captain, more likely just leaving the army, he set sail for Spain in September 1575 with letters of commendation to the king from the duque de Sessa and Don Juan himself.

On this voyage his ship was attacked and captured by Barbary corsairs, and Cervantes, together with his brother Rodrigo, was sold into slavery in Algiers, the centre of the Christian slave traffic in the Muslim world. The letters he carried magnified his importance in the eyes of his captors. This had the effect of raising his ransom price, and thus prolonging his captivity, while also, it appears, protecting his person from punishment by death, mutilation, or torture when his four daring bids to escape were frustrated. His masters, the renegade Dali Mami and later Hasan Paşa, treated him with considerable leniency in the circumstances, whatever the reason. At least two contemporary records of the life led by Christian captives in Algiers at this time mention Cervantes. He clearly made a name for himself for courage and leadership among the captive community.

At long last, in September 1580, three years after Rodrigo had earned his freedom, Miguel's family, with the aid and intervention of the Trinitarian friars, raised the 500 gold escudos demanded for his release. It was only just in time, right before Hasan Paşa sailed for Constantinople (now Istanbul), taking his unsold slaves with him. Not surprisingly, this, the most adventurous period of Cervantes's life, supplied subject matter for several of his literary works, notably the Captive's tale in *Don Quixote* and the two Algiers plays, *El trato de Argel* ("The Traffic of Algiers") and *Los baños de Argel* ("The Bagnios [an obsolete word for "prisons"] of Algiers"), as well as episodes in a number of other writings, although never in straight autobiographical form.

CIVIL SERVANT AND WRITER

Back in Spain, Cervantes spent most of the rest of his life in a manner that contrasted entirely with his decade of action and danger. He would be constantly short of money and in tedious and exacting employment; it would be 25 years before he scored a major literary success with *Don Quixote*. On his return home he found that prices had risen and the standard of living for many, particularly those of the middle class, including his family, had fallen. The euphoria of Lepanto was a thing of the past. Cervantes's war record did not now bring the recompense he expected. He applied unsuccessfully for several administrative posts in Spain's American empire. The most he succeeded in acquiring was a brief appointment as royal messenger to Oran, Algeria, in 1581. In vain he followed Philip II and the court to Lisbon in newly annexed Portugal.

About this time he had an affair with a young married woman named Ana de Villafranca (or Ana Franca de Rojas), the fruit of which was a daughter. Isabel de Saavedra, Cervantes's only child, was later brought up in her father's household. Late in 1584 he married Catalina de Salazar y Palacios, 18 years his junior. She had a small property in the village of Esquivias in La Mancha. Little is known about their emotional relationship. There is no reason to suppose that the marriage did not settle down into an adequate companionableness, despite Cervantes's enforced long absences from home.

Neither is there any special reason to suppose that Catalina was an inspiration or a model for characters in the poetry Cervantes was now writing or in his first published fiction, *La Galatea* (1585; *Galatea: A Pastoral Romance*), in the newly fashionable genre of the pastoral romance. The publisher, Blas de Robles, paid him 1,336 reales for it, a good price for a first book. The dedication of the work to Ascanio Colonna, a friend of Acquaviva, was a bid for patronage that does not seem to have been productive. Doubtless helped by a small circle of literary friends, such as the poet Luis Gálvez de Montalvo, the book did bring Cervantes's name before a sophisticated reading public. But the only later editions in Spanish to appear in the author's lifetime were those of Lisbon, 1590, and Paris, 1611. *La Galatea* breaks off in mid-narrative; judging by his repeatedly expressed hopes of writing a sequel, Cervantes evidently maintained a lasting fondness for the work.

Cervantes also turned his hand to the writing of drama at this time, the early dawn of the Golden Age of the Spanish theatre. He contracted to write two plays for the theatrical manager Gaspar de Porras in 1585, one of which, *La confusa* ("Confusion"), he later described as the best he ever wrote. Many years afterward he claimed to have written 20 or 30 plays in this period, which, he noted, were received by the public without being booed off the stage or having the actors pelted with vegetables. The number is vague; only two certainly survive from this time, the historical tragedy of *La Numancia* (1580s; *Numantia: A Tragedy*) and *El trato de Argel* (1580s; "The Traffic of Algiers"). He names nine plays, the titles of a few of which sound like the originals of plays reworked and published years later in the collection *Ocho comedias, y ocho entremeses nuevos* (1615; "Eight Plays and Eight New Interludes").

Fixed theatre sites were just becoming established in the major cities of Spain, and there was an expanding market geared to satisfying the demands of a public ever more hungry for entertainment. Lope de Vega was about to respond to the call, stamping his personal imprint on the Spanish comedia and rendering all earlier drama, including that of Cervantes, old-fashioned or inadequate by comparison. Though destined to be a disappointed dramatist, Cervantes went on trying to get managers to accept his stage works. By 1587 it was clear that he was not going to make a living from literature, and he was obliged to turn in a very different direction.

Cervantes became a commissary of provisions for the great Armada. Requisitioning corn and oil from grudging rural communities was a thankless task, but it was at least a steady job, with a certain status. It took him traveling all over Andalusia, an experience he was to put to good use in his writing. He was responsible for finances of labyrinthine complexity, and the failure to balance his books landed him in prolonged and repeated trouble with his superiors. There also was constant argument with municipal and church authorities, the latter of which more than once excommunicated him. The surviving documentation of the accountancy and negotiations involved is considerable.

After the disastrous defeat of the Armada in 1588, Cervantes gravitated to Sevilla (Seville), the commercial capital of Spain and one of the largest cities in Europe. In 1590 he applied to the Council of the Indies for any one of four major crown posts vacant in Central and South America. His petition was curtly rejected. Wrangles over his accounts and arrears of salary dragged on. He seems to have kept some contact with the literary world; there is a record of his buying certain books, and he must have managed to find time for reading. In 1592 he signed a contract to supply six plays to a theatrical manager, one Rodrigo Osorio. Nothing came of this. His commissary work continued, and the litigation came to a head; in September 1592 he was imprisoned for a few days in Castro del Río.

In 1594 Cervantes was in Madrid seeking a new post. He received an appointment that took him back to Andalusia to collect overdue taxes. Although it was in effect a promotion, the job was no more rewarding than the previous one and was similarly fraught with financial difficulties and confrontations. Cervantes was not by temperament a businessman. Probably by mutual agreement the appointment was terminated in 1596. The previous year he had won first prize (three silver spoons) in a poetry competition in Zaragoza. Back in Sevilla, he likely started seriously writing stories at about this time, not to mention a wickedly satirical sonnet on the conduct of the duque de Medina Sidonia, to be followed by one obliquely disrespectful of the recently deceased king himself. Again he met with financial troubles. In the summer of 1597 discrepancies in his accounts of three years previous landed him in the Crown Jail of Sevilla. He was confined until the end of April 1598 and perhaps conceived there the idea of *Don Quixote*, as a remark in the first prologue suggests:

> *And so, what was to be expected of a sterile and uncultivated wit such as that which I possess if not an offspring that was dried up, shriveled, and eccentric: a story filled with thoughts that never occurred to anyone else, of a sort that might be engendered in a prison where every annoyance has its home and every mournful sound its habitation?*

Information about Cervantes's life over the next four or five years is sparse. He had left Sevilla, and, perhaps for a while in Esquivias and Madrid, later for certain in Valladolid (where the royal court established itself from 1601 to 1606), he must have been writing the first part of *Don Quixote*. Early versions of two of his stories, *Rinconete y Cortadillo* ("Rinconete and Cortadillo") and *El celoso extremeño* ("The Jealous Extremaduran"), found their way into a miscellaneous compilation, unpublished, made by one Francisco Porras de la Cámara.

Publication of *Don Quixote*

In July or August 1604 Cervantes sold the rights of *El ingenioso hidalgo don Quijote de la Mancha* ("The Ingenious Hidalgo Don Quixote of La Mancha," known as *Don*

Quixote, Part I) to the publisher-bookseller Francisco de Robles for an unknown sum. License to publish was granted in September and the book came out in January 1605. There is some evidence of its content's being known or known about before publication—to, among others, Lope de Vega, the vicissitudes of whose relations with Cervantes were then at a low point. The compositors at Juan de la Cuesta's press in Madrid are now known to have been responsible for a great many errors in the text, many of which were long attributed to the author.

The novel was an immediate success, though not as sensationally so as Mateo Alemán's *Guzmán de Alfarache*, Part I, of 1599. By August 1605 there were two Madrid editions, two published in Lisbon, and one in Valencia. There followed those of Brussels, 1607; Madrid, 1608; Milan, 1610; and Brussels, 1611. Part II, *Segunda parte del ingenioso caballero don Quijote de la Mancha* ("Second Part of the Ingenious Knight Don Quixote of La Mancha"), came out in 1615. Thomas Shelton's English translation of the first part appeared in 1612. The name of Cervantes was soon to be as well known in England, France, and Italy as in Spain.

The sale of the publishing rights, however, meant that Cervantes made no more financial profit on Part I of his novel. He had to do the best he could with patronage. The dedication to the young duque de Béjar had been a mistake. He had better fortune with two much more influential persons: the conde de Lemos, to whom he would dedicate Part II and no less than three other works, and Don Bernardo de Sandoval y Rojas, archbishop of Toledo. This eased his financial circumstances somewhat. However, it is apparent that he would have liked a securer place in the pantheon of the nation's writers than he ever achieved during his lifetime—he wanted a reputation comparable to that enjoyed by Lope de Vega or the poet Luis de Góngora, for example. His sense of his own marginal position may be deduced from his *Viage del Parnaso* (1614; *Voyage to Parnassus*), two or three of the later prefaces, and a few external sources. Nevertheless, relative success, still-unsatisfied ambition, and a tireless urge to experiment with the forms of fiction ensured that, at age 57, with less than a dozen years left to him, Cervantes was just entering the most productive period of his career.

No graciousness descended on Cervantes's domestic life. A stabbing incident in the street outside the house in Valladolid, in June 1605, led ridiculously to the whole household's arrest. When they later followed the court to Madrid, he continued to be plagued by litigation over money and now, too, by domestic difficulties. The family lodged in various streets over the next few years before finally settling in the Calle de León.

Like a number of other writers of the day, Cervantes nursed hopes of a secretarial appointment with the conde de Lemos when, in 1610, the conde was made viceroy of Naples; once more Cervantes was disappointed. He had joined a fashionable religious order, the Slaves of the Most Blessed Sacrament, in 1609, and four years later he became a Franciscan tertiary, which was a more serious commitment. Students of Cervantes know, too, of some increased involvement in the literary life of the capital in the form of his attendance at the Academia Selvaje, a kind of writers' salon, in 1612.

The next year, the 12 *Exemplary Stories* were published. The prologue contains the only known verbal portrait of the author:

> *"... of aquiline countenance, with dark brown hair, smooth clear brow, merry eyes and hooked but well-proportioned nose; his beard is silver though it was gold not 20 years ago; large moustache, small mouth with teeth neither big nor little, since he has only six of them and they are in bad condition and*

worse positioned, for they do not correspond to each other; the body between two extremes, neither tall nor short; a bright complexion, more pale than dark, somewhat heavy in the shoulder and not very light of foot."

Cervantes's claim in this prologue to be the first to write original novellas (short stories in the Italian manner) in Castilian is substantially justified. Their precise dates of composition are in most cases uncertain. There is some variety in the collection, within the two general categories of romance-based stories and realistic ones. *El coloquio de los perros* ("Colloquy of the Dogs," Eng. trans. in *Three Exemplary Novels* [1952]), a quasi-picaresque novella, with its frame tale *El casamiento engañoso* ("The Deceitful Marriage"), is probably Cervantes's most profound and original creation next to *Don Quixote*. In the 17th century the romantic stories were the more popular; James Mabbe chose precisely these for the selective English version of 1640. Nineteenth- and 20th-century taste preferred the realistic ones, but by the turn of the 21st century the others were receiving again something like their critical due.

In 1614 Cervantes published *Viage del Parnaso*, a long allegorical poem in mock-mythological and satirical vein, with a postscript in prose. It was devoted to celebrating a host of contemporary poets and satirizing a few others. The author there admitted that writing poetry did not come easily to him. But he held poetry in the highest esteem as a pure art that should never be debased. Having lost all hope of seeing any more of his plays staged, he had eight of them published in 1615, together with eight short comic interludes, in *Ocho comedias, y ocho entremeses nuevos*. The plays show no shortage of inventiveness and originality but lack real control of the medium. The interludes, however, are reckoned among the very best of their kind.

It is not certain when Cervantes began writing Part II of *Don Quixote*, but he had probably not gotten much more than halfway through by late July 1614. About September a spurious Part II was published in Tarragona by someone calling himself Alonso Fernández de Avellaneda, an unidentified Aragonese who was an admirer of Lope de Vega. The book is not without merit, if crude in comparison with its model. In its prologue the author gratuitously insulted Cervantes, who not surprisingly took offense and responded, though with relative restraint if compared with the vituperation of some literary rivalries of the age. He also worked some criticism of Fernández de Avellaneda and his "pseudo" Quixote and Sancho into his own fiction from chapter 59 onward.

Don Quixote, Part II, emerged from the same press as its predecessor late in 1615. It was quickly reprinted in Brussels and Valencia, 1616, and Lisbon, 1617. Parts I and II first appeared in one edition in Barcelona, 1617. There was a French translation of Part II by 1618 and an English one by 1620. The second part capitalizes on the potential of the first, developing and diversifying without sacrificing familiarity. Most people agree that it is richer and more profound.

In his last years Cervantes mentioned several works that apparently did not get as far as the printing press, if indeed he ever actually started writing them. There was *Bernardo* (the name of a legendary Spanish epic hero), the *Semanas del jardín* ("Weeks in the Garden"; a collection of tales, perhaps like Boccaccio's *Decameron*), and the continuation to his *Galatea*. The one that was published, posthumously in 1617, was his last romance, *Los trabaios de Persiles y Sigismunda, historia setentrional* ("The Labours of Persiles and Sigismunda: A Northern Story"). In it Cervantes sought to renovate the heroic romance of adventure and love in the manner of the Aethiopica of

Heliodorus. It was an intellectually prestigious genre destined to be very successful in 17th-century France. Intended both to edify and to entertain, the Persiles is an ambitious work that exploits the mythic and symbolic potential of romance. It was very successful when it appeared; there were eight Spanish editions in two years and French and English translations in 1618 and 1619, respectively.

In the dedication, written three days before he died, Cervantes, "with a foot already in the stirrup," movingly bade farewell to the world. Clear-headed to the end, he seems to have achieved a final serenity of spirit. He died in 1616, almost certainly on April 22, not on the 23rd as had been traditionally thought. The burial certificate indicates that the latter was the day he was buried, in the convent of the Discalced Trinitarians in the Calle de Cantarranas (now the Calle de Lope de Vega). The exact spot is not marked. No will is known to have survived.

DON QUIXOTE AND CRITICAL TRADITIONS

Cervantes's masterpiece *Don Quixote* has been variously interpreted as a parody of chivalric romances, an epic of heroic idealism, a commentary on the author's alienation, and a critique of Spanish imperialism. While the Romantic tradition downplayed the novel's hilarity by transforming Don Quixote into a tragic hero, readers who view it as a parody accept at face value Cervantes's intention to denounce the popular yet outdated romances of his time. *Don Quixote* certainly pokes fun at the adventures of literary knights-errant, but its plot also addresses the historical realities of 17th-century Spain. Although no proof has been found, it is likely that Cervantes was a converso (of Jewish descent), given his father's ties to the medical profession, the family's peripatetic existence, and the government's denial of his two requests for posts in the Indies. However, the author's nuanced irony, his humanistic outlook, and his comic genius contrast notably with the melancholy, didactic tone attributed to many other Spanish converso writers.

Cervantes's strikingly modern narrative instead gives voice to a dazzling assortment of characters with diverse beliefs and perspectives. His inclusion of many differing opinions constitutes a provision called *heteroglossia* ("multiple voices") by the Russian literary critic Mikhail Bakhtin, who deemed it essential to the development of the modern novel. *Don Quixote's* comic edge illustrates another of Bakhtin's concepts, carnivalization, which favours the playfully positive aspects of the body over an ascetic rejection of the carnal. Sancho Panza's rotund shape—his name means "holy belly"—offsets Don Quixote's elongated, emaciated frame, and together they recall the medieval folkloric figures of an expansive, materialist Carnival and a lean, self-denying Lent. Yet, far from depicting illusion and reality as equal opposites, their relationship undergoes constant change: if Don Quixote assumes the lead in Part I, Sancho overtakes his master and secures his own independence in Part II.

The differences between Part I and Part II demonstrate Cervantes's awareness of the power of the printed word. *Don Quixote* history began with his obsessive reading of chivalric romances; in Part II, he realizes that his adventures are eagerly read and discussed by others. The knight's visit in Part II to a Barcelona printing shop, where he finds a spurious Part II in press and denounces it as injurious to the innocent reader and to his own rightful authorship (since he stands to lose royalties from its sales), underscores the cultural and economic impact of books of fiction. Despite his own books' popularity, Cervantes earned little from their sales. Nonetheless, his innovative reworkings of literary forms—from the pastoral novel *La Galatea* and exemplary short stories to the acclaimed novel *Don Quixote* and his one serious attempt at romance, the posthumously published *Persiles y Sigismunda*—show just how well Cervantes understood not only the 17th-century marketplace but the social effect of literature.

Importance and Influence

Cervantes's influence resonates in the popular term "quixotic" and the immediately recognizable forms of his two major protagonists, whose adventures reappear continually across the cultural landscape in theatre, film, opera, ballet, and even comic books. No study of the novel can ignore the author or his most famous work. The Hungarian theorist Gyorgy Lukács considers *Don Quixote* "the first great novel of world literature," while the Mexican author Carlos Fuentes calls Cervantes the "founding father" of Latin American literature. The novel form, according to some late 20th-century critics, has no one origin but began to exist in different countries at different times and for different reasons. Nonetheless, Cervantes's novel, with its innovations to Spanish literature, is outstanding in its creation of a new worldview. It is not coincidental that the writers most influenced by Cervantes—Daniel Defoe, Laurence Sterne, Tobias Smollett, to name only British novelists—initiated radical changes in their own literary traditions.

By illuminating the many differences in and surrounding his world, Cervantes placed in doubt the previous ways of portraying that world, whether those were literary or historical. Indeed, one of Don Quixote's main tenets is that fiction and historical truth are frequently indistinguishable, as both are dependent on the reader's perception.

Cervantes's approach is frequently dubbed "dualistic" since he often opted to express diverse modes of thought through the pairing of opposites, as with Don Quixote and Sancho Panza, the talking dogs of "Colloquy of the Dogs," or the image of the *baciyelmo* ("basinhelmet," as the narrator describes the bright object worn on a distant rider's head). Representing the opposites of reality and illusion, *baciyelmo* is Sancho's brass basin but Don Quixote's gold helmet.

The split depicted *within* Cervantes's characters— Don Quixote's "reasoned unreason," for example—has sometimes been attributed to the author's intended contrast of reality and illusion (as well as of other opposites). The question of whether the self-proclaimed knight stands for an idealism never fully attainable or for a laughably meaningless madness continues to shadow interpretations of *Don Quixote*, as it has since its introduction by the German Romantics. Opposition between idealism and realism as a leading theme in Cervantes's fiction, including the *Exemplary Stories* and his plays, remained influential as late as the mid-20th century.

Yet Cervantes was characteristically ambiguous on these issues, and this ambiguity inspired criticism of the later 20th century to reconsider previous judgments on his literary prominence. Translated almost immediately into English, French, and Italian, *Don Quixote* was viewed primarily as a comic work or a satire of Spanish customs. Ironically, it was the German Romantics, selectively reading Don Quixote as a tragic hero, who granted his author world standing. In contrast, 19th-century Spanish academics dismissed Cervantes's accomplishments, even though his style and language set the standard for modern Castilian. Not until the 20th century did the acclaim of foreign critics and Spanish expatriates finally rehabilitate Cervantes in his own country.

When Freudian psychology became popular, it engendered critical interest in the psychological force of Cervantes's fiction. European criticism was predisposed early on toward psychoanalytical approaches, which stressed the Spanish author's duality and ambiguity. From the 1970s, French and American criticism viewed Cervantes as a fragmented character not unlike his protagonists. Both the author and his characters have been perceived as psychoanalytical cases, with Don Quixote's madness attributed to his "middle-age crisis" and Cervantes's treatment of several characters to his "subconscious sympathies." As these critics worked to reveal unexpressed desires, they also analyzed the roles played by women. Feminist and gender studies have increasingly looked to Cervantes for his perceptive approach to portraying the women of 17th-century Spain. Unlike the majority of his contemporaries, Cervantes expressed great empathy toward women. Although he stops short of a "feminist" position, numerous female characters such as Marcela and Dorotea in *Don Quixote* and Isabela Castrucho in *Persiles y Sigismunda* speak forcefully in defense of women's rights.

Similarly, criticism in the late 20th century began to focus on Cervantes's preoccupations with contemporary economic and historical events. The 1609 expulsion of the Moriscos (converted Muslims), the correct governance of Spain's overseas colonies, and the exploitation of African slaves are often considered as covertly polemical topics for *Don Quixote's* alert readers. The Exemplary Stories and plays have been plumbed for their engagement with political and economic factors. Documented in *Don Quixote* and *Persiles y Sigismunda*, Cervantes's knowledge of and interest in the New World are central to his perception of a different world, one equally as cross-cultural and multilingual as that of the 21st century.

ALONSO DE ERCILLA Y ZÚÑIGA

(b. Aug. 7, 1533, Madrid, Spain—d. Nov. 29, 1594, Madrid)

The Spanish poet Alonso de Ercilla y Zúñiga is the author of *La Araucana* (1569–89), the most celebrated Renaissance epic poem written in Castilian.

Ercilla received a rigorous literary education before going to the New World in 1555. He distinguished himself as a soldier in Chile during the wars against the Araucanian Indians, and he based *La Araucana* on his experiences. He composed the whole of the poem's first part and sections of the second and third while on the field of battle; a number of stanzas were written during breaks in the action on whatever he had at hand, including pieces of leather, some too small to contain more than six lines of poetry. He finished the poem after he returned to Spain in 1563.

La Araucana consists of 37 cantos that are distributed across the poem's three parts. The first part was published in 1569; the second part appeared in 1578, when it was published with the first part; the third part was published with the first and second parts in 1589. The poem shows Ercilla to be a master of the *octava real*, the complicated stanza in which many other Renaissance epics in Castilian were written. A difficult eight-line unit of 11-syllable verses that are linked by a tight rhyme scheme, the *octava real* was a challenge few poets met. It had been adapted from Italian only in the 16th century, and it produces resonant, serious-sounding verse that is appropriate to epic themes.

La Araucana describes Spanish conquests that were not comparable in importance to those of Hernán Cortés, who conquered the Aztec empire, and Francisco Pizarro, who overthrew the Inca empire. Contrary to the epic conventions of the time, however, Ercilla placed the lesser conquests of the Spanish in Chile at the core of his poem.

La Araucana's successes—and weaknesses—as a poem stem from the uneasy coexistence of characters and situations drawn from Classical sources (primarily Virgil) and Renaissance poets (Ludovico Ariosto and Torquato Tasso) with material derived from the actions of contemporary Spaniards and Araucanians.

The mixture of Classical and Araucanian motifs in *La Araucana* often strikes the modern reader as unusual, but Ercilla's turning native peoples into ancient Greeks, Romans, or Carthaginians was a common practice of his time. For Ercilla, the Araucanians were noble and brave— only lacking, as their Classical counterparts did, the Christian faith. Caupolicán, the Indian warrior and chieftain who is the protagonist of Ercilla's poem, has a panoply of Classical heroes behind him. His valour and nobility give *La Araucana* grandeur, as does the poem's exaltation of the vanquished: the defeated Araucanians are the champions in this poem, which was written by one of the victors, a Spaniard. Ercilla's depiction of Caupolicán elevates *La Araucana* above the poem's structural defects and prosaic moments, which occur toward the end when Ercilla follows Tasso too closely and the narrative strays from the author's lived experience. Ercilla, the poet-soldier, eventually emerges as the true hero of his own poem, and he is the figure that gives the poem unity and strength.

Ercilla embodied the Renaissance ideal of being at once a man of action and a man of letters as no other in his time was. He was adept at blending personal, lived experience with literary tradition. He was widely acclaimed in Spain. In Miguel de Cervantes's 17th-century novel *Don Quixote*, Ercilla's *La Araucana* is proclaimed to be among the best poems in the heroic style ever written, good enough to compete with those of Ariosto and Tasso. La Araucana's more dramatic moments also became a source of plays. But the Renaissance epic is not a genre that has, as a whole, endured well, and today Ercilla is little known and *La Araucana* is rarely read except by specialists and students of Spanish and Latin American literatures.

FEDERICO GARCÍA LORCA

(b. June 5, 1898, Fuente Vaqueros, Granada province, Spain—d. Aug. 18 or 19, 1936, between Víznar and Alfacar, Granada province)

The Spanish poet and playwright Federico García Lorca, in a career that spanned just 19 years, resurrected and revitalized the most basic strains of Spanish poetry and theatre. He is known primarily for his Andalusian works, including the poetry collections *Romancero gitano* (1928; *Gypsy Ballads*) and *Llanto por Ignacio Sánchez Mejías* (1935; "Lament for Ignacio Sánchez Mejías," Eng. trans. *Lament for a Bullfighter*), and the tragedies *Bodas de sangre* (1933; *Blood Wedding*), *Yerma* (1934), and *La casa de Bernarda Alba* (1936; "The House of Bernarda Alba"). In the early 1930s Lorca helped inaugurate a second Golden Age of the Spanish theatre.

Spanish poet and playwright Federico García Lorca (left) sits at a restaurant with his close companion and sometime collaborator, artist Salvador Dalí, c. 1935. Apic/Hulton Archive /Getty Images

Early Years

The eldest of four children born to a wealthy landowner and his schoolteacher wife, Lorca grew up in rural Andalusia, surrounded by images and social conditions that proved to be a lifelong influence on his work. At age 10 he moved with his family to Granada, where he attended a private, secular institute in addition to a Catholic public school. Lorca enrolled in the University of Granada but was a hapless student best known for his extraordinary talents as a pianist. He took nine years to complete a bachelor's degree. Despite plans to become a musician and composer, he turned to writing in his late teens. His first experiments in prose, poetry, and drama reveal an intense spiritual and sexual malaise along with an adolescent devotion to such authors as Shakespeare, Goethe, the Spanish poet Antonio Machado, and the Nicaraguan poet Rubén Darío, father of Hispanic Modernismo, a late and decadent flowering of Romanticism.

In 1919 Lorca moved to the Residencia de Estudiantes in Madrid, a prestigious and socially progressive men's residence hall. It remained his home in the Spanish capital for the next decade. His fellow residents included the filmmaker Luis Buñuel and the artist Salvador Dalí, who later became a close companion. In Madrid, Lorca also befriended the renowned older poet Juan Ramón Jiménez and a circle of poets his own age, among them Rafael Alberti, Jorge Guillén, and Pedro Salinas.

Early Poetry and Plays

A consummate stylist, Lorca sought throughout his career to juxtapose and meld genres. His poems, plays, and prose often evoke other, chiefly popular, forms of music, art, and literature. His first book, *Impresiones y paisajes* (1918;

Impressions and Landscapes), a prose work in the modernista tradition, chronicled Lorca's sentimental response to a series of journeys through Spain as a university student. *Libro de poemas* ("Book of Poems"), an uneven collection of predominantly *modernista* poems culled from his juvenilia, followed in 1921. Both efforts disappointed Lorca and reinforced his inherent resistance to publication, a fact that led to frequent delays in the publication and production of his work. Lorca preferred to perform his poems and plays, and his histrionic recitations drew innumerable admirers.

The Spanish stage director Gregorio Martínez Sierra premiered Lorca's first full-length play, *El maleficio de la mariposa* (*The Butterfly's Evil Spell in Five Plays: Comedies and Tragi-Comedies*, 1970), a symbolist work about a lovesick cockroach, in Madrid in 1920. Critics and audiences ridiculed the drama, and it closed after four performances. Lorca's next full-length play, the historical verse drama *Mariana Pineda* (written 1923), opened in 1927 in a production with sets by Dalí and received mixed notices.

In the early 1920s, Lorca began experimenting with short, elliptical verse forms inspired by Spanish folk song, Japanese haiku, and contemporary avant-garde poetics. He wrote a prodigious series of brief poems arranged in thematic "suites," later collected and published in 1983 under the title *Suites*. (Virtually all of Lorca's poetry—that contained in the volume under discussion and in the other Spanish volumes mentioned in this biography—has been translated in *Collected Poems*, 1991). In 1922 Lorca collaborated with the eminent Andalusian composer Manuel de Falla on a festival of *cante jondo* ("deep song") in Granada. The endeavour heightened Lorca's interest in popular Andalusian song, and in a blaze of inspiration he wrote a series of poems based on songs of the Andalusian Gypsies (Roma).

Even more compressed than *Suites*, *Poema del cante jondo* (written 1921–25, published 1931; *Poem of the Deep Song*), offers a radical synthesis of the traditional and the avant-garde. The series signaled Lorca's emergence as a mature poet. His collaboration with Falla further prompted Lorca to investigate the Spanish puppet theatre tradition, and in 1923 he wrote *Los títeres de Cachiporra* ("The Billy-Club Puppets"), the first of several versions of a puppet play inspired by the classic Andalusian Grand Guignol.

From 1925 to 1928, Lorca was passionately involved with Salvador Dalí. The intensity of their relationship led Lorca to acknowledge, if not entirely accept, his own homosexuality. At Dalí's urging, the poet began to experiment more boldly with avant-garde currents in the art world, notably surrealism, although he refused to align himself with any movement. In poems such as "Oda a Salvador Dalí" (1925–26; "Ode to Salvador Dalí"), *Canciones* (written 1924, published 1926; *Songs*), and a series of abstruse prose poems, Lorca sought to create a more objective poetry, devoid of private sentiment and the "planes of reality." He joined his contemporaries in exalting Don Luis de Góngora, a 16th-century Spanish poet known for his dispassionate, densely metaphorical verse. Lorca and his fellow poets commemorated the tricentennial of Góngora's death in 1927 and became known thereafter as the Generation of 1927. Lorca also sought to articulate in public lectures his own evolving aesthetic.

Meanwhile, Lorca continued to mine the popular Spanish tradition in his plays *La zapatera prodigiosa* (written 1924, premiered 1930; *The Shoemaker's Prodigious Wife*), a classic farce, and *El amor de don Perlimplín con Belisa en su jardín* (written 1925, premiered 1933; *The Love of Don Perlimplín with Belisa in Their Garden in Five Plays: Comedies and Tragi-Comedies*, 1970), a "grotesque tragedy" partially drawn from an 18th-century Spanish comic strip. Both plays reveal themes common to Lorca's work: the capriciousness of time, the destructive powers of love and death, the phantoms of identity, art, childhood, and sex.

In 1928, with Dalí's encouragement, Lorca publicly exhibited his drawings. A gifted draughtsman blessed with a startling visual imagination, Lorca produced hundreds of sketches in his lifetime.

ROMANCERO GITANO

The publication in 1928 of *Romancero gitano* (written 1921–27; *Gypsy Ballads*), a poetry sequence inspired by the traditional Spanish romance, or ballad, catapulted Lorca into the national spotlight. A lyrical evocation of the sensual world of the Andalusian Gypsy, the collection enthralled Spanish readers, many of whom mistook Lorca for a Gypsy. The book's first edition sold out within a year. Throughout the work's 18 ballads, Lorca combines lyrical and narrative modes in fresh ways to form what he described as a tragic "poem of Andalusia." Formally, the poems embrace the conventions of medieval Spanish balladry: a nonstanzaic construction, in medias res openings, and abrupt endings. But in their wit, objectivity, and metaphorical novelty, they are brazenly contemporary. One of the collection's most famous poems, "Ballad of the Spanish Civil Guard," reads, in part:

> *Los caballos negros son.*
> *Las herraduras son negras.*
> *Sobre las capas relucen*
> *manchas de tinta y de cera.*
> *Tienen, por eso no lloran,*

de plomo las calaveras.
Con el alma de charol
vienen por la carretera.

Black are the horses,
the horseshoes are black.
Glistening on their capes
are stains of ink and of wax.
Their skulls—and this is why
they do not cry—are cast in lead.
They ride the roads
with souls of patent leather.

Lorca's sudden fame destroyed his privacy. This, coupled with the demise of his friendship with Dalí, the collapse of another love affair, and a profound spiritual crisis plunged Lorca into severe depression. He sought both release and newfound inspiration by visiting New York and Cuba in 1929–30.

LATER POETRY AND PLAYS

Lorca's stay in the United States and Cuba yielded *Poeta en Nueva York* (published 1940; *"Poet in New York"*), a series of poems whose dense, at times hallucinatory images, free-verse lines, and thematic preoccupation with urban decay and social injustice mark an audacious departure from Lorca's previous work. The collection is redolent of Charles Baudelaire, Edgar Allan Poe, T.S. Eliot, and Stephen Crane and pays homage to Walt Whitman:

... hermosura viril
que en montes de carbón, anuncios y
ferrocarriles,
soñabas ser un río y dormir como un río

con aquel camarada que pondría en tu pecho
un pequeño dolor de ignorante leopardo.

... virile beauty,
who among mountains of coal, billboards, and railroads,
dreamed of becoming a river and sleeping like a river
with that comrade who would place in your breast
the small ache of an ignorant leopard.

In Cuba, Lorca wrote *El público* ("The Audience"), a complex, multifaceted play, expressionist in technique, that brashly explores the nature of homosexual passion. Lorca deemed the work, which remained unproduced until 1978, "a poem to be hissed." On his return to Spain, he completed a second play aimed at rupturing the bounds of conventional dramaturgy, *Así que pasen cinco años* (1931; *"Once Five Years Pass"*), and he assumed the directorship of a traveling student theatre group, La Barraca (the name of makeshift wooden stalls housing puppet shows and popular fairs in Spain), sponsored by the country's progressive new Republican government.

With the 1933 premiere of his first Andalusian tragedy, *Blood Wedding*, an expressionist work that recalls ancient Greek, Renaissance, and Baroque sources, Lorca achieved his first major theatrical success and helped inaugurate the most brilliant era of Spanish theatre since the Golden Age. In 1933–34 he went to Buenos Aires, Argentina, to oversee several productions of his plays and to give a lecture series. While there he befriended the Chilean poet Pablo Neruda, with whom he collaborated on a tribute to Rubén Darío.

Despite his new focus on theatre, Lorca continued to write poetry. With others in the Generation of 1927, he embraced a "rehumanization" of poetry, as opposed to the "dehumanization" José Ortega y Gasset had described in his 1925 essay "The Dehumanization of Art." Eloquent evidence of Lorca's return to the personal are *Divan del Tamarit* (written 1931–1934, published 1940; "The Divan at Tamarit"), a set of love poems inspired by Arabic verse forms; *Seis poemas gallegos* (written 1932–1934, published 1935; "Six Galician Poems"); and *Sonetos del amor oscuro* (written 1935, published 1984; "Sonnets of Dark Love"), an 11-sonnet sequence recalling a failed love affair. The three collections underscore Lorca's abiding insistence on the interdependence of love and death.

Divan del Tamarit also expresses Lorca's lifelong interest in Arab-Andalusian (frequently referred to as "Moorish") culture, which he viewed as central to his identity as an Andalusian poet. He regarded the Catholic reconquest of Granada in 1492 as a tragic loss. *Divan del Tamarit* responds to a widespread revival of interest in Arab-Andalusian culture, especially literature, in the 1930s.

In 1934 Lorca responded to the goring and death of a bullfighter friend with the majestic *Lament for a Bullfighter*, a work famous for its incantatory opening refrain, "A las cinco de la tarde" ("At five in the afternoon"). The four-part poem, his longest, confirms Lorca as the greatest of Spain's elegiac poets.

A las cinco de la tarde.
Eran las cinco en punto de la tarde.
Un niño trajo la blanca sábana
a las cinco de la tarde.
Una espuerta de cal ya prevenida
a las cinco de la tarde.
Lo demás era muerte y sólo muerte
a las cinco de la tarde.

At five in the afternoon.
It was exactly five in the afternoon.

A boy brought the white sheet
at five in the afternoon.
A frail of lime ready preserved
at five in the afternoon.
The rest was death, and death alone
at five in the afternoon.

During the last two years of his life, Lorca premiered *Yerma* (1934), the second of his Andalusian tragedies, and completed a first draft of *The House of Bernarda Alba*, his third tragedy. Childhood events and personalities inform both *Bernarda Alba* and *Doña Rosita la soltera* (written 1934, premiered 1935; *Doña Rosita the Spinster*), the most Chekhovian of Lorca's plays, as well as *Doña Rosita's* intended sequel, the unfinished *Los sueños de mi prima Aurelia* (1936; "The Dreams of My Cousin Aurelia"). In 1935 Lorca undertook his most overtly political play, *El sueño de la vida* ("The Dream of Life"), a technically innovative work based on recent events in Spain.

Lorca was at work on *Aurelia* and *Bernarda Alba* in the summer of 1936 when the Spanish Civil War broke out. On August 16, he was arrested in Granada by Nationalist forces, who abhorred his homosexuality and his liberal views, and imprisoned without a trial. On the night of August 18 or 19 (the precise date has never been verified), he was driven to a remote hillside outside town and shot.

In 1986 the Spanish government marked the 50th anniversary of Lorca's death by erecting a monument on the site of his murder. The gesture bears witness to Lorca's stature as the most important Spanish poet and playwright of the 20th century, a man whose work continues to influence writers and artists throughout the world and to speak to readers everywhere of all that is most central to the human condition.

GARCILASO DE LA VEGA

(b. 1503, Toledo, Spain—d. Oct. 14, 1536, Nice, duchy of Savoy [now in France])

Garcilaso de la Vega was the first major poet in the Golden Age of Spanish literature (*c.* 1500–1650). Garcilaso was born into an aristocratic family that had been prominent in Spanish letters and politics for several centuries. Entering court life at an early age, he distinguished himself as a soldier, serving Emperor Charles V in Rhodes, Tunis, and Pavia. After a brief imprisonment in 1532 for conspiring to marry his brother's son to a prominent lady-in-waiting against the emperor's wishes, he was released into the service of the viceroy, the Marqués de Villafranca. Serving under the viceroy in southern France, he was mortally wounded in an assault on a fortified position and died several days later.

After writing poetry in rather conventional Spanish metres for a short period, Garcilaso had become acquainted with the poet Juan Boscán Almogáver, who quickly introduced him to Italianate metres, to the use of which he was further attracted by his close study of such Italian Renaissance poets as Petrarch, Giovanni Boccaccio, and Jacopo Sannazzaro. Garcilaso was a consummate craftsman, and he transformed the Italianate metres into Spanish verse of high lyric quality. His most important innovations in this regard were the verse stanzas of the *silva* and *liva* (both using combinations of 7- and 11-syllable lines), which allowed him a new concern with the analytical expression of thought and emotion. Garcilaso's major theme is the melancholy laments and misfortunes of romantic love as conventionally portrayed in pastoral poetry. He continually rewrote and polished his poetry, lifting his work high above that of his contemporaries and profoundly influencing the development of Spanish verse.

Garcilaso's small body of work—38 sonnets, five canciones, three eclogues, two elegies, one epistle, and eight coplas (songs)—was published with that of Boscán, by the latter's widow, in 1543. These works were soon accepted as classics and largely determined the course of lyric poetry throughout Spain's Golden Age.

LUIS DE GÓNGORA Y ARGOTE

(b. July 11, 1561, Córdoba, Spain—d. May 23, 1627, Córdoba)

Luis de Góngora y Argote was one of the most influential Spanish poets of his era. His Baroque, convoluted style, known as Gongorism (*gongorismo*), was so exaggerated by less gifted imitators that his reputation suffered after his death until it underwent a revaluation in the 20th century.

The son of a judge, Góngora profited from his father's fine library and from relatives in positions to further his education. He attended the University of Salamanca and achieved fame quickly. He took religious orders so that he might receive an ecclesiastical benefice but was not ordained priest until he was 55 years old, when he was named chaplain to the royal court in Madrid. His letters, as well as some of his satirical verse, show an unhappy and financially distressed life vexed by the animosity that some of his writings had evoked. He had strong partisans—Lope de Vega was an admirer—and equally powerful enemies, none more so than his rival Francisco de Quevedo, who outdid even Góngora in mordant and unrelenting satire.

Góngora was always successful with his lighter poetry—the *romances, letrillas,* and sonnets—but his longer works, the *Fábula de Polifemo y Galatea* (circulated in manuscript in 1613; "Fable of Polyphemus and Galatea") and the *Soledades* (circulated in manuscript in 1613;

"Solitudes"), written in an intensely difficult and purposely complex style, provoked the scorn and enmity of many. There has been a temptation to divide his work into the light-dark and easy-difficult, but 20th-century criticism has shown his compositions to have a unity that is perhaps clouded by the compactness and intensity of style in the longer ones. *Gongorismo* derives from a more general base, *culteranismo*, a Latinizing movement that had been an element in Spanish poetry since the 15th century. In the *Polifemo* and the *Soledades* Góngora elaborated his style by the introduction of numerous Latinisms of vocabulary and syntax and by exceedingly complex imagery and mythological allusions. In these long poems Góngora applied his full energies to enhancing and augmenting each device and decoration until the basically uncomplicated story was obscured. The same devices are found in his more popular lyrics.

The 19th century found little to like in the obscure and difficult Góngora, but his tercentenary in 1927 reestablished his importance. The cold beauty of his lines at last found an appreciative and receptive audience willing to see the value of verse that shunned intimate emotion but that created the purest poetry for its own sake. An English translation by R.O. Jones of selected poems was published in 1966.

JUAN RAMÓN JIMÉNEZ

(b. Dec. 24, 1881, Moguer, Spain—d. May 29, 1958, San Juan, P.R.)

The Spanish poet Juan Ramón Jiménez was awarded the Nobel Prize for Literature in 1956. After studying briefly at the University of Salamanca, Jiménez went to Madrid (1900) at the invitation of the poet Rubén Darío. His first two volumes of poetry, *Almas de violeta* ("Souls of Violet") and *Ninfeas* ("Waterlilies"), came out that same year. The two books, printed in violet and green, respectively, so embarrassed Jiménez in his later years by their excessive sentiment that he destroyed every copy he could find. A man of frail constitution, he left Madrid for reasons of health. His published volumes of that period, including *Pastorales* (1911), *Jardines lejanos* (1905; "Distant Gardens"), and *Elegías puras* (1908; "Pure Elegies"), clearly reflect the influence of Darío, with their emphasis on individuality and subjectivity expressed in free verse.

Jiménez returned to Madrid in 1912 and, for the next four years, lived at the Residencia de Estudiantes and worked as an editor of that educational institution's periodicals. In 1916 he traveled to New York City, where he married Zenobia Camprubí Aymar, the Spanish translator of the Hindu poet Rabindranath Tagore. Shortly after his return to Spain, he published *Diario de un poeta recién casado* (1917; "Diary of a Poet Recently Married"), which was issued in 1948 under the title *Diario de un poeta y mar* ("Diary of a Poet and the Sea"). That volume marked his transition to what he called "*la poesía desnuda*" ("naked poetry"), an attempt to strip his poetry of all extraneous matter and to produce it in free verse, without formal metres, of a purer nature. During the Spanish Civil War (1936–39), he allied himself with the Republican forces, until he voluntarily exiled himself to Puerto Rico, where he spent most of the rest of his life.

Although primarily a poet, Jiménez achieved popularity in the United States with the translation of his prose work *Platero y yo* (1917; Platero and I), the story of a man and his donkey. He also collaborated with his wife in the translation of the Irish playwright John Millington Synge's *Riders to the Sea* (1920). His poetic output during his life was immense. Among his better-known works are *Sonetos espirituales 1914–1915* (1916; "Spiritual Sonnets, 1914–15"),

Piedra y cielo (1919; "Stones and Sky"), *Poesía, en verso, 1917–1923* (1923), *Poesía en prosa y verso* (1932; "Poetry in Prose and Verse"), *Voces de mi copla* (1945; "Voices of My Song"), and *Animal de fondo* (1947; "Animal at Bottom"). A collection of 300 poems (1903–53) in English translation by Eloise Roach was published in 1962.

BARTOLOMÉ DE LAS CASAS
(b. August 1474, Sevilla?, Spain—d. July 17, 1566, Madrid)

Bartolomé de Las Casas, an early Spanish historian and Dominican missionary in the Americas, was the first to expose the oppression of the Indian by the European and to call for the abolition of Indian slavery. His several works include *Historia de las Indias* (first printed in 1875). A prolific writer and in his later years an influential figure of the Spanish court, Las Casas nonetheless failed to stay the progressive enslavement of the indigenous races of Latin America.

The son of a small merchant, Las Casas is believed to have gone to Granada as a soldier in 1497 and to have enrolled to study Latin in the academy at the cathedral in Sevilla (Seville). In 1502 he left for Hispaniola, in the West Indies, with the governor, Nicolás de Ovando. As a reward for his participation in various expeditions, he was given an *encomienda* (a royal land grant including Indian inhabitants), and he soon began to evangelize the Indians, serving as *doctrinero*, or lay teacher of catechism. Perhaps the first person in America to receive holy orders, he was ordained priest in either 1512 or 1513. In 1513 he took part in the bloody conquest of Cuba and, as priest-*encomendero* (land grantee), received an allotment of Indian serfs.

Although during his first 12 years in America Las Casas was a willing participant in the conquest of the Caribbean, he did not indefinitely remain indifferent to the fate of the natives. In a famous sermon on Aug. 15, 1514, he announced that he was returning his Indian serfs to the governor. Realizing that it was useless to attempt to defend the Indians at long distance in America, he returned to Spain in 1515 to plead for their better treatment. The most influential person to take up his cause was Francisco Jiménez de Cisneros, the archbishop of Toledo and future co-regent of Spain. With the help of the archbishop, the *Plan para la reformación de las Indias* was conceived, and Las Casas, named priest-procurator of the Indies, was appointed to a commission to investigate the status of the Indians. He sailed for America in November 1516.

Las Casas returned to Spain the next year. In addition to studying the juridical problems of the Indies, he began to work out a plan for their peaceful colonization by recruiting farmers as colonists. His stirring defense of the Indians before the Spanish Parliament in Barcelona in December 1519 persuaded King Charles I (the emperor Charles V), who was in attendance, to accept Las Casas's project of founding "towns of free Indians"—i.e., communities of both Spaniards and Indians who would jointly create a new civilization in America. The location selected for the new colony was on the Gulf of Paria in the northern part of present-day Venezuela. Las Casas and a group of farm labourers departed for America in December 1520. The failure to recruit a sufficient number of farmers, the opposition of the *encomenderos* of Santo Domingo, and, finally, an attack by the Indians themselves all were factors that brought disaster to the experiment in January 1522.

Upon his return to Santo Domingo, the unsuccessful priest and political reformer abandoned his reforming activities to take refuge in religious life; he joined the Dominican order in 1523. Four years later, while serving as prior of the convent of Puerto de Plata, a town in northern Santo Domingo, he began to write the *Historia apologética*.

One of his major works, the *Apologética* was to serve as the introduction to his masterpiece, the *Historia de las Indias*. The *Historia*, which by his request was not published until after his death, is an account of all that had happened in the Indies just as he had seen or heard of it. But, rather than a chronicle, it is a prophetic interpretation of events. The purpose of all the facts he sets forth is the exposure of the "sin" of domination, oppression, and injustice that the European was inflicting upon the newly discovered colonial peoples. It was Las Casas's intention to reveal to Spain the reason for the misfortune that would inevitably befall her when she became the object of God's punishment.

Las Casas interrupted work on the book only to send to the Council of the Indies in Madrid three long letters (in 1531, 1534, and 1535), in which he accused persons and institutions of the sin of oppressing the Indian, particularly through the *encomienda* system. After various adventures in Central America, where his ideas on the treatment of the natives invariably brought him into conflict with the Spanish authorities, Las Casas wrote *De único modo* (1537; "Concerning the Only Way of Drawing All Peoples to the True Religion"), in which he set forth the doctrine of peaceful evangelization of the Indian. Together with the Dominicans, he then employed this new type of evangelization in a "land of war" (a territory of still-unconquered Indians)—Tuzutlan, near the Golfo Dulce (Sweet Gulf) in present-day Costa Rica. Encouraged by the favourable outcome of this experiment, Las Casas set out for Spain late in 1539, arriving there in 1540.

While awaiting an audience with Charles V, Las Casas conceived the idea of still another work, the *Brevísima relación de la destrucción de las Indias* ("A Short Account of the Destruction of the Indies"), which he wrote in 1542 and in which the historical events described are in themselves of less importance than their theological interpretation:

"The reason why the Christians have killed and destroyed such an infinite number of souls is that they have been moved by their wish for gold and their desire to enrich themselves in a very short time."

Las Casas's work finally seemed to be crowned with success when King Charles signed the so-called New Laws (Leyes Nuevas). According to these laws, the *encomienda* was not to be considered a hereditary grant; instead, the owners had to set free their Indians after the span of a single generation. To ensure enforcement of the laws, Las Casas was named bishop of Chiapas in Guatemala, and in July 1544 he set sail for America, together with 44 Dominicans. Upon his arrival in January 1545, he immediately issued *Avisos y reglas para confesores de españoles* ("Admonitions and Regulations for the Confessors of Spaniards"), the famous *Confesionario*, in which he forbade absolution to be given to those who held Indians in *encomienda*. The rigorous enforcement of his regulations led to vehement opposition on the part of the Spanish faithful during Lent of 1545 and forced Las Casas to establish a council of bishops to assist him in his task. But soon his uncompromisingly pro-Indian position alienated his colleagues, and in 1547 he returned to Spain.

Las Casas then entered upon the most fruitful period of his life. He became an influential figure at court and at the Council of the Indies. In addition to writing numerous *memoriales* (petitions), he came into direct confrontation with the learned Juan Ginés de Sepúlveda, an increasingly important figure at court by reason of his *Democrates II* ("Concerning the Just Cause of the War Against the Indians"), in which he maintained, theoretically in accordance with Aristotelian principles, that the Indians "are inferior to the Spaniards just as children are to adults, women to men, and, indeed, one might even say, as apes are to men." Las Casas finally confronted him in 1550 at the Council of Valladolid, which was presided over by famous theologians. The argument was continued in 1551, and its repercussions were enormous.

The servitude of the Indians was already irreversibly established, and, despite the fact that Sepúlveda's teachings had not been officially approved, they were, in effect, those that were followed in the Indies. But Las Casas continued to write books, tracts, and petitions, testimony to his unwavering determination to leave in written form his principal arguments in defense of the American Indian.

During his final years Las Casas came to be the indispensable adviser both to the Council of the Indies and to the king on many of the problems relating to the Indies. In 1562 he had the final form of the *Prólogo* to the *Historia de las Indias* published, although in 1559 he had left written instructions that the work itself should be published only "after forty years have passed, so that, if God determines to destroy Spain, it may be seen that it is because of the destruction that we have wrought in the Indies and His just reason for it may be clearly evident." At the age of 90 Las Casas completed two more works on the Spanish conquest in the Americas. Two years later he died in the Dominican convent of Nuestra Señora de Atocha de Madrid, having continued to the end his defense of his beloved Indians, oppressed by the colonial system that Europe was organizing.

At the suggestion of Francisco de Toledo, the viceroy of Peru, the king ordered all the works, both published and unpublished, of Las Casas to be collected. Although his influence with Spain and the Indies declined sharply, his name became well known in other parts of Europe, thanks to the translations of the *Destrucción* that soon appeared in various countries. In the early 19th century the Latin American revolutionary Simón Bolívar himself was inspired by some of the letters of Las Casas in his struggle against Spain, as were some of the heroes of Mexican independence. His name came into prominence again in the latter half of the 20th century, in connection with the so-called Indigenistas movements in Peru and Mexico. The modern significance of Las Casas lies in the fact that he was the first European to perceive the economic, political, and cultural injustice of the colonial or neocolonial system maintained by the North Atlantic powers since the 16th century for the control of Latin America, Africa, and Asia.

The most complete edition of Las Casas's works is Juan Antonio Llorente (ed.), *Colección de las obras del venerable obispo de Chiapas don Bartolomé de Las Casas* (1822, reprinted 1981).

BENITO PÉREZ GALDÓS

(b. May 10, 1843, Las Palmas, Canary Islands, Spain—d. Jan. 4, 1920, Madrid.

Benito Pérez Galdós is regarded as the greatest Spanish novelist since Miguel de Cervantes. His enormous output of short novels chronicling the history and society of 19th-century Spain earned him comparison with Honoré de Balzac and Charles Dickens. Born into a middle-class family, Pérez Galdós went to Madrid in 1862 to study law but soon abandoned his studies and took up journalism. After the success of his first novel, *La fontana de oro* (1870; "The Fountain of Gold"), he began a series of novels retelling Spain's history from the Battle of Trafalgar (1805) to the restoration of the Bourbons in Spain (1874). The entire cycle of 46 novels would come to be known as the *Episodios nacionales* (1873–1912; "National Episodes"). In these works Galdós perfected a unique type of historical fiction that was based on meticulous research using memoirs, old newspaper articles, and eyewitness accounts. The resulting novels are vivid, realistic, and accurate accounts of historical events as they must have appeared to those par-ticipating in them. The Napoleonic occupation of Spain and the struggles between liberals and absolutists preced-ing the death of Ferdinand VII in 1833 are respectively treated in the first two series of 10 novels each, all com-posed in the 1870s.

In the 1880s and 1890s Pérez Galdós wrote a long series of novels dealing with contemporary Spain, begin-ning with *Doña Perfecta* (1876). Known as the *Novelas españolas contemporáneas* ("Contemporary Spanish Novels"), these books were written at the height of the author's lit-erary maturity and include some of his finest works, notably *La des he re da da* (1881; *The Disinherited Lady*) and his masterpiece, the four-volume novel *Fortunata y Jacinta* (1886–87), a study of two unhappily married women from different social classes. Pérez Galdós's earlier novels in the series show a reforming liberal zeal and an intransigent opposition to Spain's ubiquitous and powerful clergy, but after the 1880s he displayed a newly tolerant acceptance of Spain's idiosyncracies and a greater sympathy for his coun-try. He demonstrated a phenomenal knowledge of Madrid, of which he showed himself the supreme chronicler. He also displayed a deep understanding of madness and abnormal psychological states. Pérez Galdós gradually came to admit more elements of spirituality into his work, eventually accepting them as an integral part of reality, as evident in the important late novels *Nazarín* (1895) and *Misericordia* (1897; *Compassion*).

Financial difficulties prompted Pérez Galdós in 1898 to begin a third series of novels (covering the Carlist wars of the 1830s) in the *Episodios nacionales,* and he eventually went on to write a fourth series (covering the period from 1845 to 1868) and begin a fifth, so that by 1912 he had brought his history of Spain down to 1877 and retold events of which he himself had been a witness. The books of the fifth series, however, and his last works showed a decline in mental powers compounded by the blindness that overtook him in 1912.

Pérez Galdós also wrote plays, some of which were immensely popular, but their success was largely owing to the political views presented in them rather than to their artistic value.

JUAN RUIZ

(b. c. 1283, Alcalá, Spain—d. c. 1350)

Libro de buen amor (1330; expanded in 1343; *The Book of Good Love*), the masterpiece of the poet and cleric Juan Ruiz, is perhaps the most important long poem in the literature of medieval Spain.

Almost nothing is known of Ruiz's life apart from the information he gives in the *Libro:* he was educated at Toledo and by 1330 had finished writing the *Libro* while serving as archpriest in the village of Hita, near Alcalá. He also apparently earned some fame from the popular songs he composed.

The *Libro de buen amor* is a long poem composed mainly in the form known as *cuaderna vía,* although verses in many other metrical forms are found scattered throughout the work. The *Libro* contains 12 narrative poems, each describing a different love affair. The work's title refers to the distinction the author makes between *buen amor (i.e.,* love of God) and *loco amor (i.e.,* carnal love). But while the author frequently indulges in sententious passages praising spiritual love, his narratives describe in great detail a male hero's attempts to obtain carnal love through his wooings and unsuccessful seductions of various women. The work also contains a parody of a sermon along with other anticlerical satires, several love songs, and a song in praise of small women.

Besides its realistic and high-spirited descriptions of attempted amorous conquests, the book is remarkable for its satirical glimpses of Spanish medieval life. It contains vigorous descriptions of basic character types from the lower classes, including one of the first major comic personages in Spanish literature, the old panderess Trotaconventos. The author shows a mastery of popular speech and offers folk sayings and proverbs along with bits of obscure but impressive learning.

Ruiz derived his material from a wide range of literary and other sources, including the Bible, Spanish ecclesiastical treatises, Ovid and other ancient authors, the medieval goliard poets, the fabliaux, various Arabic writings, and popular poetry and songs, impressing upon all these the cheerful cast of mind of a worldly, ribald, curiously learned priest.

TIRSO DE MOLINA

(b. March 9?, 1584, Madrid, Spain—d. March 12, 1648, Soria)

Tirso de Molina (the pseudonym of Gabriel Téllez) was one of the outstanding dramatists of the Golden Age of Spanish literature.

Tirso studied at the University of Alcalá and in 1601 was professed in the Mercedarian Order. As the order's official historian he wrote *Historia general de la orden de la Merced* in 1637. He was also a theologian of repute. Guided to drama by an inborn sense of the theatrical and inspired by the achievements of Lope de Vega, creator of the Spanish *comedia,* Tirso built on the "free-and-easy" prescriptions that Vega had propounded for dramatic construction. In his plays he sometimes accentuated the religious and philosophical aspects that attracted his theological interest; at other times he drew on his own topographical and historical knowledge, gained while traveling for his order through Spain, Portugal, and the

West Indies. Sometimes he borrowed from the vast common stock of Spanish stage material, and at other times he
relied on his own powerful imagination.

Three of his dramas appeared in his *Ciga rra les de Toledo*
(1621; "Weekend Retreats of Toledo"), a set of verses, tales,
plays, and critical observations that, arranged after the
Italian fashion in a picturesque framework, affect to provide a series of summer recreations for a group of friends.
Otherwise his extant output of about 80 dramas—a frag-
ment of the whole—was published chiefly in five *Partes*
between 1627 and 1636. The second part presents apparently insoluble problems of authenticity, and the
authorship of certain other of his plays outside this part
has also been disputed.

The most powerful dramas associated with his name
are two tragedies, *El burlador de Sevilla* ("The Seducer of
Seville") and *El condenado por desconfiado* (1635; *The Doubted
Damned*). The first introduced into literature the hero-vil-
lain Don Juan, a libertine whom Tirso derived from
popular legends but re-created with originality. The figure
of Don Juan subsequently became one of the most famous
in all literature through Wolfgang Amadeus Mozart's
opera *Don Giovanni* (1787). *El burlador* rises to a majestic
climax of nervous tension when Don Juan is confronted
with the statue-ghost of the man he has killed, and deliberately chooses to defy this emanation of his diseased
conscience. *El condenado por desconfiado* dramatizes a theological paradox. It presents the case of a notorious evildoer
who has kept and developed the little faith he had and is
granted salvation by an act of divine grace, contrasted with
the example of a hitherto good-living hermit, eternally
damned for allowing his one-time faith to shrivel.

Tirso was at his best when portraying the psychological conflicts and contradictions involved in these master
characters. At times he reaches Shakespearean standards

of insight, tragic sublimity, and irony. The same qualities are found in isolated scenes of his historical dramas, for example in *Antona García* (1635), which is notable for its objective analysis of mob emotion; in *La prudencia en la mujer* (1634; "Prudence in Woman"), with its modern interpretation of ancient regional strife; and in the biblical *La venganza de Tamar* (1634), with its violently realistic scenes.

When inspired, Tirso could dramatize personality and make his best characters memorable as individuals. He is more stark and daring than Vega but less ingenious, more spiritually independent than Pedro Calderón de la Barca but less poetic. His plays of social types and manners, such as *El vergonzoso en palacio* (written 1611, published 1621; "The Bashful Man in the Palace"), are animated, varied in mood, and usually lyrical. At the same time, however, Tirso's style is erratic and sometimes trite. In pure comedy he excels in cloak-and-sword situations; and in, for example, *Don Gil de las calzas verdes* (1635; "Don Gil of the Green Stockings"), he manipulates a complex, rapidly moving plot with exhilarating vitality. His tragedies and comedies are both famous for their clowns, whose wit has a tonic air of spontaneity. Naturalness in diction suited his dramatic purpose better than the ornamental rhetoric then coming into vogue, and generally he avoided affectations, remaining in this respect nearer to Vega than to Calderón. Tirso was not as consistently brilliant as these great contemporaries, but his finest comedies rival theirs, and his best tragedies surpass them.

MIGUEL DE UNAMUNO

(b. Sept. 29, 1864, Bilbao, Spain—d. Dec. 31, 1936, Salamanca)

The essays of the educator, philosopher, and author Miguel de Unamuno y Jugo had considerable influence in early 20th-century Spain.

Unamuno was the son of Basque parents. After attending the Vizcayan Institute of Bilbao, he entered the University of Madrid in 1880 and in four years received a doctorate in philosophy and letters. Six years later he became professor of Greek language and literature at the University of Salamanca.

In 1901 Unamuno became rector of the university, but he was relieved of his duties in 1914 after publicly espousing the Allied cause in World War I. His opposition in 1924 to General Miguel Primo de Rivera's rule in Spain resulted in his forced exile to the Canary Islands, from which he escaped to France. When Primo de Rivera's dictatorship fell, Unamuno returned to the University of Salamanca and was reelected rector of the university in 1931, but in October 1936 he denounced General Francisco Franco's Falangists, was removed once again as rector, and was placed under house arrest. He died of a heart attack two months later.

Spanish author, educator, and philosopher Miguel de Unamuno. Popperfoto/Getty Images

Unamuno was an early existentialist who concerned himself largely with the tension between intellect and emotion, faith and reason. At the heart of his view of life was his personal and passionate longing for immortality. According to Unamuno, man's hunger to live on after death is constantly denied by his reason and can only be satisfied by faith, and the resulting tension results in unceasing agony.

Although he also wrote poetry and plays, Unamuno was most influential as an essayist and novelist. If his vigorous and iconoclastic essays have any common theme, it is that of the need to preserve one's personal integrity in the face of social conformity, fanaticism, and hypocrisy. His first published work was the essays collected in *En torno al casticismo* (1895), in which he critically examined Spain's isolated and anachronistic position in western Europe at the time. His *Vida de Don Quijote y Sancho* (1905; *Life of Don Quixote and Sancho*) is a detailed analysis of Miguel de Cervantes's literary characters. Unamuno's mature philosophy found its fullest expression in *Del sentimiento trágico de la vida en los hombres y en los pueblos* (1913; *The Tragic Sense of Life in Men and Peoples*), in which he stressed the vital role spiritual anxiety plays in driving man to live the fullest possible life. This and other themes were explored in *La agonía del cristianismo* (1925; *The Agony of Christianity*).

Unamuno's novels are intensely psychological depictions of agonized characters who illustrate and give voice to his own philosophical ideas. His most famous novel is *Abel Sánchez: una historia de pasión* (1917; *Abel Sanchez*), a modern re-creation of the biblical story of Cain and Abel, which centres on the painfully conflicting impulses of the character representing Cain. His other novels include *Amor y pedagogía* (1902; "Love and Pedagogy"), which describes a father's attempt to raise his son scientifically, ending in failure and the son's ruin; *Niebla* (1914; *Mist*); and *San Manuel Bueno, mártir* (1933; "Saint Manuel the Good, Martyr"), the story of an unbelieving priest. Unamuno's *El Cristo de Velázquez* (1920; *The Christ of Velázquez*), a study in poetic form of the great Spanish painter, is regarded as a superb example of modern Spanish verse.

LOPE DE VEGA

(b. Nov. 25, 1562, Madrid, Spain—d. Aug. 27, 1635, Madrid)

Lope de Vega was an outstanding dramatist of the Spanish Golden Age, author of as many as 1,800 plays and several hundred shorter dramatic pieces, of which 431 plays and 50 shorter pieces are extant.

LIFE

Lope de Vega was the second son and third child of Francisca Fernandez Flores and Félix de Vega, an embroiderer. He was taught Latin and Castilian in 1572–73 by the poet Vicente Espinel, and the following year he entered the Jesuit Imperial College, where he learned the rudiments of the humanities. Captivated by his talent and grace, the bishop of Ávila took him to the Alcalá de Henares (Universidad Complutense) in 1577 to study for the priesthood, but Vega soon left the Alcalá on the heels of a married woman.

Vega acquired a humanistic education from his abundant though haphazard readings in erudite anthologies. In 1583 he took part in the Spanish expedition against the Azores. By this time he had established himself as a playwright in Madrid and was living from his *comedias* (tragicomic social dramas). He also exercised an undefined role as gentleman attendant or secretary to various nobles, adapting his role as servant or panderer according to the situation.

Also by this time, the poet's life was already launched on a course of tempestuous passion. The "remote beauty" who took him from the Alcalá was followed by Elena Osorio, an actress of exceptional beauty and maturity. His romantic involvement with her was intense, violent, and marred by Vega's jealousy over Elena's liaison with

Lope de Vega wrote thousands of plays and hundreds of short dramatic pieces that made him the premier Spanish dramatist of his age. Boyer/Roger Viollet/Getty Images

the powerful gallant Don Francisco Perrenot de Granvelle, nephew of the cardinal de Granvelle. Finally, when Elena abandoned the poet, he wrote such fierce libels against her and her family that he landed in prison. The libel continued in a court case in 1588, which sent him into exile from Castile for eight years. In the middle of this incredible court scandal, Vega abducted Isabel de Urbina (the "Belisa" of many of his poems), the beautiful 16-year-old sister of Philip II's earl marshal. They were forced to marry, and the new husband immediately departed with the Spanish Armada against England.

On his return, he passed the remainder of his exile in Valencia, at that time a centre of considerable dramatic activity, and took to the serious writing of plays. Here, too, he engaged in writing *romanceros,* or ballad poetry, which had become fashionable. In 1590 he was appointed secretary to the duke of Alba, whom he followed to Toledo and then to the ducal estate at Alba de Tormes, where his wife died in childbirth in 1595. He auctioned off everything he owned and left for Madrid, where his public concubinage with the widow Antonia Trillo de Armenta caused him another lawsuit (1596).

He had left the duke's service in 1595, and in 1598 he went to the home of the marqués de Sarriá, with whom he remained until 1600. Sometime around 1595 he also met the illiterate and singularly beautiful actress Micaela de Luján, who was to be for nearly 20 years the poet's most peaceful love; she was the "Camila Lucinda" of numerous magnificent verses composed for her by Vega. He took a second wife, Juana de Guardo, the daughter of a wealthy pork butcher, by whom he had two children, Carlos Félix and Feliciana. He was mercilessly pilloried by his literary enemies for such an opportunistic union.

Height of Literary Productivity

From 1605 until his death, Vega remained a confidential secretary and counselor to the duke of Sessa, with whom he maintained a voluminous and revealing correspondence. In 1608 he was also named to a sinecure position as a familiar of the Inquisition and then prosecutor (*promotor fiscal*) of the Apostolic Chamber. By this time, Vega had become a famous poet and was already regarded as the "phoenix of Spanish wits." In 1609 he published *Arte nuevo de hacer comedias en este tiempo* ("New Art of Writing Plays in This Time"), a poetic treatise in which he defended his own plays with more wit than effectiveness.

In 1610, in the midst of full literary production—on the road to his 500 *comedias*—Vega moved his household definitively from Toledo to Madrid. In Madrid, Vega was afflicted by painful circumstances that complicated his life in a period when he was still very creative. Juana became ill, miscarried, and lived in precarious health under Vega's constant care; Carlos Félix, his favourite son, also became ill and died, in 1612. Juana died in childbirth with Feliciana, and Micaela de Luján must also have died during that time, since Vega took into his own home the children remaining from this relationship, Marcela and Lope Félix, or Lopito.

These heartbreaks moved the poet to a deep religious crisis. In 1609 he entered the first of several religious orders. From this time on he wrote almost exclusively religious works, though he also continued his theatrical work, which was financially indispensable. In 1614 he entered the priesthood, but his continued service as secretary and panderer to his patron, the duke of Sessa, hindered him from obtaining the ecclesiastical benefits he sought. The duke, fearful of losing Vega's services, succeeded in having one of the poet's former lovers, the actress Lucia de

Salcedo, seduce Vega. The duke thus permanently recovered his secretary. Vega thereafter became involved in new and scandalous romantic relationships.

In 1627, his verse epic on the life and execution of Mary, queen of Scots, *La corona trágica,* which was dedicated to Pope Urban VIII, brought in reward a doctorate in theology of the Collegium Sapientiae and the cross of the Order of Malta, out of which came his proud use of the title *Frey* ("Brother"). His closing years were full of gloom. His last lover, Marta de Nevares, who shared his life from 1619 until her death in 1632, lost first her sight and then her sanity in the 1620s. The death at sea of his son Lope Félix del Carpio y Luján and the abduction and abandonment of his youngest daughter, Antonia Clara, both in 1634, were blows that rent his soul. His own death in Madrid in August 1635 evoked national mourning.

WORKS

Vega became identified as a playwright with the *comedia,* a comprehensive term for the new drama of Spain's Golden Age. Vega's productivity for the stage, however exaggerated by report, remains phenomenal. He claimed to have written an average of 20 sheets a day throughout his life and left untouched scarcely a vein of writing then current. Cervantes called him "the prodigy of nature." Juan Pérez de Montalván, his first biographer, in his *Fama póstuma* (1636), attributed to Vega a total of 1,800 plays, as well as more than 400 *autos sacramentales* (short allegorical plays on sacramental subjects). The dramatist's own first figure of 230 plays in 1603 rises to 1,500 in 1632; more than 100, he boasts, were composed and staged in 24 hours. The titles are known of 723 plays and 44 autos, and the texts survive of 426 and 42, respectively.

The earliest firm date for a play written by Vega is 1593. His 18 months in Valencia in 1589–90, during which he was writing for a living, seem to have been decisive in shaping his vocation and his talent. The influence in particular of the Valencian playwright Cristóbal de Virués (1550–1609) was obviously profound. Toward the end of his life, in *El laurel de Apolo,* Vega credits Virués with having, in his "famous tragedies," laid the very foundations of the comedia. Virués's five tragedies, written between 1579 and 1590, do indeed display a gradual evolution from a set imitation of Greek tragedy as understood by the Romans to the very threshold of romantic comedy. In the process the five acts previously typical of Spanish plays have become three; the classical chorus has given way to comment within the play, including that implicit in the expansion of a servant's role to that of confidant; the unities of time, place, and action have disappeared, leaving instead to each act its own setting in time and space; and hendecasyllabic blank verse has yielded to a metrical variety that, seeking to reflect changing moods and situations, also suggests the notable degree of lyricism soon to permeate the drama. The Spanish drama's confusing of tragic effect with a mere accumulation of tragic happenings has deflected the emphasis from in-depth character portrayal to that of complexity of plot, action, and incident, and the resulting emphasis on intrigues, misunderstandings, and other devices of intricate and complicated dramatic plotting have broken down the old divisions between dramatic genres in favour of an essentially mixed kind, tragicomedy, that would itself soon be known simply as *comedia*. Finally, from initially portraying kings and princes of remote ages, Virués began to depict near-contemporary Spain and ordinary men and women.

There can be no claiming that Vega learned his whole art from Virués. Bartolomé de Torres Naharro at the beginning of the 16th century had already adumbrated the cloak and sword (*cape y espada*) play of middle-class manners. A decade before Virués, Juan de la Cueva had discovered the dramatic interest latent in earlier Spanish history and its potential appeal to a public acutely responsive to national greatness. In the formation of the comedia this proved another decisive factor on which Vega fastened instinctively.

It was at this point that Vega picked up the inheritance and, by sheer force of creative genius and fertility of invention, gave the *comedia* its basic formula and raised it to a peak of splendour. The *comedia*'s manual was Vega's own poetic treatise, *El arte nuevo de hacer comedias en este tiempo*, in which he firmly rejected the Classical and Neoclassical "rules," opted for a blend of comedy and tragedy and for metrical variety, and made public opinion the ultimate arbiter of taste.

The *comedia* was essentially, therefore, a social drama, bringing a thousand changes on the accepted foundations of society: respect for crown, for church, and for the human personality, the latter being symbolized in the "point of honour" (*pundonor*) that Vega commended as the best theme of all "since there are none but are strongly moved thereby." This "point of honour" was a matter largely of convention, "honour" being equivalent, in a very limited and brittle sense, to social reputation; men were expected to be brave and proud and not to put up with an insult, while "honour" for women basically meant maintaining their chastity (if unmarried) or their fidelity (if married). It followed that this was a drama less of character than of action and intrigue that rarely, if ever, grasped the true essence of tragedy.

Few of the plays that Vega wrote were perfect, but he had an unerring sense for the theme and detail that could move an audience conscious of being on the crest of its country's greatness to respond to a mirroring on the stage of some of the basic ingredients of that greatness. Because of him the *comedia* became a vast sounding board for every chord in the Spanish consciousness, a "national" drama in the truest sense.

In theme Vega's plays range over a vast horizon. Traditionally his plays have been grouped as religious, mythological, classical, historical (foreign and national), pastoral, chivalric, fantastic, and of contemporary manners. In essence the categories come down to two, both Spanish in setting: the heroic, historical play based on some national story or legend, and the cloak-and-sword drama of contemporary manners and intrigue.

For his historical plays Vega ransacked the medieval chronicle, the *romancero,* and popular legend and song for heroic themes, chosen for the most part as throwing into relief some aspect either of the national character or of that social solidarity on which contemporary Spain's greatness rested. The conception of the crown as fount of justice and bulwark of the humble against oppression inspires some of his finest plays. *Peribáñez y el comendador de Ocaña (Peribáñez and the Commander of Ocaña), El mejor alcalde, el rey (The King, the Greatest Alcalde),* and *Fuente Ovejuna (All Citizens Are Soldiers)* are still memorable and highly dramatic vindications of the inalienable rights of the individual, as is *El caballero de Olmedo (The Knight from Olmedo)* on a more exalted social plane. In *Fuente Ovejuna* the entire village assumes responsibility before the king for the slaying of its overlord and wins his exoneration. This experiment in mass psychology, the best known outside Spain of all his plays, evoked a particular response from audiences in tsarist Russia.

Vega's cloak-and-sword plays are all compounded of the same ingredients and feature the same basic situations: gallants and ladies falling endlessly in and out of love, the "point of honour" being sometimes engaged, but very rarely the heart, while servants imitate or parody the main action and one, the *gracioso,* exercises his wit and common sense in commenting on the follies of his social superiors. *El perro del hortelano* (*The Gardener's Dog*), *Por la puente Juana* (*Across the Bridge, Joan*), *La dama boba* (*The Lady Nit-Wit*), *La moza de cántaro* (*The Girl with the Jug*), and *El villano en su rincón* (*The Peasant's House Is His Castle*) are reckoned among the best in this minor if still-entertaining kind of play.

All Vega's plays suffer from haste of composition, partly a consequence of the public's insatiable desire for novelty. His first acts are commonly his best, with the third a hasty cutting of knots or tying up of loose ends that takes scant account both of probability and of psychology. There was, too, a limit to his inventiveness in the recurrence of basic themes and situations, particularly in his cloak-and-sword plays. But Vega's defects, like his strength, derive from the accuracy with which he projected onto the stage the essence of his country and age. Vega's plays remain true to the great age of Spain into which he had been born and which he had come to know, intuitively rather than by study, as no one had ever known it before.

Vega's nondramatic works in verse and prose filled 21 volumes in 1776–79. Much of this vast output has withered, but its variety remains impressive. Vega wrote pastoral romances, verse histories of recent events, verse biographies of Spanish saints, long epic poems and burlesques upon such works, and prose tales, imitating or adapting works by Ariosto and Cervantes in the process. His lyric compositions—ballads, elegies, epistles, sonnets (there are 1,587 of these)—are myriad. Formally they rely much on the conceit, and in content they provide a running commentary on the poet's whole emotional life.

Among specific nondramatic works that deserve to be mentioned are the 7,000-line *Laurel de Apolo* (1630), depicting Apollo's crowning of the poets of Spain on Helicon, which remains of interest as a guide to the poets and poetasters of the day; *La Dorotea* (1632), a thinly veiled chapter of autobiography cast in dialogue form that grows in critical esteem as the most mature and reflective of his writings; and, listed last because it provides a bridge and key to his plays, the *Arte nuevo de hacer comedias en este tiempo.* This verse apology rested on the sound Aristotelian principle that the dramatist's first duty is to hold and satisfy his audience: the comedia, he says in effect, had developed in response to what the Spanish public demanded of the theatre. The treatise provides a clear picture of the principles and conventions of a drama entitled to be called national in its close identification with the social values and emotional responses of the age.

CHAPTER 5

LATIN AMERICAN LITERATURE

The term *Latin American literature* embraces the national literatures of the Spanish-speaking countries of the Western Hemisphere. Historically, it also includes the literary expression of the highly developed American Indian civilizations conquered by the Spaniards. Over the years, Latin American literature has developed a rich and complex diversity of themes, forms, creative idioms, and styles.

THE COLONIAL PERIOD

When the sails of Christopher Columbus's ships rose above the horizon on Oct. 12, 1492, the peoples of what the Europeans would call the New World possessed their own forms of artistic verbal expression: from prayers, hymns, and myths to theatre of various kinds. But even the most advanced pre-Columbian civilizations lacked alphabetic writing, so their "literature" was exclusively oral (if one includes various mnemonic ideographs and pictographs), kept by the memory of individuals entrusted with that task and by the collectivity. A substantial number of these oral narratives were preserved, thanks to the efforts of friars, priests, and chroniclers, as well as native historians who learned to read and write. The narratives' themes, characters, topics, and even metaphors have been periodically adopted by Latin American literature. In the latter half of the 20th century, much work was done to recover and study pre-Columbian literature, including that part of it created in the aftermath of the European invasion.

The first European poetry to be heard in the New World was most surely the ballads sung by Columbus's sailors in their settlements on the island of Hispaniola (now comprising the states of Haiti and the Dominican Republic). These romances (narrative poems with eight-syllable lines), which harkened back to the Middle Ages, continued to be composed and sung in all areas where the Spaniards settled. More sophisticated poetry, following Italian Renaissance metres and themes, began to be written shortly thereafter in the capitals of the viceroyalties (or vice-kingdoms) of Mexico and Peru. These cities became the centres of European culture in America. The viceroyalty comprising what is today roughly Mexico, parts of the southwestern United States, and Central America was called the Viceroyalty of Nueva España (New Spain), and the one centred in Peru was the Viceroyalty of Peru. Because the viceregal capitals were organized like European courts, literary activity thrived there throughout the colonial period. There were poetic contests, theatre, public recitations, and literary gatherings like those of the academies and universities of Europe.

With the development of the printing press in the 15th century, the Spanish empire depended more and more on the written word. Writing in all areas, particularly in law and religious doctrine, became paramount in the empire's daily life. The creation of a native elite, able to write and imbued with Western culture, was crucial to the empire's functioning, so colleges and universities were founded: a college in Mexico in 1536 and a university in 1551, a university in 1538 in Hispaniola, and a university in Lima in 1551.

El Almirante Christoval Colon Descubre la Isla Española, ij haze poner una Cruz, etc.

Christopher Columbus meets with the natives of Hispaniola. The descriptions Columbus wrote in his letters and reports to Spain of his voyages served as the basis for later accounts of the New World. Library of Congress Rare Book and Special Collections Division

For learning purposes, large numbers of *cartillas*, or alphabet cards, were shipped from Spain.

THE EARLIEST LITERARY ACTIVITY

Although there must have been some early stirrings in Hispaniola, literary activity in the Western sense—that is, written forms that had a conscious literary purpose and employed an alphabetic language—began with the Hispanicization of Mexico City. The former Aztec capital was already a major metropolis when the Spaniards took over, and they strove earnestly to compete with the institutions of the vanquished, particularly in religion but also in theatre, poetry, and all forms of oral literature. Mexico City soon became a cultural centre, with poets, many of them born in Spain, who were attuned to every trend back in Europe. Poets already recognized in Spain, such as the Sevillian Gutierre de Cetina and Diego Hurtado de Mendoza, lived in Mexico, as did Spanish-born prose writers such as the famous author of picaresque novels Mateo Alemán. The first Mexican-born poet to attain renown was Francisco de Terrazas, who composed fine sonnets in the Petrarchan style, probably during the last half of the 16th century.

The most distinguished composition to issue from these endeavours was *Grandeza mexicana* (1604; "Mexican Greatness" or "The Magnificence of Mexico City"), a long poem in praise of Mexico City by Bernardo de Balbuena. A highly elaborate piece, Balbuena's poem celebrates Mexico City as the crossroads of all worlds, a global centre through which flowed goods coming from Spain's Asian imperial outpost in the Philippines (and brought to Mexico's Pacific shores by the Manila Galleon) on their way to Veracruz, where they were picked up by the fleets that would take them, via Havana, to Seville, Spain.

Focusing on the economic richness brought about by so much trade, Balbuena exults in the beauty of the city's horses, monuments, markets, fruit, and pageants.

The epic form proved to be the most important manifestation of Renaissance-style poetry in the first century of the colonial period. More specifically, these were poems written in the manner of Ludovico Ariosto's *Orlando furioso* and Torquato Tasso's *Gerusalemme liberata*. The best of all the epics written about the conquest of the New World was by far Alonso de Ercilla y Zúñiga's *La Araucana* (1569–89; *The Araucaniad*). The young soldier and courtier began the poem while engaged in campaigns against the Araucanian Indians of what is today Chile. While the poem has been praised for the authenticity lent by the fact that the poet was a participant in the wars he describes, and also for the very positive portrayal of the Araucanians, its deepest value lies in the poetic genius Ercilla brought to it. He was a powerful and refined poet, the supreme master of the eight-line octava real stanza in the Spanish language, and he had a great sense of the dramatic. Praised by Miguel de Cervantes in *Don Quixote*, Ercilla is considered a major writer in both the Spanish and Latin American canons.

Pedro de Oña's *Arauco domado* (1596; *Arauco Tamed*) was a worthy successor on the same theme, though it is both rhetorical and derivative. Oña, a native of the region, is named in conventional histories of literature as the first great Chilean poet. He has never achieved the popularity of Ercilla, however.

A Caribbean example of this epic tradition is *Espejo de paciencia* (1608; "Model of Patience"). Written in Cuba by the Canarian Silvestre de Balboa y Troya de Quesada, it is about the defeat of a French pirate who abducts a local ecclesiastic for ransom, and it reflects anti-Protestant fervour in the Spanish empire.

Chronicles of Discovery and Conquest

Yet what has been commonly considered, retrospectively, the most important 16th-century writing in the Americas is the chronicles of the discovery and conquest of the New World. This group of documents includes narrative accounts, legal documents (depositions, reports, arguments, etc.), and full-fledged histories. Because of their foundational aura, the most celebrated of the texts are Columbus's letters and reports to the Catholic Monarchs and their functionaries. There is an added charm in Columbus's awkwardness of style (Spanish was not his native tongue), his difficulties in describing objects unknown to Europeans, and his huge mistakes. In spite of these often attractive flaws, his accounts constitute a substantial legacy in the discourse of the West. The most egregious of Columbus's errors was, of course, his belief that he had arrived somewhere in Asia, which led to his adopting the name "Indies" for the lands he "discovered." Hence the misnomer "Indians" for all the natives of the American continent.

Columbus's letters and reports were quickly disseminated in the original and in Latin translations. Using these and other early accounts, the Italian humanist Peter Martyr d'Anghiera wrote, during the last years of the 15th and early years of the 16th century, the first history of the New World, *De Orbe Novo decades* (1516; *De Orbe Novo: The Eight Decades of Peter Martyr d'Anghiera*). Whereas Columbus was a navigator who could write a little, Peter Martyr was steeped in culture; during the 16th century his elegant Latin tract enjoyed a wide readership all over Europe.

While the discovery of the Caribbean was an astonishing event to Europeans, the discovery of Mexico was dazzling. Here were hitherto unknown civilizations that not only were populous and spread over vast territories but also had splendid cities and complex forms of government, arts, crafts, and religious practices. Knowledge of the conquest of Mexico was provided by its Spanish protagonist Hernán Cortés, whose *Cartas de relación* (1519–26; *Letters from Mexico*) told of the tortuous campaign by which a few hundred Spaniards took over the powerful Aztec empire, aided by gunpowder, horses, cunning, and the resentful peoples who were subject to Aztec rule. Cortés was a vigorous writer, with a flair for the dramatic and an eye for the kind of details that would captivate the European reader. He described battles but also customs, costumes, rituals, and the elaborate protocol of the Aztec court.

Cortés was a master at self-dramatization and self-promotion. His haughty attitude provoked one of his soldiers, Bernal Díaz del Castillo, to write a prolix account of the conquest 50 years after the event. He wanted to give the common soldier's perspective. Díaz del Castillo's prodigious memory allowed him to recall vividly many of his companions, down to the names and colours of their horses. *The Historia verdadera de la conquista de la Nueva España* (1632; *The True History of the Conquest of Mexico*) is a monumental volume written by a man who claimed to have little formal education, which may explain the book's particular immediacy and charm. It is an invaluable source of information on both the common lives of the soldiers and the customs of the natives they defeated. Most memorable is Díaz del Castillo's description of the astonishment Spaniards felt at the sight of Mexico City, which he likens to the marvels found in the romances of chivalry. While not literary in the formal sense of Renaissance poetics, the *Historia verdadera* is literature in a modern sense in that it places authenticity above all rules of style or decorum. Nothing escapes the author's

Bernal Díaz del Castillo. © Visual & Written/SuperStock

gaze; no detail is too insignificant or even repulsive. Of all the books to have come out of colonial Latin America, his is the one still most read.

But no book coming from the Spanish dominions attained a wider readership at the time than Bartolomé de Las Casas's *Brevísima relación de la destrucción de las Indias* (1542; *A Short Account of the Destruction of the Indies*). Originally a Spanish settler, Las Casas was appalled at the treatment of the Indians by the rapacious Spaniards. He became a Dominican friar, steeped himself in the law, and began to write bitter denunciations of the conquistadors' actions. These he directed to the Spanish crown, whom he considered innocently unaware of what was being perpetrated in the monarch's name.

In 1526 Las Casas also commenced the *Historia de las Indias* (selections appear in *History of the Indies*), a voluminous history of the conquest of the New World. It was not published in his lifetime, but Las Casas did publish a summary, the *Brevísima relación*, as a polemic, hoping that it would have an immediate and telling impact. It did, probably beyond his expectations. Las Casas's accusations were a factor in the issuance of the "New Laws" that went some way toward ending hereditary Spanish grants of land and Indians, thus limiting the Spaniards' use of natives for labour. His little book took on a life of its own abroad, being translated into several European languages and used by Spain's enemies to elaborate what has come to be known as the "Black Legend," a lurid account of what occurred to the Indians at the hands of the Spaniards. *Brevísima relación* became, in short, part of the religious polemics and wars between Spain and countries under the sway of the Protestant Reformation. Written in a dramatic style and perhaps exaggerating the atrocities perpetrated on the Indians, it was both a polemic and an appeal. Las Casas is known as "the Apostle of the Indians" and is revered in Latin America. He remained a controversial figure in Spain until the 20th century.

Historians of the New World

By the turn of the 17th century, most of the conquest of America had been accomplished, and historians, some appointed by the Spanish crown, attempted to provide a comprehensive overview of the event. Whereas at first chroniclers had prevailed—some of whom, such as Columbus and Cortés, had been protagonists—now the historians took over. Other than Las Casas, Gonzalo Fernández de Oviedo and official court historian Antonio de Herrera y Tordesillas continued the work that Peter Martyr had begun. The most significant among these new writers, however, was Garcilaso de la Vega, El Inca, the son of a Spanish conquistador and an Inca woman of noble lineage. Because of his combined heritage, Garcilaso, who was born in Peru but spent most of his adult life in Spain, is commonly considered to be the first truly Latin American writer. His masterpiece is *Los comentarios reales de los Incas* (1609, 1617; *Royal Commentaries of the Incas*, with a foreword by Arnold J. Toynbee), whose second part is called *Historia general del Perú* (*General History of Peru*).

The *Comentarios reales* tells the history of the Inca empire, providing a detailed description of all aspects of Inca culture. It is also the story of Garcilaso's maternal family, based on his own recollections of what his relatives told him and on the oral and written testimony of others. Garcilaso's avowed purpose is to correct the Spanish histories of the conquest of the Andes (hence the title "commentaries"), which were written by men who did not even know the Quechuan languages spoken by the natives of Peru. He gives a dramatic account that combines autobiography, ethnography, and history, all cast in an elegant and precise prose style. The *Historia general del Perú* relates the tale of the Spanish conquest and the civil wars among the Spanish, in which Garcilaso's father played a prominent, though controversial, role (he was accused of aiding those rebelling against the crown). It is the story of Garcilaso's paternal family, told in excruciating detail for it was intended to clear his father's name before the Spanish authorities.

Garcilaso is the most prominent of the native historians of the conquest because his book is of such a high literary quality and also because of his mixed heritage. In the 20th century his fellow Peruvian Felipe Guamán Poma de Ayala was also intensively studied. Guamán Poma's lengthy and wide-ranging *El primer nueva corónica y buen gobierno* (1612–15; "The First New Chronicle and Good Government," translated in abridgment as *Letter to a King*) is written in a very faulty Spanish, laced with Quechua words and troubled by Quechuan syntax, which gives his work an authentic and dramatic tone. The book is illustrated with Guamán Poma's primitive but trenchant full-page drawings of the events he narrates. Its author accuses the Spaniards of not abiding by their own Christian doctrine, which he himself has adopted, and demands the restoration of native leaders to local rule. The *Primer nueva corónica* is a laboriously told history that includes lore and descriptions of native customs and practices. Guamán Poma did not have much impact on Latin American literature and historiography because his manuscript was not discovered and published until the 20th century.

While historians were interpreting the events of the conquest and debating their consequences, literary life in the Spanish empire continued unabated. Renaissance poetry, as well as other cultural manifestations, soon evolved into Baroque forms, particularly in the viceroyalties of Mexico and Peru. A distinctive kind of Baroque art developed in colonial Latin America, a style that has come to be known as the Barroco de Indias, or "Baroque of the Indies," arguably the first authentic artistic style to emerge in the region.

The Barroco de Indias

In poetry, the Barroco de Indias begins with a gleeful acceptance of the manner originated by Luis de Góngora y Argote, the great Spanish Baroque poet, who had brought about a veritable revolution in poetic language. Góngora's poetry is difficult, laden with mythological allusions, bristling with daring metaphors that strain the limits of the language, and syntactically complex. He soon had numerous and ardent praisers and detractors in Spain and the viceroyalties. Among the poets, whatever their status, he was mostly admired and imitated. In fact, gongorismo is practically a whole poetic movement in colonial Latin America, affecting poetry through the 17th century and well into the 18th.

Baroque poetry is known for its vicious satires. Góngora, for example, delighted in heaping invective on his literary rivals. Viceregal courts outdid the Spanish court in pomposity, constantly providing ample targets for their poets to exercise satirical wit. Whereas Balbuena's *Grandeza mexicana* (1604) praised Mexico City, Mateo Rosas de Oquendo's *Sátira hecha por Mateo Rosas de Oquendo a las cosas que pasan en el Pirú año de 1598* (1598; "Satire Written by Mateo Rosas de Oquendo About Things Happening in Peru in the Year 1598") satirized Peru. The Spanish-born wanderer lived for some time in Tucuman and Lima, where he turned a caustic eye on colonial society. Lima itself, profiting from silver mines in Potosí, now had literary academies, luxurious goods, and various forbidden pleasures, all of which called forth an elaborate invective from Rosas de Oquendo.

He was surpassed in his criticism of colonial doings, however, by Juan del Valle y Caviedes, a shopkeeper who was also Spanish-born. Caviedes, the best-known satirical poet of the Barroco de Indias, focused on the frailties of the human body, to the extent that some readers believed him to be syphilitic as well as misanthropic. His most important work was *Diente del Parnaso* ("The Tooth of Parnassus"), a collection of 47 poems not published until 1873. These are given over to ridiculing the hapless doctors of Lima, who killed more often than they cured. Caviedes, as did other poets of the Barroco de Indias, found the scholastic "science" of the time lacking and showed a modern impatience with its crude methods of observation and reliance on received authority.

Probably the best practitioner of Gongorist poetry in colonial Latin America was Hernando Domínguez Camargo, a Jesuit born in Bogotá. Domínguez Camargo wrote a voluminous epic, *Poema heroico de San Ignacio de Loyola* (1666; "Heroic Poem in Praise of St. Ignatius Loyola"), praising the founder of the Jesuit order, but he is best remembered for a short ballad titled *A un salto por donde se despeña el arroyo de Chillo* ("To a Waterfall Where the Chillo Brook Crashes"). The said brook is portrayed as a bolting horse that smashes himself against rocks at the bottom of a waterfall, presenting an image of grotesque beauty typical of the Baroque.

The Barroco de Indias peaks in the poetry of Sor Juana Inés de la Cruz, who has become a canonical figure in Spanish-language literature. Sor Juana's life was dramatic. She rose to fame from illegitimacy and a precarious childhood. Invited to the viceregal court, she shone there and was later admitted to a convent, where she suffered a saintly death while assisting the victims of an epidemic.

Despite all misguided efforts to make her a heretic, Sor Juana was a pious Catholic nun.

As a writer, she was versatile, putting forth poetry, prose, and plays. Her extended philosophical poem *Primero sueño* (1692; "First Dream," Eng. trans. *Sor Juana's Dream*) ranked alongside Góngora's *Soledades* in the

Sor Juana Inés de la Cruz, portrait by Fray Miguel de Herrera, 18th century. Private Collection/Art Resource, NY

breadth and depth of its aspirations. The *Respuesta a Sor Filotea* (written 1691; "Answer to Sor Filotea," included in *Sor Juana Inés de la Cruz: Poems*, 1985) is an early instance of feminism in its argument that women should be permitted to have intellectual interests. Sor Juana's love sonnets manage to be at the same time playful and profound. Her secular and religious plays are well-crafted. Along with Garcilaso de la Vega, but surpassing his literary accomplishments in both quality and quantity, Sor Juana stands at the apex of colonial letters. Her modern perspectives foreshadow the work of the 18th century and beyond.

THE 18TH CENTURY

Following the War of the Spanish Succession (1701–14), the first Spanish Bourbons set out to put their kingdoms in order and to win the hearts and minds of their subjects. Philip V (1700–24, 1724–46), Luis I (1724), and Ferdinand VI (1746–59) enacted new tax laws, overhauled domestic and international defense, converted the aristocracy into a service nobility, and enlisted the literati to frame these changes as a return to Castilian tradition. The culmination of their vision was the reign of Charles III (1759–88), who pursued fiscal and political changes in Spanish America known as the Caroline reforms and expelled the Jesuits in 1767.

The Viceroyalty of New Granada (now Colombia, Venezuela, and parts of Ecuador and Peru) became an important centre for scientific study and commerce. It had foundered after its initial founding in 1717, was suppressed in 1723, and was reestablished in 1739. Numerous Spanish and other European scientists traveled to New Granada and the other viceroyalties of Spanish America during the first half of the century. There they measured and categorized plants, stones, and animals, led by the

Enlightenment impulse to dominate nature through intellectual rather than physical force. Spanish merchants, too, flocked to the viceregal capitals, where they hoped to enrich themselves, marry wealthy Creole women, and become members of the ruling clans. Before and after their expulsion, the Jesuit humanists (like 18th-century Italian and Spanish humanists in general) looked to Renaissance authorities on rhetoric and poetics. They traced a continuum between the earlier humanists and contemporary authorities on physics and optics. Exiled to northern Italy, some of these Jesuits were among the first Spanish Americans to issue calls for independence.

HISTORIOGRAPHIES

In addition to the accounts of Spanish America earlier penned by European explorers, philosophers, and naturalists, important historiographical works were written by Creoles or by Spaniards who had lived most of their lives in one or more of the viceroyalties. José Gumilla, a Jesuit missionary along the banks of the Orinoco River, wrote the first modern account of the flora, fauna, and humans in that region. Demonstrating a humanist's command of Classical and Renaissance rhetoric and a philosopher's understanding of modern physics and geography, *El Orinoco ilustrado* (1741–45; "The River Orinoco Illustrated") circulated throughout the Americas and Europe in several languages. Another Jesuit, Juan José de Eguiara y Eguren, put together a literary history of New Spain. His incomplete *Bibliotheca mexicana* (1755; "Mexicana Library") brings together the manuscripts and published works of authors there. Six decades later the counterrevolutionary Mexican Mariano Beristáin de Souza advanced the humanist's project in his own *Biblioteca hispanoamericana septentrional* (1816–21; "Northern Spanish American Library").

José Martín Félix de Arrate y Acosta finished his *Llave del Nuevo Mundo, antemural de las Indias Occidentales: La Habana descripta* ("Key to the New World, Holding Wall of the Indies: Havana Described") in 1761, though it was first published in 1827. Alongside his defense of Creoles in Havana, Arrate laid out economic statistics and policies for Cuba inspired by modern economic theorists. Steeped in Classical erudition, José Eusebio de Llano Zapata corresponded with humanists throughout Europe after he left Peru at midcentury. He authored treatises on formal logic and physics and a carefully researched and written natural history, *Memorias histórico-físicas-apologéticas de la América Meridional* (1761; "Apologetic Historico-Physical Memoirs of South America"), of which only one volume has been published. The economy of expression in Llano Zapata's *Memorias* and his access to the publications of academies of science in London, Paris, Vienna, and Amsterdam make previous natural histories of South America appear unscientific.

A very different sort of historiography was practiced by the Spaniard Alonso Carrió de Lavandera, who left Spain for New Spain and later moved to Peru, where he spent nearly 40 years. A merchant and provincial magistrate whom the Spanish crown commissioned to escort the Jesuits out of Peru in 1767, he conducted an inspection of the postal system of the viceroyalty in 1771–73. His satirical account of that tour, *El lazarillo de ciegos caminantes* (1775?; "Guide for Roving Blindmen" or "Guide for Blind Rovers," Eng. trans. *El Lazarillo: A Guide for Inexperienced Travelers Between Buenos Aires and Lima*), was published under a pseudonym and is perhaps the best-known Latin American work of the 18th century. Its most obvious debt is to Menippean satire, since it parodies elements of the travelogue, almanac, natural history, newspaper, and memoir. Carrió condemns the moral and political blindness of apparently enlightened crown and church officials from Guatemala—through which he passed on his way to the Viceroyalty of Peru—to Argentina.

In the late 18th century Juan de Velasco wrote *Historia del reino de Quito en la América meridional* ("History of the Kingdom of Quito in South America"), a comprehensive account of pre-Columbian and colonial Quito, not published until well into the 19th century. The Jesuit Francisco Javier Clavijero wrote numerous chronicles, including the formidable *Storia antica del Messico* (1780–81; "Ancient History of Mexico," Eng. trans. *The History of Mexico*). Translated into Spanish as *Historia antigua de México* in the early 19th century, it manifests the Classical erudition of Jesuits in Mexico City and signals the evolution of Creole consciousness.

A lawyer and theologian, Antonio Sánchez Valverde wrote important essays on medicine, philosophy, and history, as well as several tomes of Neoclassical sermons. For his invectives against the Spanish crown and church officials in Santo Domingo, he was harassed and imprisoned. He fled to Spain, where he became a member of the economic society of Madrid. (Formed to foment local economies, economic societies in Latin America became heavily involved in pro-independence movements.) He is best known for his 1785 essay *Idea del valor de la Isla Española* ("An Idea of Hispaniola's Value").

The Cuban Ignacio José de Urrutia y Montoya, a distinguished jurist who had studied in Mexico City, left unfinished his *Teatro histórico, jurídico, y político militar de la Isla Fernandina de Cuba* (1789; "Historical, Legal, Political, and Military Theatre of the Island of Cuba"). The introduction manifests his command of Neoclassical rhetoric while it glosses the major jurists of the western European Enlightenment.

A controversial figure, the Mexican friar José Servando Teresa de Mier Noriega y Guerra lived and wrote in Spain, France, and other European countries. In *Memorias* (probably first published in 1856 in a book about Servando Teresa de Mier; *The Memoirs of Fray Servando Teresa de Mier*) and *Historia de la revolución de Nueva España* (1813; "History of the Revolution in New Spain"), he revealed the political and religious justifications for Mexican independence. No less significant is the brief *Carta a los españoles americanos* ("Letter to American Spaniards"), written in 1791 by the Peruvian Juan Pablo Viscardo y Guzmán. It was published first in French (1799) and then in Spanish (1801). Viscardo claimed that rapacious adventurers had transformed a shining conquest of souls into the shame of the Spanish name and that Spanish rule was tyranny. His accusations went beyond those of Bartolomé de Las Casas. Viscardo called on Creoles to lift the yoke of tyranny by separating from Spain. Both the Mexican and the Peruvian emboldened actors of the independence movements and created nightmarish visions of Spanish colonial rule that would be repeated by Neoclassicists and Romantics in the republics of Spanish America.

PLAYS

Although elites in Spanish America did not embrace Enlightenment ideals until the last years of the 18th century, authors began much earlier to explore the new ways of thinking about nature and to develop new ways of imitating it in fiction and new ways of viewing their societies. The exaggeration of Baroque tendencies marks much of the literature from the first half of the century. In some authors' works, a swollen Gongorism mixes with the rationalism prescribed by French Neoclassicists to produce an

incipient Rococo period of intense preciosity. This is especially true of the works of those authors who wrote
occasional theatre and poetry—that is, dramas and poems
that celebrated the arrivals or birthdays of archbishops
and viceroys, military victories, and so on.

Unlike the historiographers, those agents of revolution and republicanism, playwrights throughout the 18th
century imagined spectacles of royal power in which hier-
archies of estate, caste, and gender were reinforced for
literate and illiterate spectators alike. Reworkings of plays
by Calderón and Lope de Vega competed with original
dramas that glorified the reconquest of Spain from Muslim
invaders and the conquest of America.

Fernando de Orbea, whose family occupied government positions throughout the Viceroyalty of Peru, wrote
one of the few surviving plays from what is today Colombia.
In *La conquista de Santa Fé de Bogotá* ("The Conquest of
Santa Fé de Bogotá [an early name for the city of Bogotá],"
which may have been first performed in 1710), arias and
recitative in Spanish and in Quechua present a vision of
the Spanish conquest that was modeled after Virgil's
Aeneid and several colonial chronicles.

In Lima the dramas of Pedro de Peralta Barnuevo
ranged from adaptations of French Neoclassical plays to
librettos for operas at the viceregal palace. A mathematician, poet, attorney, accountant, and historian, Peralta
dazzled European visitors to Lima. *La Rodoguna* (written
about 1719) is a free adaptation of Pierre Corneille's drama
Rodogune (the name of the play's heroine); it is more
Neoclassical than Peralta's occasional plays. The best of
the latter is *El Mercurio galante* ("The Gallant Mercury"),
an operetta performed in 1720 between the acts of *Afectos
vencen finezas* ("Feelings Conquer Finery"). A spoof of the
courting devices of Spaniards from different kingdoms, *El
Mercurio galante* was Peralta's rejoinder to the tales of

Spanish suitors and seductresses published in the light-hearted Parisian magazine *Mercure galant*.

Eusebio Vela, a transplanted Spanish actor and playwright, wrote plays that were popular in Mexico City. *El apostolado en las Indias y martirio de un cacique* ("The Apostolate in the Indies and Martyrdom of a Chief"), first performed in 1732, presents a somewhat sanitized account of the Spanish conquest of the Aztec empire. While the plot and diction owe much to Spanish Baroque theatre, the hero Cortés foreshadows the rational, sensitive leaders that came to dominate the Spanish and Italian stage during the second half of the century.

Santiago de Pita, an army officer from Havana, wrote *El príncipe jardinero y fingido Cloridano* (*c*. 1730; "The Gardener-Prince and Feigned Cloridano"), a musical play on love and kingship that was inspired by Italian operas. It was performed in Spain during the 18th century. Francisco del Castillo, a blind Mercedarian friar who was called "El Ciego de la Merced," was a favourite at the viceregal court. His *La conquista del Perú* (performed in 1748; "The Conquest of Peru") and his tragedy *Mitrídates, rey del Ponto* (before 1749; "Mithridates, King of Pontus") show his range as a dramatist who, like Peralta, was negotiating the Spanish Baroque and French Neoclassicism. Castillo's complete works were published in the 20th century.

POETRY

Lyrical and spiritual poems have survived, although they are of uneven quality. Mother Francisca Josefa de la Concepción de Castillo y Guevara, who wrote a prose autobiography, *Vida* (published 1817; "Life"), at the behest of her confessor, also composed the poetry in *Afectos espirituales* (written mostly in the early and mid-1700s; published 1843; "Spiritual Feelings"). Both these works are notable for their mystic reflection. The Jesuit Juan Bautista Aguirre wrote spiritual, lyrical, and satirical poetry that was published after his death. His *A una rosa* ("To a Rose") and *Descripción del Mar de Venus* ("Description of Venus's Sea") illustrate the prolonged transition from late Baroque to Neoclassical aesthetics that characterizes the Rococo. Manuel de Zequeira y Arango, a Cuban Neoclassical poet, is best known for his idyllic portrait of Cuba, *A la piña* ("To the Pineapple"), which was written sometime before 1821 and published posthumously.

Epic poetry was not often attempted in Spanish during the first half of the 18th century. Pedro de Peralta Barnuevo's *Lima fundada; o, conquista del Perú* (1732; "Lima Founded; or, Conquest of Peru") illustrates the promise and the pitfalls of the genre. While Peralta's occasional poetry often confirms the staying power of Góngora, *Lima fundada* blends Alonso de Ercilla's poetics with French Neoclassical prescriptions for epic and bucolic poetry. Intellectual achievements interested Peralta more than military feats; continuous footnotes on men of letters in Spain and Peru dwarf the descriptions of battles, and Francisco Pizarro goes missing for pages. Some two decades later, in Mexico City, Francisco Ruiz de León created a Cortés who appears less a conqueror than a courtier in *Hernandia* (1755; "Ferdinand"). The frequent appearance in *Hernandia* of the Italian scena (a form of solo vocal composition in which the recitative is followed by arias) and several allusions to soft music and song during battles are firmly Rococo and confirm his debts to opera, which had been popular in the viceregal courts of Spanish America since the late 17th century.

An exiled Jesuit, Rafael Landívar, wrote *Rusticatio mexicana* (1782; *The Rusticatio Mexicana of Rafael Landívar*), a Latin poem that owes much to the bucolic poetry published in France and England a century earlier. *Rusticatio mexicana* exalts the animals, plants, and minerals native to New Spain, detailing the agricultural, textile, and mining practices of the region.

Satirical poetry was much more common. Friar Castillo's salty *Conversaciones* ("Conversations") reveal tears in the social fabric of Lima. Miscegenation, smuggling, prostitution, fashion, and feigned nobility are all targeted in the tradition of Rosas de Oquendo and Caviedes. The Andalusian Esteban de Teralla y Landa, who lived in Mexico City before he moved to Lima about 1782, contrasted appearances and realities in a manner reminiscent of Juvenal. Written under the pseudonym Simón Ayanque, *Lima por dentro y fuera* (1797; "Lima Inside and Out") is his best-known work. In a style representative of Rococo poetics he lays waste to Lima's enlightened facade.

EARLY NOVELS

The late 18th century saw the rise of the Latin American novel. In these early novels, one encounters at every turn the Neoclassical conviction that society would be reformed by a combination of informed individual choice and state regulation. Francisco Javier Eugenio de Santa Cruz y Espejo, son of a Quechua father and a Spanish mother, penned satirical novels, treatises on medical and religious matters, and legal papers. His novel *El nuevo Luciano de Quito* (written in 1779; "The New Lucian of Quito") and its sequel *La ciencia blancardina* (written in 1780; "Blancardian Science") ridiculed the schoolmen's educational program. He proposed cultural reforms that borrowed from Thomas Hobbes, Sir Francis Bacon, Voltaire, Adam Smith, and Neoclassical authorities from France, Spain, Italy, and Portugal. Espejo was active in Santa Fé de Bogotá's economic society, and in 1792 he founded Quito's first newspaper, *Primicias de la cultura de*

Quito ("Seedlings of Civilization in Quito"). His satires circulated widely in manuscript but were not published until the 20th century.

The Peruvian Pablo Antonio José de Olavide y Jáuregui was the quintessential Enlightenment reformer. Among other things, he worked at establishing immigrant colonies to expand the agricultural sector and reinforce the notion that manual labour was not dishonourable, and he was one of those who aimed at teaching trades and persuading the aristocracy to use trained workers on their lands. In his early 20s, Olavide bought a seat on the royal court in Lima. Within a year he faced legal sanctions for his role in the reconstruction efforts that followed the massive earthquake of 1746. He fled to Spain, where he married a wealthy middle-aged widow. His *Paulina* (1828), *Sabina* (1828), and other sentimental novels and short stories were influenced by Samuel Richardson, Voltaire, and Jean-Jacques Rousseau. After several years of working on immigration and economic projects, Olavide was persecuted for his unorthodox religious views and took refuge in France. His eventual disavowal of such views is fictionalized in the melancholic tale of fall and redemption *El Evangelio en triunfo; o, historia de un filósofo desengañado* (1797; "The Gospel in Triumph; or, History of an Undeceived Philosopher") and explored further in *Poemas cristianos* (1797; "Christian Poems"). Olavide's poetry and prose maintained the didacticism of Neoclassicism while they foreshadowed the tenebrism of Romanticism.

The most famous literary figure of late colonial New Spain is the novelist, poet, and journalist José Joaquín Fernández de Lizardi. His acerbic wit and wide-ranging interests are evident in his best-known novels, *El periquillo sarniento* (vol. 1–3 were published in 1816; vol. 4 was suppressed, probably for "offense to public morals," until 1830–31; *The Itching Parrot*) and *La educación de las mujeres; o,*

La Quijotita y su prima (incomplete edition 1818–19; complete edition 1831–32; "The Education of Women; or, Miss Quixote and Her Cousin"). The first is a raucous journey through late 18th-century Mexico in the form of an elderly man's picaresque life story. Its successor asks prospective female readers to look in the two mirrors that are its two female principals and to rid themselves of the same vices that they see in the ill-fated Quijota. Lizardi's novels present a sometimes patronizing, always rationalist perspective on lives that do not measure up to Enlightenment ideals.

For late 18th-century authors and their crown and church patrons, Neoclassicism represented both the spirit of their age and the destined fate of society under their tutelage. But by the fourth decade of the 19th century, many of Spain's American dominions had achieved political independence, and authors elected to wrap Neoclassical forms around the goal of cultural independence or to discard them altogether as unwanted remnants of the crown.

Cuban Literature

A recognizably Cuban literature first began to emerge after the end of the 18th century. In the early 19th century, several writers gained prominence espousing intellectualism and the concept of freedom. These ideas gained perhaps their greatest intensity in the writings of José Martí, a Cuban of modest Spanish background who led the Modernist movement in Cuban literature. He inspired an entire school of writing devoted to winning freedom from Spain. Writers whose works reflected social protest in the pre-Castro period include Nicolás Guillén, a leader in founding the Afro-Cuban school of literature, and Jose Z. Tallet, both activist poets.

In the 20th century, short stories became the predominant prose form, but exceptional novels were also produced, such as Alejo Carpentier's *¡Ecué-Yamba-Ó!* (1933; "Lord, May You Be Praised!"), which is a tribute to Afro-Cuban life and culture, and *El siglo de las luces* (1962; *Explosion in a Cathedral*, 1963), which portrays the violence and chaos wrought on the Caribbean during the French Revolution. The works of the poet, novelist, and essayist José Lezama Lima have also been influential. In addition, the works of the American writer Ernest Hemingway are deeply admired on the island, which was his home for many years and the setting for *The Old Man and the Sea* (1952) and *Islands in the Stream* (1970). Cuban writers such as Reinaldo Arenas, Guillermo Cabrera Infante, Leonardo Padura Fuentes, and Ronaldo Menedez have earned international attention in the postrevolutionary era. However, many such writers have been exiled after falling afoul of government censors. By the early 21st century, Cuban writers had published large numbers of major novels and literary magazines.

ROMANTICISM

The first Latin Americans to write under the sway of Romanticism were poets such as the Cuban José María de Heredia, who had begun by mastering Neoclassical poetic forms. Heredia still wrote odes in the Neoclassical manner, but the emotional charge of his poetry, the presentation of a self astonished by the beauty and power of nature, and his espousal of the cause for national independence were Romantic to the core. Romanticism in Latin America was coeval with the movements that brought about independence from Spain to all Latin American countries, save, ironically, Heredia's Cuba and the rest of the Caribbean.

The Venezuelan Andrés Bello, who was imbued with the Neoclassical spirit, had written *Silva a la agricultura de la zona tórrida* (1826; "Ode to Agriculture in the Torrid

Zone"), a Virgilian poem that lauds nature for its generous sustenance of man. The Ecuadorian José Joaquín de Olmedo wrote in praise of the heroes of South American independence, as in his 1825 ode "La victoria de Junín: canto a Bolívar" ("The Victory at Junín: A Song to Bolívar"). Heredia, on the other hand, wrote a Romantic ode to Niagara Falls, "Oda al Niágara" ("Ode to Niagara"), whose theme is the water's violent beauty. A similar poem addressed to a hurricane, "En una tempestad" ("In a Storm"), expressed his awe and fear before the wantonly destructive wind. An exile who lived in the United States and Mexico and died young, Heredia was the very embodiment of the Romantic outcast, horrified by the abuses of established authority, which in this case was the Spanish government of Cuba. In his "Himno del desterrado" ("Hymn of the Exile") he sings about the clash between Cuba's physical beauty and the outrages committed in its immoral political life.

In contrast to Heredia, the Argentine Esteban Echeverría, who had left his country voluntarily, returned in the early 1830s from studying in Paris to become an active promoter of democracy and Romantic literature. Argentina, of course, had become an independent country, but, as happened elsewhere in the continent, it had gone from foreign rule to domestic despotism. Echeverría became an opponent of the Juan Manuel de Rosas dictatorship (1835–52). In 1837 he founded the Asociación de Mayo ("May Association," after the month of Argentina's independence), a group of liberal intellectuals who sought a national literature reflective of their culture and society. By 1841 Echeverría had to leave Argentina as an exile. He went to Uruguay, where he remained until his early death. Though a prolific writer and pamphleteer, Echeverría's place in literary history is secured by a poem and a short story. The poem, "La cautiva" ("The Captive," included in

Rimas [1837]), is about a white couple, María and Brian, abducted by Indians. His story "El matadero" ("The Slaughterhouse") was written between 1838 and 1840, but it was not published until 30 years later, after Echeverría's death. It is a political allegory directed against Rosas: a cultivated young man, liberal in manner and dress, is brutally slain by thugs who frequent the Buenos Aires slaughterhouse.

But the towering figure of Argentine—and Latin American—literature of the mid-19th century was Domingo Faustino Sarmiento. His *Civilización y barbarie: Vida de Juan Facundo Quiroga* (1845; *Life in the Argentine Republic in the Age of the Tyrants; or, Civilization and Barbarism*) is arguably the most important book ever written by a Latin American. It was written during Sarmiento's second exile in Chile, as a political pamphlet against Rosas. But the book, which grew in subsequent editions, was a wide-ranging meditation on Argentine culture, centred on the figure of strongman Facundo Quiroga, whom Sarmiento offers as the prototype of the rural strong man who might evolve into a Rosas.

Sarmiento is attracted and repulsed by the gauchos, the Argentine cowboys from whose midst Facundo emerged. His loving descriptions of the Argentine plain, the Pampas, and of the nomadic gauchos are among the most powerful in Latin American literature. But Sarmiento wanted Argentina to be modern, to adopt the ways of his admired United States, and to reject the barbaric gaucho culture that led to a tyrant like Rosas. The clash between barbarism (rural, native culture) and civilization (urban, European-influenced culture) that Sarmiento saw at the core of Argentine life became a formula for characterizing all of Latin American culture. It is, with his great book, Sarmiento's most enduring legacy. Sarmiento was elected president of Argentina in 1868, and he remained in power until 1874, beginning a tradition of important writers becoming presidents that endures in Latin America to the present day.

Domingo Faustino Sarmiento's fierce nationalistic pride is evidenced in Life in the Argentine Republic in the Age of the Tyrants, or, Civilization and Barbarism *written more than two decades before he was elected Argentina's president.* Three Lions/Hulton Archive/Getty Images

The Romantic preference for national themes, local landscapes, and regional human types continued with an epic poem by Juan Zorrilla de San Martín, *Tabaré* (1886; *Tabaré: An Indian Legend of Uruguay*), which depicted the fate of the Charrúa Indians, defeated by the Spanish invaders. The high point of this trend of portraying native types was reached in Argentina by José Hernández in the gaucho epic *Martín Fierro* (1872–79; *Martín Fierro: An Epic of the Argentine*, also translated as *The Gaucho Martin Fierro*). It was the best of the gaucho literature genre, inaugurated unwittingly by Sarmiento's *Facundo*—a body of literature that included Rafael Obligado's *Santos Vega* (1887), on a famous minstrel, and the comical *Fausto* (1866; *Faust*) by Estanislao del Campo.

The Caribbean counterpart of this literature was the Cuban antislavery novel, in which the wretched living conditions of African slaves toiling in the production of sugar are depicted. The Romantic Gertrudis Gómez de Avellaneda, a celebrated lyric poet, published *Sab* (1841; *Sab: An Autobiography*), about a house slave in love with his white mistress; and Anselmo Suárez y Romero wrote his powerful *Francisco* (1839). The masterpiece of this group of novels was Cecilia Valdés (1882; *Cecilia Valdés; or, Angel's Hill: A Novel of Cuban Customs*), by the Cuban exile Cirilo Villaverde, perhaps the best Latin American novel of the 19th century.

Villaverde's only competition comes from two other novels named after their women protagonists: *María* (1867; *María: A South American Romance*), by the Colombian Jorge Isaacs, and Amalia (1851–55; *Amalia: A Romance of the Argentine*), by the Argentine José Mármol. Villaverde's vast narrative centres on the heroine, Cecilia, a mulatto so light-skinned that she can pass for white, who is in love with Leonardo, white, rich, and, unbeknownst to them, her half-brother. *Cecilia Valdés* is rich in details of Cuban life under Spanish domination, and it is a scathing denunciation of slavery. Romantic in spirit, the novel is cast in the mold of 19th-century Realism, a combination that in Latin America produced a version of a peculiar new genre, the cuadro de costumbres, or "sketch of local customs" (a form of costumbrismo). These brief, descriptive essays depicted the lives of rural folk, or of poor urban dwellers, whose traditional customs differed from the modern ways of those writing them.

A uniquely Peruvian version was created by Ricardo Palma, whose sketches are often brief narratives that he called *tradiciones*. Volumes of his *Tradiciones peruanas* appeared between 1872 and 1910. They occupy a prominent place in Latin American literary history. (English-language selections from them appear in *The Knights of the Cape and Thirty-seven Other Selections from the Tradiciones Peruanas of Ricardo Palma* [1945].)

MODERNISMO

By the end of Palma's career as a writer, a new literary movement had swept through Latin America, the first since the Barroco de Indias to have a distinctly New World inflection—Modernismo. The movement's leader was the Nicaraguan Rubén Darío, the first great poet in the Spanish language since Sor Juana Inés de la Cruz. Darío's slim volume of poetic prose and poetry "Azul" (1888; "Blue") is a watershed for both Latin American and Spanish literature. Darío, who had been reading French Symbolist poetry, took seriously Rimbaud's injunction that "one must be absolutely modern." In that spirit Darío chose "Modernism" as the name for his movement. This meant writing poetry of uncompromising aesthetic beauty and discarding the sentimentality and the rhetoric of Romanticism, which in Spanish had not yielded great poetic works. Darío experimented with metrics, with the accentuation of verse, the inner rhythm of prose, rhyme, and asymmetrical stanzas to create a sonorous, musical language. His themes were often erotic, in daring, decadent fashion. Exoticism, particularly "Oriental" subjects and objects, obsessed him.

Darío led a bohemian, cosmopolitan life, sometimes accepting the patronage of minor Central American tyrants and always the accolades of the rich and powerful. He spread his poetic gospel by traveling and living in various Latin American countries—Chile, Argentina, Cuba—and inflamed the Spanish literary scene during his sojourns in the mother country. His "Prosas profanas" (1896; "Lay Prose," Eng. trans. in *Prosas Profanas and Other Poems*) was scandalous, beginning with the misleading and daring title. The verses were a profanation in subject and form. They project a sense of aristocracy born of good taste and a disdain for those lacking it. By 1905, when he published "Cantos de vida y esperanza" ("Songs of Life and Hope"), Darío was less haughty and more reflective, sober, sombre, and mature. Here he introduces political topics, assuming in one memorable poem ("Oda a Roosevelt") an anti-American, anti-Protestant stance while proclaiming a pan-Hispanic identity (a position generally apparent in the English-language volume titled *Selected Poems* [1965]).

Darío's fellow modernistas include the Cubans José Martí and Julián del Casal, the Colombian José Asunción Silva, and the Mexicans Manuel Gutiérrez Nájera and Amado Nervo. All died relatively young, which curtailed the reach and duration of the movement. They were all remarkable poets, but Martí, because of his political activities organizing the war of Cuban independence and his heroic death in the field of battle, became a figure rivaling Darío in importance. He was not a poet of the same

Panamanian Literature

Anthropologists and folklorists have published many stories and poems of the Kuna, a Chibchan-speaking Indian people, in the process creating one of the best-documented bodies of Native American literature. Apart from Panama's indigenous arts and oral traditions, few artistic achievements were produced in the region prior to independence in 1903. The themes of earlier works were mostly European or church-related. Some progress has been made in national expression since that time, by poets and fiction writers such as Gaspar Octavio Hernández, Ricardo Miró, and Gloria Guardia, among others.

stature, but, as a journalist and orator, Martí had no equal. He wrote perceptive sketches of American life (he spent many years in New York City) and numerous pieces for Latin American periodicals as well as for his own *Patria*, a newspaper he edited in New York. His *Versos libres* ("Free Verses"), published posthumously, and *Versos sencillos* (1891; "Simple Verses," Eng. trans. *Versos sencillos*) were innovative, subtle, and powerful. Some stanzas of the brief, haiku-like "simple verses" have attained wide currency put to song in the popular Guantanamera. His essay *Nuestra América* (1891; *Our America*, Eng. trans. in *Tres documentos de nuestra América* [1979]) is a manifesto in favour of Latin American cultural and political independence.

THE VANGUARDIA

Eventually the innovations of Modernismo became routine, and poets began to look elsewhere for ways to be original. The next important artistic movement in Latin America was the avant-garde, or the *vanguardia*, as it is known in Spanish. This movement reflected several

European movements, especially Surrealism. It can be safely said that the repercussions of Surrealism in Latin America lasted throughout the 20th century. The Latin American variants were distinctive and rich and produced several masterworks, not only in literature but also in the plastic arts, painting in particular. Modernismo had been a renovation of poetic form and techniques, extending to the use of free verse. But, on the whole, the experiments remained within accepted and traditional prosodic molds. The *vanguardia*, on the other hand, instituted a radical search for new, daring, confrontational themes and shockingly novel forms. These changes occurred at different paces in the various genres.

The most daring and quick to adapt was poetry, clearly because it was aimed at a smaller, more sophisticated and receptive audience. During the first half of the 20th century, Latin American literature was blessed with many fine poets: Chileans Gabriela Mistral, Vicente Huidobro, Nicanor Parra, and Pablo Neruda; Mexican Octavio Paz; Cubans Nicolás Guillén and José Lezama Lima; Puerto Rican Luis Palés Matos; Argentines Jorge Luis Borges and Oliverio Girondo; and Nicaraguan Ernesto Cardenal. Gabriela Mistral, Pablo Neruda, and Octavio Paz won Nobel Prizes. In the wake of Modernismo and against its by now worn innovations and aspirations, *vanguardista* poetry freed itself from prosodic constraints and the pursuit of sublime beauty, choosing instead to seek the poetic in the prosaic and to delve into the inner recesses of the self, no matter how dark. The premier poets of the whole group were Neruda and Paz, though cases can be made for Jorge Luis Borges and José Lezama Lima.

Neruda's *Residencia en la Tierra* (1925–35; *Residence on Earth*) set the tone. It is a torrent of poetry poured from a self untrammeled by decorum, using what appear to be

Chilean poet Pablo Neruda, 1952. As a key member of the vanguardia, *Neruda produced verse that ignored convention and shocked readers with its raw emotion.* Keystone/Hulton Archive/Getty Images

Surrealist free-association techniques, flowing in a blank verse that nevertheless sounds more Shakespearean than anything else in its extravagant and fertile imagery. Sexual impulses are sometimes evident and sometimes lurk just beneath the surface, as metaphors pile upon each other with apparent disregard for order or limit. It is a poetry at times expressing the deep despair of city dwellers seeking a more direct contact with nature and the purer sources of life.

Neruda was able to focus his poetic impulses after a political conversion brought about by the Spanish Civil War (1936–39). After this event, he sought a collective voice, less focused on the individual self and more attuned to the vast injustices of history, which he gives a biblical dimension requiring biblical punishments and atonements. All this led Neruda to his masterpiece, the *Canto general* (1950; Eng. trans. *Canto General*), an epic poem that encompasses the sweep of Latin American history from pre-Columbian times to the mid-20th century. It is a "General Song," Whitman-like in scope and Americanist thematics, but precisely *general*, not a "song of myself." Yet, the poetic voice of Neruda is the protagonist of this vast retelling (with commentary) of the various atrocities and injustices visited upon the downtrodden in Latin America. It is a poem oblivious to its weaknesses and to its moments of prosaic pamphleteering, which include a paean to Soviet dictator Joseph Stalin (Neruda had become a member of the Chilean Communist Party), and able to overcome them by its sheer poetic thrust, attaining the magnificence of such sections as "Alturas de Macchu Picchu" ("Heights of Machu Picchu")—an ascent to the ancient Inca citadel that ranks with the greatest poetry of the Western canon, including that of Dante and John Milton. Toward the end of his career, the versatile Neruda turned to simple forms on simple topics—

namely, his *Odas elementales* (1954; *Elementary Odes*), in which he sings the praises of an artichoke, wood, and the like.

Paz was a much more cerebral poet, but he shared with Neruda an epic flair in poems such as *Piedra de Sol* (1957; Sun Stone) and also a penchant for erotic themes. Like Neruda, he too was a Republican activist during the Spanish Civil War, but the war experience turned him away from communism and all other political utopian movements. Paz's major poetic work is contained in the 1960 edition of "Libertad bajo palabra" (first published in 1949; "Freedom Under Parole"). The poems that appear in the 1960 edition are included in the English-language volume *The Collected Poems of Octavio Paz*, 1957–1987 (1987). In *Piedra de Sol* Paz ponders time, in terms of the Aztec calendar, and time's nemesis, love or eros, which seeks to perpetuate the fleeting moment in the ecstasy of pleasure but fails and falls to death.

Paz was obsessed by the projection of the past into the present; thus he was fascinated by ruins, those of ancient Mexico and the Classical ruins in Sicily, where the Greco-Roman past seems to live (in, for example, "Himno entre ruinas" ["Hymn Among Ruins"]). But not even the hard stones can resist time's relentless passing, and the consolation of poetic beauty and love are transient. Paz has a Classical mind; the present repeats the past, and what seem to be obsolete forms reappear in new contexts. Greeks and Aztecs expressed the same yearnings. The present is the delusion of difference; everything is the same, only our individual consciousness is dissolved by death. Paz can often convey this feeling of melancholy in exquisite brief poems, such as *Certeza* ("Certainty"), and can also sustain it in longer compositions, such as *Entre lo que veo y digo* ("Between What I See and What I Say").

Literature in Time of War

El Salvador's elite has long prized the arts, especially literature. But any kind of antigovernment literature was an extremely dangerous enterprise during the civil war years. One of the country's most widely respected poets, Roque Dalton, was assassinated in 1975 after having written several books that criticized the ruling party, and many other Salvadoran writers, artists, and intellectuals fled the country. Few have returned, but those who have, including poets Manlio Argueta and Francisco Rodriguez, give frequent readings before large audiences.

THE MODERN NOVEL

In prose fiction, the *vanguardia* did not arrive as quickly. The first step was a renovation of the novel but within accepted 19th-century Realist forms. The first novels to be considered modern—that is, contemporary—in Latin American fiction were those written during and about the Mexican Revolution (1910–20). While adhering to conventional forms, these novels presented an unsentimental, harsh, and action-packed world of wanton cruelty, with crisp plots in which the characters seem to be propelled by superior forces, as in Classical tragedy. The best and best-known by far was *Los de abajo* (1915; *The Underdogs*), by Mariano Azuela.

While the Mexican Revolution as theme continued to dominate Mexican fiction for a good part of the 20th century, in the rest of Latin America there appeared a host of novels that came to be grouped under the *rubric novelas de la tierra*, or *novela criollista* (regionalist novels; "novels of local colour"). These novels were widely read and attained some international recognition. The most notable were three by authors who acquired prominent places in Latin

American literary history: *Don Segundo Sombra* (1926; *Don Segundo Sombra*) by the Argentine Ricardo Güiraldes, *Doña Bárbara* (1929; *Doña Bárbara*) by the Venezuelan Rómulo Gallegos, and *La vorágine* (1924; *The Vortex*) by the Colombian José Eustasio Rivera.

All three are set in rural contexts and depict man's struggle to tame nature and make it subservient and bountiful. Each, as is the case with other contemporary novels published in various Latin American countries, describes toil within a given national industry: *Doña Bárbara* and *Don Segundo Sombra* depict cattle ranching in the Venezuelan and Argentine plains (the llano and the pampa, respectively), and *La vorágine* describes rubber prospecting in the Colombian jungle. The mighty struggle against nature reaches transcendental proportions and in all cases approaches allegory and myth: man against nature, civilization against barbarism, good against evil. These are powerful novels, with memorable characters, such as the old gaucho Don Segundo Sombra and the alluring and controlling Doña Bárbara, the "Devourer of Men." In *La vorágine* the jungle, a relentless, merciless force, is the protagonist.

The regionalist novel dramatized the Latin American quest to define its culture as deriving from, yet antagonistic to, the continent's natural forces. This productive and dramatic contradiction made the *novela de la tierra* the literary tradition within which and counter to which new novelistic projects were measured.

A complementary tradition, attuned to the rebelliousness, skepticism, and contentiousness of the avant-garde, emerged mostly in Argentina, Uruguay, and Paraguay, and its leader was Jorge Luis Borges. Whereas the regionalist novel aspired to give a direct, unmediated version of Latin American reality, Borges furnished one that was avowedly bookish and thus derived from the Western tradition.

Borges saw in gaucho tales the repetition of Greek and biblical myths—not fresh stories from a new world but reiterations of the same old world. He mastered the tale based on apocryphal references and sources and programmatically rejected long fiction, declaring that some novels are as boring as life itself.

His first collection of short stories was *Historia universal de la infamia* (1935; A Universal History of Infamy), in which he began to experiment with apocryphal attributions and bogus bibliographies. Deceptively simple, the stories are about adventuresome and variously criminal protagonists, crime and villainy being a constant in Borges's fiction. But Borges's decisive collection was *Ficciones* (1944; English trans. *Ficciones*), which contains some of his classics, such as *Tlön, Uqbar, Orbis Tertius, La muerte y la brújula* ("Death and the Compass"), and *Pierre Menard, autor del Quijote* ("Pierre Menard, Author of the *Quijote*"). These are texts that so unsettle the norms of realist fiction from within that they made regionalist novels appear obsolete. In fact, in *Tlön, Uqbar, Orbis Tertius* he seems to parody the procedures of the regionalist novel by inventing a country—as, Borges would claim, regionalist novelists themselves really did, despite their disingenuous claims of faithfully reflecting reality. In any case, by 1944 regionalist fiction was retreating. Avant-garde narrative forms, some drawn from sources belonging to African or Indian cultures, began to prevail.

One of the main impulses of the avant-garde in all the arts was to incorporate indigenous and African artistic traditions into the mainstream of Latin American life. In painting, this trend led to Mexican mural paintings. In literature, it meant recovering African or Indian stories and either retelling them in Spanish or weaving them into larger narratives. In 1930 the Guatemalan Miguel Ángel Asturias published in Paris his *Leyendas de Guatemala*

("Legends of Guatemala"), in which he retold Maya stories drawn from the oral tradition of his country. The Cuban Lydia Cabrera brought out her *Cuentos negros de Cuba* (1940; "African Stories from Cuba"). These were but two of the many narrative projects in this vein. Larger projects, such as the Ecuadorean Jorge Icaza's *Huasipungo* (1934; *Huasipungo: The Villagers*), had a more decidedly political edge, depicting the Indians as victims of brutal oppression and economic exploitation.

The regionalist and vanguardista trends merge more successfully in two landmark Latin American novels that inaugurated what has come to be known as "magic realism": Asturias's *El señor presidente* (1946; *The President*) and Alejo Carpentier's *El reino de este mundo* (1949; *The Kingdom of This World*). Asturias's novel, about the dictatorship of *Manuel Estrada Cabrera* in Guatemala, employs Surrealist techniques to create an aura of fear and the sense that events are guided by supernatural forces, echoing Native American beliefs. Carpentier writes about Haiti from 1750 to 1820, including the Haitian revolution at the end of the 18th century, which was carried out by slaves in commerce with, the novel relates, the supernatural forces of nature harnessed by their leaders. Instances of the fantastic occur and are believed to be real by the slaves. Magic realism consists in the depiction of the fantastic from the point of view of those who, whether their religion be Roman Catholic or some doctrine of indigenous or African origin, accept as true the extranatural aspects of their faith in the context of a narrative that is otherwise realistic according to traditional standards.

In 1955 Carpentier published an influential collection of stories that he had written in the 1940s and early 1950s, *Guerra del tiempo* (*War of Time*), a work that is the quintessential expression of magic realism. Asturias and Carpentier, who thus successfully combined regionalist and avant-garde trends, are the bridge to the new Latin American novel of the 1960s and 1970s, the years of the so-called "boom" of the Latin American novel.

Another transitional figure was the Mexican Juan Rulfo, but his work is of such high quality that it would be unfair to confine him to that limited role. The short stories in his collection *El llano en llamas* (1953; "The Plain in Flames," Eng. trans. in *The Burning Plain and Other Stories*) and his novel, *Pedro Páramo* (1955; Eng. trans. *Pedro Páramo*), are among the best works of fiction ever published in Latin America. Rulfo's rural characters live in the aftermath of the Mexican Revolution, the victims of those who had presumably fought to save them. In the stories, laconic narrators tell about their stark, violent lives, reduced to dramatic situations so primal that they approximate myths. *Pedro Páramo* is a brief masterpiece about the lives affected by a despotic country chieftain whose money and power are not enough to satisfy his boundless ambitions. The story is told by multiple narrators, some of whom speak from their graves, and it is redolent with violence, unbridled lust, and incest. It is

Bolivian Literature: *Nocturno Paceño*

Nocturno paceño (2006; "Night in La Paz") by Bolivian Manuel Vargas is a novel that consists of 16 accounts that can be read independently and that oscillate between realism and surrealism. Set during the seven years of Hugo Bánzer's dictatorship after the coup of 1971, the work has the night as its leitmotiv. The protagonists are university students in La Paz who risk their welfare in both love and politics, share the night hours with various shady characters, and attempt to escape the repressive dictatorship.

like a small-scale *Inferno*, presented through techniques such as stream of consciousness, flashbacks, and the employment of various narrators whose voices are sometimes difficult to identify. Rulfo was such a perfectionist that, in addition to a collection of film scripts, he published only these two books, which secured his place in Latin American literary history.

During the second half of the 20th century, the poets Pablo Neruda (Chile) and Octavio Paz (Mexico) and the novelists Miguel Ángel Asturias (Guatemala) and Gabriel García Márquez (Colombia) received Nobel Prizes. Argentine Jorge Luis Borges was widely accepted as a modern classic; Cuba's Alejo Carpentier and novelists Juan Rulfo (Mexico) and João Guimarães Rosa (Brazil) were also internationally recognized. But the boom involved chiefly García Márquez, Argentina's Julio Cortázar, the Mexican Carlos Fuentes, and the Peruvian Mario Vargas Llosa, to whom could also be added the Uruguayan Juan Carlos Onetti, the Chilean José Donoso, and the Cubans José Lezama Lima and Guillermo Cabrera Infante.

The common feature of the novels produced by these writers was the adoption of the style and techniques of the modern European and American novel—that is to say, the

Costa Rican Literature

Costa Ricans have been marginally active in the field of literature. Roberto Brenes Mesén and Ricardo Fernández Guardia were widely known in the early 20th century as independent thinkers in the fields of education and history, respectively. Fabián Dobles and Carlos Luis Fallas have attracted international attention as writers of novels with social protest themes. Carmen Naranjo is one of several noted female writers.

works of Marcel Proust, James Joyce, Franz Kafka, John Dos Passos, William Faulkner, and Ernest Hemingway. Stream of consciousness, multiple and unreliable narrators, fragmented plots, interwoven stories, a strong influence of the cinema, and other modern techniques, ignored by the regionalist novelists, were now adopted and adapted to Latin American themes, stories, and situations. The new techniques and styles gave these novels a poetic aura that had been generally absent from Latin American prose fiction, save for the short stories. Another element that had hitherto been relatively infrequent was humour, which appeared particularly in works by Cortázar, García Márquez, and Cabrera Infante; yet another was a frankness in sexual themes, heretofore rare in Latin American literature.

THE "BOOM" NOVELS

Among the works that brought recognition to these writers and that are now considered the epicentre of the boom is *Cien años de soledad* (1967; *One Hundred Years of Solitude*), by García Márquez, a world-class masterpiece that has entered the canon of Western literature. This novel tells the story of Macondo, a small town in the jungle, from its foundation to its being razed by a hurricane a century later. A second novel central to the boom is *Rayuela* (1963; *Hopscotch*), by Cortázar. The first of the boom novels to acquire international recognition, it follows the antics and adventures of an Argentine bohemian exiled in Paris and his return to Buenos Aires. *La muerte de Artemio Cruz* (1962; *The Death of Artemio Cruz*), by Fuentes, revisits the theme of the Mexican Revolution, exploring its aftermath of corruption and power struggles among the revolutionaries. *La ciudad y los perros* (1963; *The Time of the Hero*), by Vargas Llosa, won the prestigious Seix Barral

Prize in Spain and centres on the brutal life of cadets in a military school.

Among other important novels of the period are Onetti's *El astillero* (1961; *The Shipyard*), a dark tale about a pimp with ambitions; *Coronación* (1962; *Coronation*) by Donoso, a sardonic chronicle of the Chilean middle to upper-middle class; *Tres tristes tigres* (1967; *Three Trapped Tigers*), by Cabrera Infante, a hilariously funny yet sombre portrayal of Havana on the eve of the Cuban Revolution; and Lezama Lima's *Paradiso* (1966), a deeply poetic novel of education that created a scandal because of its homoerotic thematics. Some of these works have not aged well, and, in the cases of Fuentes, Vargas Llosa, and Donoso, later novels turned out to be better or more significant. Fuentes's *Terra Nostra* (1975), for instance, is more ambitious than anything else that he has written; Donoso's *El obsceno pájaro de la noche* (1970; *The Obscene Bird of Night*) is more daring than his earlier or later fiction; and Vargas Llosa's *La guerra del fin del mundo* (1981; *The War of the End of the World*) is of epic proportions and ambitions. In fact, Vargas Llosa's and Fuentes's production after the boom was, on the whole, considerably better than their earlier work.

Close on the heels of the boom writers were an Argentine and a Cuban—Manuel Puig and Severo Sarduy, respectively—whose innovations and originality differed but whose themes were similar. Puig and Sarduy dealt often, though not exclusively, with the most taboo of topics in Latin America: homosexuality. Puig, whose use of popular culture (film, song, serial novels) was masterful, published a series of excellent works beginning with *La traición de Rita Hayworth* (1968; *Betrayed by Rita Hayworth*). His best work was probably *El beso de la mujer araña* (1976; *The Kiss of the Spider Woman*), a masterpiece that became a widely acclaimed film. In it, a political activist and a gay man share a cell in an Argentine jail and come to know each other by talking about movies. It is a profoundly touching novel in dialogue that makes powerful statements about Latin American culture.

More theoretically inclined than Puig, Sarduy—who lived in exile in Paris and was involved with the Structuralist group Tel Quel, active there in the 1960s and 1970s—wrote less-accessible novels whose protagonists were often transvestites. Tightly woven and written in an elaborate yet playful prose, Sarduy's works such as *De donde son los cantantes* (1967; *From Cuba with a Song*), *Cobra* (1972; Eng. trans. *Cobra*), and *Maitreya* (1978; Eng. trans. *Maitreya*) are books of exquisite, disturbing beauty, written with a sense of global doom.

A third writer, younger than Puig and Sarduy, who made an original contribution was the Cuban Miguel Barnet, whose *Biografía de un cimarrón* (1966; *Biography of a Runaway Slave*) began an entire narrative trend, the so-called "testimonial narrative." In these books, a writer interviews a person from a marginal social group and transcribes the result in the first person. Many such books were produced, but none attained the well-deserved acclaim of Barnet's transcription of the centenarian former slave and Maroon Esteban Montejo.

"POST-BOOM" WRITERS

In the 1980s and 1990s—a period that some have called the "post-boom"—the major novelists had little competition. In fact, with the early deaths of Puig and Sarduy, they encountered no young rivals of their quality. Those who had made a name for themselves in the 1960s continued to publish works of considerable value. Fuentes, for instance, published *La campaña* (1990; *The Campaign*), an excellent novel about the independence period in Latin America, and Vargas Llosa wrote *La fiesta del chivo* (2000; *The Feast of*

Isabel Allende at a 2009 press conference promoting her book La isla bajo el mar (Island Beneath the Sea). *Allende is considered one of the most successful woman novelists from Latin America.* Javier Soriano/AFP/ Getty Images

the Goat), which dealt with Rafael Trujillo's dictatorship in and Vargas Llosa wrote *La fiesta del chivo* (2000; *The Feast of the Goat*), which dealt with Rafael Trujillo's dictatorship in the Dominican Republic. Both books are remarkable not only because of their literary quality, but also because their authors ventured beyond their own countries (Mexico and Peru, respectively) to find their historical themes. García Márquez, on the other hand, returned to a favourite topic in his *Del amor y otros demonios* (1994; *Of Love and Other Demons*). But he also made a most unexpected turn back to journalism, his original profession, with *Noticia de un secuestro* (1996; *News of a Kidnapping*), the chronicle of a kidnapping in a troubled Colombia beset by drug and guerrilla wars.

The most significant literary development in the last few decades of the 20th century was the emergence of a host of recognized women writers, mostly novelists. Chilean Isabel Allende found a niche, particularly in Europe. Her *La casa de los espíritus* (1982; *The House of Spirits*) was widely acclaimed, though it closely resembles García Márquez's *Cien años de soledad* in the magical world it describes and even in the sound of the prose. Argentine Luisa Valenzuela had some success, though more abroad than at home, with the exception of her *Novela negra con argentinos* (1990; *Black Novel with Argentines*). Chilean Diamela Eltit found a following mostly among academic critics for her highly experimental fiction. Her most discussed novel is *Lumpérica* (1983; *E. Luminata*), a text laden with stylistic games and a vague plot. With Puerto Ricans Ana Lydia Vega and Rosario Ferré, Eltit became part of an established group of women writers who were quickly accepted into the Latin American canon.

Younger women novelists such as Cubans Mayra Montero (settled in Puerto Rico), Daína Chaviano (settled in Miami), and Zoé Valdés (settled in France) and Mexican

Angeles Mastretta outstripped their predecessors in originality and independence. In fact, at the turn of the 21st century, Cuban women writers in exile were highly popular in Latin America, Spain, and other parts of Europe. Chaviano won an important award in Spain. Montero, Valdés, and Chaviano shared a common preference for sexual themes as such (as opposed to "gender issues"). They dealt with sexuality without guilt or reticence while straightforwardly denouncing the many sexual biases remaining in Cuba and elsewhere. In fact, were it not for the humour and irony invested in their works, Montero and Valdés might be viewed as pornographers, presenting heterosexual feminine desires, fantasies, and practices in a fashion previously limited to male authors.

La última noche que pasé contigo (1991; *The Last Night I Spent with You*) is Montero's best-known novel. Its hilarious plot involves couples who meet during a Caribbean cruise. Chaviano's *El hombre la hembra y el hambre* (1998; "Man, Woman, and Hunger") is about a young woman in contemporary Cuba who works as a prostitute to support herself. She lives a double life whose parallel tracks converge in a surprise ending. Mastretta's very successful *Arráncame la vida* (1985; *Mexican Bolero*) ironically revisits the most hallowed theme of 20th-century Mexican fiction: the Revolution. But Mastretta portrays revolutionary Mexico from a woman's perspective, which gives the whole process a subtly ironic twist that sometimes turns into outright humour.

Montero's and Mastretta's titles are drawn from popular songs, not just to follow the trend started by others such as Sarduy, Barnet, and Puig, but to mock the melodramatic, teary tone of Latin American romantic music, always about men's woes in their relationships with women. Though none of these works is of the literary quality of those by Vargas Llosa, Fuentes, or García

Márquez, they are far from negligible, constituting a discernible trend as the 21st century had neared.

THE MODERN ESSAY

All of this literary production was accompanied by a strong essayistic tradition whose main topic was the distinctiveness of Latin American culture and, within that culture, the individual cultures of the various countries. Many of the poets and fiction writers mentioned before also wrote essays in this vein: Carpentier, Paz, Borges, Lezama Lima, and Sarduy, for example. But there also were writers whose chief production was the essay. They includ the Uruguayan José Enrique Rodó, the Peruvian José Carlos Mariátegui, the Mexicans José Vasconcelos and Alfonso Reyes, the Dominican Pedro Henríquez Ureña, the Venezuelan Mariano Picón Salas, the Cuban Fernando Ortiz, the Argentine Ezequiel Martínez Estrada, the Puerto Rican Antonio Pedreira, and the Colombian Germán Arciniegas.

In many cases the issue these writers tackled was how to incorporate marginal cultures (African, Indian) within Latin America into the mainstream culture of the area and of each individual country. The most important and influential of these essays was *Ariel* (1900) by Rodó. In the wake of Spain's humiliating defeat by the United States in the Spanish-American War, Rodó muses about the differences between the cultures of North and South America. In reply to Sarmiento's glorification of North American culture, he calls for adherence to the spiritual, artistic values of Latin American culture, against the pragmatism and utilitarianism of the great new power to the north. His essay had such a positive reception that "Ariel clubs" were founded in various Latin American countries.

Most of the essayistic tradition either followed Rodó or argued against him. In the 1920s Mariátegui proposed a Marxist interpretation of Peruvian society and culture in his "7 ensayos de interpretación de la realidad peruana" (1928; "Seven Interpretive Essays on Peruvian Reality"). Written in a lively style and surprisingly devoid of cant, Mariátegui's essay argued in favour of an alliance between the political and artistic avant-gardes. A more scholarly approach was that of Ureña, whose elegant and profound "Seis ensayos en busca de nuestra expresión" (1928; "Six Essays in Search of Our Mode of Expression") provides a broad-ranging interpretation of Latin American culture going back to colonial times. In a similar vein, Mariano Picón Salas published in 1944 his "De la conquista a la independencia: tres siglos de historia cultural hispanoamericana" ("A Cultural History of Spanish America, from Conquest to Independence"). These essays were incorporated into the curricula of universities throughout the world.

At midcentury a powerful essay by the Mexican poet Octavio Paz, "El laberinto de la soledad" (1950; "The Labyrinth of Solitude"), offered an existentialist and psychoanalytic interpretation of Mexican culture. It had an enormous influence on Mexican fiction and poetry and was imitated by Latin American essayists elsewhere.

At the turn of the 21st century, Latin American literature seemed to be shifting from the modern to the postmodern. The line of demarcation remains unclear. Postmodern literature avails itself of most of the techniques introduced by modern literature, particularly self-consciousness of its own status as literature. The difference, perhaps, is that postmodern literature does not aspire to be profound or pretend that it can make momentous pronouncements about the self, society, the nation, or humankind. It instead tends toward playfulness. The herald of postmodern change had been Severo Sarduy. No writer of his stature or that of his predecessors (Borges, Cortázar, García Márquez, etc.) emerged to solidify this tendency. The most significant statement on postmodernism itself was provided by Cuban exile novelist, short-story writer, and essayist Antonio Benítez Rojo (1931), published in his "La isla que se repite: el Caribe y la perspectiva postmoderna" (1989; "The Repeating Island"), a worthy successor to the essayistic tradition sketched before.

CHAPTER 6

MAJOR LATIN AMERICAN WRITERS

The following writers represent a selection of the most important shapers of what is today called Latin American literature. As these biographies demonstrate, however, restricting Latin American literature to those works produced in Latin America would exclude works by writers who were born in Latin America but who left (or were forced from) their home countries. So, too, restricting Latin American literature to those who were born in Latin America would exclude the Spanish-born writers of the early colonial period. The novelists, dramatists, poets, and nonfiction writers described here were born in a variety of countries and produced their works while living in various places around the world. They range from those who wrote during the 17th century to those who continue to publish today.

ISABEL ALLENDE
(b. Aug. 2, 1942, Lima, Peru)

Isabel Allende is a Chilean American writer in the magic realist tradition who became one of the first successful woman novelists from Latin America.

Allende was born in Peru to Chilean parents. She worked as a journalist in Chile until she was forced to flee to Venezuela after the assassination (1973) of her uncle,

Chilean Pres. Salvador Allende. In 1981 she began writing a letter to her terminally ill grandfather that evolved into her first novel, *La casa de los espíritus* (1982; *The House of the Spirits*). It was followed by the novels *De amor y de sombra* (1984; *Of Love and Shadows*), *Eva Luna* (1987), and *El plan infinito* (1991; *The Infinite Plan*) and the collection of stories *Cuentos de Eva Luna* (1990; *The Stories of Eva Luna*). All are examples of magic realism, in which realistic fiction is overlaid with elements of fantasy and myth. Her concern in many of these works is the portrayal of South American politics, and her first four works reflect her own experiences and examine the role of women in Latin America. *The Infinite Plan*, however, is set in the United States, and its protagonist is male.

Allende followed those works of fiction with the novels *Hija de la fortuna* (1999; *Daughter of Fortune*), about a Chilean woman who leaves her country for the California gold rush of 1848–49, and *Retrato en sepia* (2000; *Portrait in Sepia*), about a woman tracing the roots of her past. *El Zorro* (2005; *Zorro*) is a retelling of the well-known legend, and *Inés del alma mía* (2006; *Inés of My Soul*) tells the fictionalized story of Inés Suárez, the mistress of conquistador Pedro de Valdivia.

Allende's first nonfiction work, *Paula* (1994), was written as a letter to her daughter, who died of a hereditary blood disease in 1992. A more lighthearted book, *Afrodita: cuentos, recetas, y otros afrodisíacos* (1997; *Aphrodite: A Memoir of the Senses*), shared her personal knowledge of aphrodisiacs and included family recipes. *Mi país inventado* (2003; *My Invented Country*) recounted her self-imposed exile after the Sept. 11, 1973, revolution in Chile and her feelings about her adopted country, the United States—where she has lived since the early 1990s—after the September 11 attacks of 2001. She published another memoir about her extended family, *La suma de los dias* (*The Sum of Our Days*), in 2007.

In 1996 Allende used the profits from *Paula* to fund the Isabel Allende Foundation, which supports nonprofit organizations targeting issues that women and girls in Chile and the San Francisco Bay Area face.

RAMÓN AMAYA AMADOR

(b. April 29, 1916, Olanchito, Hond.—d. Nov. 24, 1966, near Bratislava, Czech.)

The Honduran author Ramón Amaya Amador is best known for his social novels, many of them historical in nature, and for his politically charged nonfiction works.

Amaya Amador grew up outside of the Standard Fruit Company's banana plantations in his native department of Yoro. As an adult, he spent time as a schoolteacher before working on the plantations himself. There he became politically involved and worked as a union organizer on behalf of the plantation workers.

He began his writing career as a journalist for the La Ceiba-based newspaper *El Atlántico* ("The Atlantic") in the early 1940s. In 1943 Amaya Amador founded a weekly newspaper, *Alerta* ("Alert"), that served as a mouthpiece for the interests of the Honduran working class. His leftist views led to persecution by the regime of Gen. Tiburcio Carías Andino, and Amaya Amador fled to Guatemala in 1947. In exile, he wrote his best-known work, *Prisión verde* (1950; "Green Prison"), a novel that depicts the exploitative working conditions of the typical Honduran banana plantation in the 1930s and 1940s.

Amaya Amador became known throughout Latin America as a prominent communist intellectual, and in 1954 he helped found a clandestine Honduran Communist

Party. From then on he spent the rest of his life residing in Argentina and Czechoslovakia, with occasional short return trips to his home country when the changing political climate allowed it. He worked for a variety of progressive publications and wrote a number of historical novels (which were usually published posthumously), including *El señor de la sierra* (1987; "The Man from the Mountains") and *Con la misma herradura* (1993; "With the Same Tool"), before dying in a plane crash at age 50.

REINALDO ARENAS

(b. July 16, 1943, Holguín, Oriente, Cuba—d. Dec. 7, 1990, New York, N.Y., U.S.)

Reinaldo Arenas was a Cuban-born writer of extraordinary and unconventional novels who fled persecution and immigrated to the United States.

As a teenager Arenas joined the revolution that brought Fidel Castro to power in 1959. He moved to Havana in 1961 and became a researcher in the José Martí National Library (1963–68), an editor for the Cuban Book Institute (1967–68), and a journalist and editor for the literary magazine *La Gaceta de Cuba* (1968–74).

His first novel, the award-winning *Celestino antes del alba* (1967; *Singing from the Well*), was the only one of his novels to be published in Cuba. His second and best-known novel, *El mundo alucinante* (1969; *Hallucinations: Being an Account of the Life and Adventures of Friar Servando Teresa de Mier;* also published as *The Ill-Fated Peregrinations of Fray Servando*), was smuggled out of the country and first published in French. During the 1970s, Arenas was imprisoned for his writings and open homosexuality.

In 1980 Arenas escaped (during the mass exodus from the port of Mariel) to the United States. There he finally published *Otra vez el mar* (1982; *Farewell to the Sea*), the manuscript of which had been confiscated by the Cuban government. His other novels included *La vieja Rosa* (1980; *Old Rosa*); *Necesidad de liberdad* (1986), a book of lectures and essays; *La loma del ángel* (1987; *Graveyard of the Angels*); and *El portero* (1988; *The Doorman*).

Suffering from AIDS, Arenas committed suicide in 1990. Some of his posthumously published works are *Viaje a La Habana: novela en tres viajes* (1990; "Journey to Havana: A Novel in Three Trips") and *Antes que anochezca: autobiografía* (1992; *Before Night Falls*).

MIGUEL ÁNGEL ASTURIAS

(b. Oct. 19, 1899, Guatemala City, Guat.—d. June 9, 1974, Madrid, Spain)

The writings of the Guatemalan poet, novelist, and diplomat Miguel Ángel Asturias, which combine the mysticism of the Maya with an epic impulse toward social protest, are seen as summing up the social and moral aspirations of his people. Asturias won the Nobel Prize for Literature in 1967 and the Soviet Union's Lenin Peace Prize in 1966.

In 1923, after receiving his degree in law from Guatemala's University of San Carlos, Asturias settled in Paris, where he studied ethnology at the Sorbonne and became a militant Surrealist under the influence of the French poet and movement leader André Breton. His first major work, *Leyendas de Guatemala* (1930; "Legends of Guatemala"), describes the life and culture of the Maya before the arrival of the Spanish. It brought him critical acclaim in France as well as at home.

On his return to Guatemala, Asturias founded and edited *El diario del aire*, a radio magazine. During this period he published several volumes of poetry, beginning with *Sonetos* (1936; "Sonnets"). In 1946 he embarked upon a diplomatic career, continuing to write while serving in several countries in Central and South America. From

1966 to 1970 Asturias was the Guatemalan ambassador in Paris, where he took up permanent residence.

In the 1940s Asturias's talent and influence as a novelist began to emerge with his impassioned denunciation of the Guatemalan dictator Manuel Estrada Cabrera, *El señor presidente* (1946; "The President"). In *Hombres de maíz* (1949; *Men of Maize*), the novel generally considered his masterpiece, Asturias depicts the seemingly irreversible wretchedness of the Indian peasant. Another aspect of that misery—the exploitation of Indians on the banana plantations—appears in the epic trilogy that comprises the novels *Viento fuerte* (1950; "The Cyclone"), *El papa verde* (1954; *The Green Pope*), and *Los ojos de los enterrados* (1960; *The Eyes of the Interred*). Asturias's writings are collected in the three-volume *Obras completas* (1967).

ANDRÉS BELLO

(b. Nov. 29, 1781, Caracas [now in Venezuela]—d. Oct. 15, 1865, Santiago, Chile)

The poet and scholar Andrés Bello is regarded as the intellectual father of South America.

His early reading in the classics, particularly Virgil, influenced his style and theories. At the University of Venezuela in Caracas he studied philosophy, jurisprudence, and medicine. Acquaintanceship with the German naturalist and traveller Alexander von Humboldt (1799) led to the interest in geography so apparent in his later writings. He was a friend and teacher of the South American liberator Simón Bolívar, with whom he was sent to London in 1810 on a political mission for the Venezuelan revolutionary junta. Bello elected to stay there for 19 years, acting as secretary to the legations of Chile and Colombia and spending his free time in study, teaching, and journalism.

Bello's position in literature is secured by his *Silvas americanas*, two poems, written during his residence in England, which convey the majestic impression of the South American landscape. These were published in London (1826–27) and were originally projected as part of a long, never-finished epic poem, *América*. The second of the two, *Silva a la agricultura de la zona tórrida*, is a poetic description of the products of tropical America, extolling the virtues of country life in a manner reminiscent of Virgil. It is one of the best-known poems in 19th-century Spanish-American letters.

In 1829 he accepted a post in the Chilean Ministry of Foreign Affairs, settled in Santiago, and took a prominent part in the intellectual and political life of the city. He was named senator of his adopted country—he eventually became a Chilean citizen—and founded the University of Chile (1843), of which he was rector until his death. Bello was mainly responsible for the Chilean Civil Code, promulgated in 1855, which was also adopted by Colombia and Ecuador and had much the same influence throughout South America as the Code Napoléon in Europe.

Bello's prose works deal with such varied subjects as law, philosophy, literary criticism, and philology. Of the last, the most important is his *Gramática de la lengua castellana* (1847; "Grammar of the Spanish Language"), long the leading authority in its field.

ANTONIO BENÍTEZ ROJO

(b. March 14, 1931, Havana, Cuba—d. Jan. 5, 2005, Northampton, Mass., U.S.)

The short-story writer, novelist, and essayist Antonio Benítez Rojo was one of the most notable Latin American writers to emerge in the second half of the 20th century. His first book, the short-story collection *Tute de reyes*

("King's Flush"), won Cuba's major literary award, the Casa de las Américas Prize, in 1967, and in 1969 he won the Writers' Union annual short-story prize with his volume *El escudo de hojas secas* ("The Shield of Dry Leaves").

Benítez Rojo studied economics and accounting at the University of Havana and did not become involved in literary life until his mid-30s. He spent parts of his childhood in Panama and Puerto Rico, and he studied for a year in Washington, D.C. Learning English enabled him to read American and British literature in the original. At the outset of the Cuban Revolution, Benítez Rojo worked in the Ministry of Labour. He won an official contest with the very first short story he wrote and switched to the cultural bureaucracy, where he rose to the rank of director of the Caribbean Studies Centre of Casa de las Américas. Disaffected with Castro's regime, he abandoned Cuba in 1980. He traveled to the United States and took a position as professor of Spanish at Amherst College in Amherst, Mass.

His novel *El mar de las lentejas* (1979; *Sea of Lentils*) is set in the Caribbean during the colonial period. His prizewinning collection of essays *La isla que se repite: el Caribe y la perspectiva posmoderna* (1989; *The Repeating Island: The Caribbean and the Postmodern Perspective*) has become widely influential. The collection of stories *El paso de los vientos* (1999; "Windward Passage") contains some pieces that are set in colonial times.

Benítez Rojo's stories follow two main themes: Caribbean history and the disintegration of the Cuban bourgeoisie in the aftermath of the revolution. The former deals with the emergence of the Caribbean from the clashes between the white colonizers and their black slaves who seek freedom. The latter explores the uncanny in the manner of Edgar Allan Poe, Horacio Quiroga,

Jorge Luis Borges, and Julio Cortázar. By far Benítez Rojo's best story, and one of the best ever from Latin America, is *Estatuas Sepultadas* (*Buried Statues*), which narrates the isolation of a formerly well-to-do family in an enclosed mansion, where they can barely hear and must intuit the transcendental transformations taking place around them.

ADOLFO BIOY CASARES

(b. Sept. 15, 1914, Buenos Aires, Arg.—d. March 8, 1999, Buenos Aires)

Adolfo Bioy Casares was an Argentine writer and editor known both for his own work and for his collaborations with Jorge Luis Borges. His elegantly constructed works are oriented toward metaphysical possibilities and employ the fantastic to achieve their meanings.

Born into a wealthy family, Bioy Casares was encouraged in his writing, publishing (with the help of his father) his first book in 1929. In 1932 he met Borges, a meeting that resulted in lifelong friendship and literary collaboration. Together they edited the literary magazine *Destiempo* (1936).

Bioy Casares published several books before 1940, including collections of short stories (such as *Caos* [1934; "Chaos"] and *Luis Greve, muerto* [1937; "Luis Greve, Deceased"]), but he did not win wide notice until the publication of his novel *La invención de Morel* (1940; *The Invention of Morel*). A carefully constructed and fantastic work, it concerns a fugitive (the narrator) who has fallen in love and strives to establish contact with a woman who is eventually revealed to be only an image created by a film projector. The novel formed the basis for Alain Robbe-Grillet's film script for *Last Year at Marienbad* (1961). The novel *Plan de evasión* (1945; *A Plan for Escape*) and the six short stories of *La trama celeste* (1948; "The Celestial Plot") further explore imaginary worlds, tightly constructed to adhere to a fantastic logic.

In the novel *El sueño de los héroes* (1954; *The Dream of Heroes*), Bioy Casares examines the meaning of love and the significance of dreams and memory to future actions. The novel *Diario de la guerra del cerdo* (1969; *Diary of the War of the Pig*) is a mixture of science fiction and political satire.

Other works by Bioy Casares, who used the pseudonyms Javier Miranda and Martin Sacastru, include the collections of short stories *El gran serafín* (1967; "The Great Seraphim"), *Historias de amor* (1972; "Love Stories"), *Historias fantásticas* (1972; "Fantastic Stories"), and the novels *Dormir al sol* (1973; *Asleep in the Sun*) and *La aventura de un fotógrafo en La Plata* (1985; *The Adventure of a Photographer in La Plata*).

In their collaborative efforts, Bioy Casares and Borges often employed the pseudonyms Honorio Bustos Domecq, B. Suarez Lynch, and B. Lynch Davis. Together they published *Seis problemas para Don Isidro Parodi* (1942; *Six Problems for Don Isidro Parodi*) and *Crónicas de Bustos Domecq* (1967; Chronicles of Bustos Domecq), both of which satirize a variety of Argentine personalities. The two also edited *Los mejores cuentos policiales* (1943; "The Greatest Detective Stories"), a two-volume book of gaucho poetry (*Poesía gauchesca*, 1955), and other works. Bioy Casares collaborated with his wife, the poet Silvina Ocampo, and Borges to edit *Antología de la literatura fantástica* (1940; "Anthology of Fantastic Literature"; Eng. trans. *The Book of Fantasy*) and *Antología poética argentina* (1941; "Anthology of Argentine Poetry").

In 1990 Bioy Casares was awarded the Cervantes Prize for Literature, the highest honour of Hispanic letters.

JORGE LUIS BORGES

(b. Aug. 24, 1899, Buenos Aires, Arg.—d. June 14, 1986, Geneva, Switz.)

The works of the Argentine poet, essayist, and short-story writer Jorge Luis Borges have become classics of 20th-century world literature.

LIFE

Borges was reared in the then-shabby Palermo district of Buenos Aires, the setting of some of his works. His family, which had been notable in Argentine history, included

Argentine author Jorge Luis Borges, receiving the French Legion of Honour in 1983. Many of Borges's works are considered modern classics. Joel Robine/AFP/Getty Images

British ancestry, and he learned English before Spanish. The first books that he read—from the library of his father, a man of wide-ranging intellect who taught at an English school—included *The Adventures of Huckleberry Finn*, the novels of H.G. Wells, *The Thousand and One Nights*, and *Don Quixote*, all in English. Under the constant stimulus and example of his father, the young Borges from his earliest years recognized that he was destined for a literary career.

In 1914, on the eve of World War I, Borges was taken by his family to Geneva, where he learned French and German and received his B.A. from the Collège de Genève.

Leaving there in 1919, the family spent a year on Majorca and a year in mainland Spain, where Borges joined the young writers of the Ultraist movement, a group that rebelled against what it considered the decadence of the established writers of the Generation of 1898.

Returning to Buenos Aires in 1921, Borges rediscovered his native city and began to sing of its beauty in poems that imaginatively reconstructed its past and present. His first published book was a volume of poems, *Fervor de Buenos Aires, poemas* (1923; "Fervour of Buenos Aires, Poems"). He is also credited with establishing the Ultraist movement in South America, though he later repudiated it. This period of his career, which included the authorship of several volumes of essays and poems and the founding of three literary journals, ended with a biography, *Evaristo Carriego* (1930).

During his next phase, Borges gradually overcame his shyness in creating pure fiction. At first he preferred to retell the lives of more or less infamous men, as in the sketches of his *Historia universal de la infamia* (1935; "A Universal History of Infamy"). To earn his living, he took a major post in 1938 at a Buenos Aires library named for one of his ancestors. He remained there for nine unhappy years.

In 1938, the year his father died, Borges suffered a severe head wound and subsequent blood poisoning, which left him near death, bereft of speech, and fearing for his sanity. This experience appears to have freed in him the deepest forces of creation. In the next eight years he produced his best fantastic stories, those later collected in *Ficciones* ("Fictions") and the volume of English translations titled *The Aleph and Other Stories*, 1933–69 . During this time, he and another writer, Adolfo Bioy Casares, jointly wrote detective stories under the pseudonym

H. Bustos Domecq (combining ancestral names of the two writers' families), which were published in 1942 as *Seis problemas para Don Isidro Parodi* (*Six Problems for Don Isidro Parodi*). The works of this period revealed for the first time Borges's entire dreamworld, an ironical or paradoxical version of the real one, with its own language and systems of symbols.

When the dictatorship of Juan Perón came to power in 1946, Borges was dismissed from his library position for having expressed support of the Allies in World War II. With the help of friends, he earned his way by lecturing, editing, and writing. A 1952 collection of essays, *Otras inquisiciones* (1937–1952) (*Other Inquisitions*, 1937–1952), revealed him at his analytic best. When Perón was deposed in 1955, Borges became director of the national library, an honorific position, and also professor of English and American literature at the University of Buenos Aires. By this time, Borges suffered from total blindness, a hereditary affliction that had also attacked his father and had progressively diminished his own eyesight from the 1920s onward. It had forced him to abandon the writing of long texts and to begin dictating to his mother or to secretaries or friends.

The works that date from this late period, such as *El hacedor* (1960; "The Doer," Eng. trans. *Dreamtigers*) and *El libro de los seres imaginarios* (1967; *The Book of Imaginary Beings*), almost erase the distinctions between the genres of prose and poetry. His later collections of stories include *El informe de Brodie* (1970; *Dr. Brodie's Report*), which deals with revenge, murder, and horror, and *El libro de arena* (1975; *The Book of Sand*), both of which are allegories combining the simplicity of a folk storyteller with the complex vision of a man who has explored the labyrinths of his own being to its core.

Assessment

After 1961, when he and Samuel Beckett shared the Formentor Prize, an international award given for unpublished manuscripts, Borges's tales and poems were increasingly acclaimed as classics of 20th-century world literature. Prior to that time, Borges was little known, even in his native Buenos Aires, except to other writers, many of whom regarded him merely as a craftsman of ingenious techniques and tricks. By the time of his death, the nightmare world of his "fictions" had come to be compared to the world of Franz Kafka and to be praised for concentrating common language into its most enduring form. Through his work, Latin American literature emerged from the academic realm into the realm of generally educated readers.

JUAN BOSCH

(b. June 30, 1909, La Vega, Dom.Rep. — d. Nov. 1, 2001, Santo Domingo)

The Dominican writer, scholar, and politician Juan Bosch Gaviño was elected president of the Dominican Republic in 1962 but deposed less than a year later.

Bosch, an intellectual, was an early opponent of Rafael Trujillo's dictatorial regime. He went into exile in 1937 and in 1939 founded the leftist Dominican Revolutionary Party (Partido Revolucionario Dominicano; PRD). The PRD was the first well-organized political party of the Dominican Republic and the only one with a constructive program ready to implement after Trujillo's death in 1961. Bosch, a dazzling and charismatic orator, won a landslide victory in the elections of Dec. 20, 1962. He was the first politician to directly address the peasantry, a heretofore ignored group that gave him an overwhelming majority in the election. Bosch not only appealed to the poor but also cut across class lines to win the favour of the middle class and intellectuals.

Entering office on Feb. 27, 1963, Bosch faced serious problems at the outset of his term. The United States was at odds with Fidel Castro's government in Cuba and leery of the slightest hint of leftist politics in the Caribbean. This fear was fed by damaging reports of the new regime from a skeptical U.S. ambassador in the Dominican Republic. Bosch's constitution of April 29, liberal and democratic, alienated four powerful groups in the country: landholders, even small ones, were frightened by his prohibition against *latifundia* (large plantation-type farms); the Roman Catholic church was angered by the secular nature of the constitution; industrialists felt the constitution was worker-oriented; and the military considered that its powers were curtailed. On Sept. 25, 1963, the military deposed Bosch. Two years later his followers staged a rebellion in hopes of returning Bosch to power. The United States, fearful of a Communist revolution, sent troops to end the revolt.

After a two-year exile in Puerto Rico (Sept. 28, 1963– September 1965), Bosch was allowed to return and reluctantly agreed to take part in the new elections. Fearful for his safety, he campaigned half-heartedly, making no public appearances, and lost to Joaquín Balaguer, the conservative candidate with heavy backing from the United States. Bosch and his party abstained from participating in the 1970 elections, but by 1973 the PRD wanted to rejoin the political process. Bosch resigned from the PRD and formed a third party, the Party of Dominican Liberation (Partido de la Liberación Dominicana). In subsequent presidential elections, Bosch repeatedly lost but claimed vote fraud. He last ran for president in 1994, finishing third.

His term in office was too short for a judgment of his effectiveness as president, but Bosch's contribution to his country's political development was of paramount importance. After 31 years of dictatorship, Bosch created a genuine political party, forcing the opposition to do the same and enabling his country to have legitimate, representative elections.

Bosch was a respected historian and essayist, having written mostly on Dominican and Caribbean politics. He also wrote novels and a biography, *Simón Bolívar* (1960).

ERNESTO CARDENAL

(b. Jan. 20, 1925, Granada, Nic.)

The revolutionary Nicaraguan poet and Roman Catholic priest Ernesto Cardenal is considered to be the second most important Nicaraguan poet, after Rubén Darío.

He was educated first at Jesuit schools in Nicaragua, then in Mexico and at Columbia University. Having undergone a religious conversion, in 1957 he entered the Trappist monastery at Gethsemane, Ky., transferred to the Benedictine monastery of Cuernavaca, Mex., and, after studying theology in a seminary at La Ceja, Colom., was ordained a priest in 1965 in Nicaragua.

His early poems, collected in *Epigramas* (1961), denounce the senseless violence of the Somoza regime in Nicaragua, while others are love poems written with a fine sense of irony. *La hora o* (1960; *Zero Hour and Other Documentary Poems*), a long documentary poem denouncing the effects of domestic tyranny and American imperialism in Central American history, is a masterpiece of protest poetry. In subsequent works Cardenal began to use empty phrases and commercial slogans as symbols of an alienating world.

The poems in *Salmos* (1964; *The Psalms of Struggle and Liberation*) represent Cardenal's rewriting of the biblical psalms of David and condemn modern-day evils. These poems, like many of his others, express the tension between his revolutionary political fervour and his religious faith. The book culminates in an apocalyptic view of the world, a theme that becomes an obsession in later works.

In *Oración por Marilyn Monroe y otros poemas* (1965; *Marilyn Monroe, and Other Poems*), the earlier prophetic tone is linked to contemporary events: the death of the film actress Marilyn Monroe serves as an example of what Cardenal sees as the dehumanizing corruption of the capitalist system. Clichés, slogans, newspaper clippings, and advertisements in the poem become symbols of noncommunication.

Among his other volumes of poetry is *El estrecho dudoso* (1966; "The Doubtful Strait"), *Homenaje a los indios americanos* (1969; *Homage to the American Indians*), and *Oráculo sobre Managua* (1973; "Oracles About Managua"). *Vida en el amor* (1970; *To Live Is to Love*), a book of philosophical essays, and *En Cuba* (1972; *In Cuba*), recollections of his visit there in 1970, comprise his prose work. Volumes of his poetry have been translated into all the major European languages.

Cardenal took an active part in the Sandinista revolution that ousted Anastasio Somoza in July 1979, and he became minister of culture in the new government. In this post he sponsored popular workshops in poetry and theatre and promulgated Sandinista political ideals. His later works of poetry include *Nueva Antología poética* (1978), *Vuelos de victoria* (1985; *Flights of Victory*), and *Cántico cósmico* (1989; *Cosmic Canticles*).

ALEJO CARPENTIER

(b. Dec. 26, 1904, Lausanne, Switz.—d. April 24, 1980, Paris, France)

Alejo Carpentier y Valmont, considered one of the best novelists of the 20th century, was also a musicologist, an essayist, and a playwright. Among the first practitioners of the style known as magic realism, he exerted a decisive influence on the works of younger Latin American writers such as Gabriel García Márquez.

Though born in Lausanne to a French father and a Russian mother, Carpentier claimed throughout his life that he was Cuban-born. He was taken to Havana as an infant. The language that he spoke first was his father's, however, which left him with a French accent in Spanish. In Havana he acquired a superb education in private schools, his father's library, and the University of Havana. In the 1920s Carpentier was among the founders of the Afro-Cuban movement that sought to incorporate African forms into avant-garde art, particularly music, dance, and the theatre. Carpentier wrote several opera librettos and ballet pieces with Afro-Cuban themes, and in 1933 he published a novel, *¡Ecue-Yamba-O!* ("Praised Be God!"), in the same vein.

In 1928 Carpentier had fled Cuban dictator Gerardo Machado's repressive regime and settled in Paris. He remained in France until 1939, when he returned to Havana. In 1945 he left Havana again, this time for Caracas, Venezuela. The next year he published *La música en Cuba* ("The Music of Cuba"), based on extensive archival research. Using that documentation, he began to publish short stories with historical background and instances of the fantastic. This combination became the hallmark of his work and the formula for magic realism. *Viaje a la semilla* (1944; *Journey Back to the Source*), for instance, set in 19th-century Cuba, is told in reverse, from the protagonist's death to his return to the womb. This and other stories would be collected in the important volume *Guerra del tiempo* (1958; *War of Time*).

Carpentier's second novel, and the first to enjoy wide acclaim, was *El reino de este mundo* (1950; *The Kingdom of This World*); it is about the Haitian revolution. In the prologue to this work, Carpentier expounds on magic realism, which he defines as the representation of "marvelous American reality." His novel *Los pasos perdidos* (1953; *The Lost Steps*), his best-known work, is the first-person account of a character who travels to the Orinoco jungle in search of the meaning of life and the origins of time.

In 1959 Carpentier returned to Havana to join the victorious Cuban Revolution. He would remain faithful to Castro's regime, serving as a Cuban diplomat in Paris from the middle 1960s until his death. In 1962 Carpentier published another historical novel, *El siglo de las luces* (*Explosion in a Cathedral*), which chronicles the impact of the French Revolution on Caribbean countries. It was very successful and there were calls to award Carpentier a Nobel Prize, something that eluded him. In his final years Carpentier turned to lighter, sometimes humorous fiction, as in Concierto barroco (1974; Eng. trans. *Concierto barroco*), *El recurso del método* (1974; *Reasons of State*), and *El arpa y la sombra* (1979; *The Harp and the Shadow*). In the latter, the protagonist is Christopher Columbus, involved in a love affair with the Catholic Queen Isabel of Castile. Carpentier's last novel, *La consagración de la primavera* (1979; "The Consecration of Spring"), deals with the Cuban Revolution.

JULIO CORTÁZAR

(b. Aug. 26, 1914, Brussels, Belg.—d. Feb. 12, 1984, Paris, France)

Julio Cortázar was an Argentine novelist and short-story writer who combined existential questioning with experimental writing techniques in his works.

Cortázar, who used the pseudonym Julio Denis, was the son of Argentine parents and was educated in Argentina, where he taught secondary school and worked as a translator. *Bestiario* (1951; "Bestiary"), his first short-story collection, was published the year he moved to Paris, an act motivated by dissatisfaction with the Perón government and what he saw as the general stagnation of the Argentine middle class. He remained in Paris, where he received French citizenship in 1981, though he kept his Argentine citizenship as well. He also traveled widely.

Another collection of short stories, *Final del juego* (1956; "End of the Game"), was followed by *Las armas secretas* (1958; "Secret Weapons"). Some of those stories were translated into English as *End of the Game, and Other Stories* (1967). The main character of *El perseguidor* ("The Pursuer"), one of the stories in *Las armas secretas*, embodies many of the traits of Cortázar's later characters. The metaphysical anguish that he feels in his search for artistic perfection and in his failure to come to grips with the passage of time, coupled with his rejection of 20th-century values, was among Cortázar's central preoccupations.

Another story, "Las babas del diablo" (1958; "The Devil's Drivel"), served as the basis for Michelangelo Antonioni's motion picture *Blow-up* (1966). Cortázar's masterpiece, *Rayuela* (1963; *Hopscotch*), is an open-ended novel, or anti-novel; the reader is invited to rearrange the different parts of the novel according to a plan prescribed by the author. A series of playful and humorous stories written between 1952 and 1959 were published in *Historias de cronopios y de famas* (1962; *Cronopios and Famas*). His other works include Todos los fuegos el fuego (1966; *"All Fires the Fire"*) and *Libro de Manuel* (1973; *A Manual for Manuel*).

SOR JUANA INÉS DE LA CRUZ

(b. Nov. 12, 1651?, San Miguel Nepantla, Viceroyalty of New Spain [now in Mexico]—d. April 17, 1695, Mexico City)

The poet, dramatist, scholar, and nun who became known as Sor Juana Inés de la Cruz was an outstanding writer of the Latin American colonial period and of the Hispanic Baroque.

Juana Ramírez de Asbaje was born out of wedlock to a family of modest means in either 1651 or, according to a baptismal certificate, 1648 (there is no scholarly consensus on her birth date). Her mother was a Creole and her father Spanish. Juana thirsted for knowledge from her earliest years and throughout her life. As a girl, she had little access to formal education and would be almost entirely self-taught. Her mother sent the gifted child to live with relatives in Mexico City. There her prodigious intelligence attracted the attention of the viceroy, Antonio Sebastián de Toledo, marquis de Mancera. He invited her to court as a lady-in-waiting in 1664 and later had her knowledge tested by some 40 noted scholars.

In 1667, given what she called her "total disinclination to marriage" and her wish "to have no fixed occupation which might curtail my freedom to study," Sor (Spanish: "Sister") Juana began her life as a nun with a brief stay in the order of the Discalced Carmelites. She moved in 1669 to the more lenient Convent of Santa Paula of the Hieronymite order in Mexico City, and there she took her vows. Sor Juana remained cloistered in the Convent of Santa Paula for the rest of her life.

Convent life afforded Sor Juana her own apartment, time to study and write, and the opportunity to teach music and drama to the girls in Santa Paula's school. She also functioned as the convent's archivist and accountant. In her convent cell, Sor Juana amassed one of the largest private libraries in the New World, together with a collection of musical and scientific instruments. She was able to continue her contact with other scholars and powerful members of the court. The patronage of the viceroy and vicereine of New Spain, notably that of the marquis and marquise de la Laguna from 1680 to 1688, helped her maintain her exceptional freedom. They visited her, favoured her, and had her works published in Spain. For her part, Sor Juana, though cloistered, became the unofficial court poet in the 1680s. Her plays in verse, occasional poetry, commissioned religious services, and writings for state festivals all contributed magnificently to the world outside the convent.

Sor Juana's success in the colonial milieu and her enduring significance are due at least in part to her mastery of the full range of poetic forms and themes of the Spanish Golden Age. She was the last great writer of the Hispanic Baroque and the first great exemplar of colonial Mexican culture. Her writings display the boundless inventiveness of Lope de Vega, the wit and wordplay of Francisco de Quevedo, the dense erudition and strained syntax of Luis de Góngora, and the schematic abstraction of Pedro Calderón de la Barca. Sor Juana employed all of the poetic models then in fashion, including sonnets, romances (ballad form), and so on. She drew on a vast stock of Classical, biblical, philosophical, and mythological sources. She wrote moral, satiric, and religious lyrics, along with many poems of praise to court figures. Though it is impossible to date much of her poetry, it is clear that, even after she became a nun, Sor Juana wrote secular love lyrics.

Her breadth of range—from the serious to the comical and the scholarly to the popular—is equally unusual for a nun. Sor Juana authored both allegorical religious dramas and entertaining cloak-and-dagger plays. Notable in the popular vein are the *villancicos* (carols) that she composed to be sung in the cathedrals of Mexico City, Puebla, and Oaxaca. Sor Juana was as prolific as she was encyclopaedic. The authoritative modern edition of her complete works, edited by Alfonso Méndez Plancarte and Alberto G. Salceda, runs to four lengthy volumes.

Sor Juana placed her own stamp on Spanish 17th-century literature. All of the nun's poetry, however densely Baroque, exhibits her characteristically tight logic. Her philosophical poems can carry the Baroque theme of the deceptiveness of appearances into a defense of empiricism that borders on Enlightenment reasoning. She celebrated woman as the seat of reason and knowledge rather than passion. Her famous poem "Hombres necios" ("Foolish Men") accuses men of the illogical behaviour that they criticize in women. Her many love poems in the first person show a woman's *desengaño* (disillusionment) with love, given the strife, pain, jealousy, and loneliness that it occasions.

Other first-person poems have an obvious autobiographical element, dealing with the burdens of fame and intellect. Sor Juana's most significant full-length plays involve the actions of daring, ingenious women. Sor Juana also occasionally wrote of her native Mexico. The short play that introduces her religious drama *El divino Narciso* (1689; *"The Divine Narcissus,"* in a bilingual edition) blends the Aztec and Christian religions. Her various carols contain an amusing mix of Nahuatl (a Mexican Indian language) and Hispano-African and Spanish dialects.

Sor Juana's most important and most difficult poem, known as the *Primero sueño* (1692; *First Dream*, published in *A Sor Juana Anthology*, 1988), is both personal and universal. The date of its writing is unknown. It employs the convoluted poetic forms of the Baroque to recount the torturous quest of the soul for knowledge. In the poem's opening, as night falls, the soul is unchained from the body to dream. Over the course of the night's dreaming, the soul attempts unsuccessfully to gain total knowledge by following the philosophical paths of Neoplatonism and Scholasticism. As the sun rises and routs the night, the dream fades and the body awakens, but the soul determines to persist in its efforts. The last lines of the poem refer to a female "I," which associates the foregoing quest with its author. In fact, the entire 975-line poem, thick with erudition, attests to the nun's lifelong pursuit of learning.

The prodigiously accomplished Sor Juana achieved considerable renown in Mexico and in Spain. With renown came disapproval from church officials. She broke with her Jesuit confessor, Antonio Núñez de Miranda, in the early 1680s because he had publicly maligned her. The nun's privileged situation began definitively to collapse after the departure for Spain of her protectors, the marquis and marquise de la Laguna. In November 1690, Manuel Fernández de Santa Cruz, bishop of Puebla, published without Sor Juana's permission her critique of a 40-year-old sermon by the Portuguese Jesuit preacher António Vieira. Fernández de Santa Cruz entitled the critique *Carta atenagórica* ("Letter Worthy of Athena"). Using the female pseudonym of Sister Filotea, he also admonished Sor Juana to concentrate on religious rather than secular studies.

Sor Juana responded to the bishop of Puebla in March 1691 with her magnificent self-defense and defense of all women's right to knowledge, the *Respuesta a sor Filotea de la Cruz* ("Reply to Sister Filotea of the Cross"; translated in *A Sor Juana Anthology*, 1988). In the autobiographical section of the document, Sor Juana traces the many obstacles that her powerful "inclination to letters" had forced her to surmount throughout her life. Among the obstacles she discusses is having been temporarily forbidden by a prelate to read, which caused her to study instead "everything that God has created, all of it being my letters." Sor Juana famously remarks, quoting an Aragonese poet and also echoing St. Teresa of Ávila: "One can perfectly well philosophize while cooking supper." She justifies her study of "human arts and sciences" as necessary to understand sacred theology. In her defense of education for women in general, Sor Juana lists as models learned women of biblical, Classical, and contemporary times. She uses the words of Church Fathers such as St. Jerome and St. Paul, bending them to her purposes, to argue that women are entitled to private instruction. Throughout the *Respuesta*, Sor Juana concedes some personal failings but remains strong in supporting her larger cause. Similarly, in the same year of 1691, Sor Juana wrote for the cathedral of Oaxaca some exquisite carols to St. Catherine of Alexandria that sing the praises of this learned woman and martyr.

Yet by 1694 Sor Juana had succumbed in some measure to external or internal pressures. She curtailed her literary pursuits. Her library and collections were sold for alms. She returned to her previous confessor, renewed her religious vows, and signed various penitential documents. Sor Juana died while nursing her sister nuns during an epidemic.

Her story and accomplishments, however, have helped her live on. She now stands as a national icon of Mexico and Mexican identity; her former cloister is a centre for higher education, and her image adorns Mexican currency. Because of rising interest in feminism and women's writing, Sor Juana came to new prominence in the late 20th century as the first published feminist of the New World and as the most outstanding writer of the Spanish American colonial period. A woman of genius who, to paraphrase Virginia Woolf's famous recommendation for the female author, succeeded under hostile circumstances in creating a "room of her own," Sor Juana remains avidly read and deeply meaningful to the present day.

RUBÉN DARÍO

(b. Jan. 18, 1867, Metapa, Nic.—d. Feb. 6, 1916, León)

Rubén Darío, the pseudonym of Félix Rubén García Sarmiento, was an influential Nicaraguan poet, journalist, and diplomat. As a leader of the Spanish American literary movement known as Modernismo, which flourished at the end of the 19th century, he revivified and modernized poetry in Spanish on both sides of the Atlantic through his experiments with rhythm, metre, and imagery. Darío developed a highly original poetic style that founded a tradition.

LIFE AND WORK

Precocious and prolific, from the age of 14 he signed the name Rubén Darío to his poems and stories of love, heroism, and adventure, which, although imitative in form, showed a strikingly vivid imagination. In 1886 he left Nicaragua, beginning the travels that continued throughout his life. He settled for a time in Chile, where in 1888 he published his first major work, *Azul* ("Blue"), a collection of short stories, descriptive sketches, and verse. This volume was soon recognized in Europe and Latin America as the herald of a new era in Spanish American literature.

Darío had only recently become acquainted with French Parnassian poetry, and *Azul* represents his attempt to apply to Spanish the tenets of that stylistic movement. In the prose works in *Azul* he discarded the traditional long and grammatically complex Spanish sentence structure, replacing it with simple and direct language. Both the prose and poetry in this volume are generally concerned with objective description, and both deal with exotic subjects, chiefly classical mythology, France, and Asia. As a whole, the volume exhibits Darío's concern with "art for art's sake," and it reveals little interest in everyday life.

After his return to Central America in 1889 and two brief marriages (the first ended by his wife's death and the other by separation), he left to take up an appointment in 1893 as Colombian consul in Buenos Aires, where he found the cosmopolitan atmosphere stimulating. Young writers there hailed him as their leader, and the modernist movement organized around him. Darío's next significant work, *Prosas profanas y otros poemas* (1896; "Profane Hymns and Other Poems"), a collection of verse, continued the innovative stylistic trends of *Azul* but treated its exotic scenes and personages in a manner more symbolic than objective, for it was influenced by the contemporary French Symbolist poets.

Darío went to Europe in 1898 as a correspondent for the Buenos Aires newspaper *La Nación*. Based in Paris and Majorca, he traveled extensively on the European continent on journalistic and diplomatic missions. By this time, world events and his own advancing age had brought about a profound change in his outlook on life. He became vitally concerned with the world outside the realm of art: the possible threat of North American imperialism after the defeat of Spain in 1898, the solidarity of Spanish-speaking peoples, the future of Spanish America after the collapse of Spain's empire in the New World, and the age-old problems of human existence. The collection that is generally considered to be his masterpiece, *Cantos de vida y esperanza* (1905; "Songs of Life and Hope"), reflects these concerns and is the culmination of his technical experimentation and his artistic resourcefulness.

On the outbreak of World War I in 1914, Darío left Europe, physically ill and on the brink of poverty. In an attempt to alleviate his financial difficulties, he began a lecture tour of North America, but he developed pneumonia in New York and died shortly after his return to his homeland.

Among the many editions of Darío's work in Spanish is *Obras completas*, 2 vol. (1971), edited by A.M. Plancarte. *Selected Poems,* translated by Lysander Kemp (1965), contains an introduction by Octavio Paz and a tribute—originally given before the Buenos Aires Pen Club in 1933—by Federico García Lorca and Pablo Neruda.

ASSESSMENT

In addition to the three major collections on which his greatest fame rests, Darío wrote approximately 100 short stories and tales, several volumes of poetry and penetrating literary criticism, and the journalistic articles that appeared in *La Nación* and elsewhere.

From the standpoint of artistic resourcefulness and technical perfection, Darío is considered by many to be one of the greatest poets who ever wrote in Spanish. Throughout his career he boldly experimented with many forms of verse, and he probably introduced more metrical innovations than any other Spanish-language poet. Darío's poetry is notable for its remarkable musicality, grace, and sonority, and he had a masterly command of rhyme and metrical structure. His earlier anecdotal and descriptive poems treat faraway places, mythology, and other exotic subjects with a rich lyricism, while the later poems in *Cantos de vida* contain a pronounced philosophical note and exhibit a poignant and powerful sense of the tragic side of life.

CARLOS FUENTES
(b. Nov. 11, 1928, Panama City, Pan.)

The experimental novels of Carlos Fuentes, a Mexican novelist, short-story writer, playwright, critic, and diplomat, won him an international literary reputation.

Carlos Fuentes received the first International Don Quijote de la Mancha Award, in the outstanding career category, in 2008. The award recognizes contributions to the promotion and spread of Spanish culture and language. Pierre-Philippe Marcou/AFP/Getty Images

The son of a Mexican career diplomat, Fuentes was born in Panama and traveled extensively with his family in North and South America and in Europe. He learned English at age four in Washington, D.C. As a young man, he studied law at the University of Mexico in Mexico City and later attended the Institute of Advanced International Studies in Geneva. Fuentes was a member of the Mexican delegation to the International Labour Organization (ILO) in Geneva (1950–52), was in charge of cultural dissemination for the University of Mexico (1955–56), was cultural officer of the ministry (1957–59), and was ambassador to France (1975–77). He also cofounded and edited several periodicals, including *Revista Mexicana de literatura* (1954–58; "Mexican Review of Literature").

Rebelling against his family's middle-class values early in the 1950s, Fuentes became a communist, but he left the party in 1962 on intellectual grounds while remaining an avowed Marxist. His first collection of stories, *Los días enmascarados* (1954, 2nd ed. 1966; "The Masked Days"), re-creates the past realistically and fantastically. His first novel, *La región más transparente* (1958; *Where the Air Is Clear*), which treats the theme of national identity and bitterly indicted Mexican society, won him national prestige. The work is marked by cinematographic techniques, flashbacks, interior monologues, and language from all levels of society, showing influences from many non-Spanish literatures. After this, Fuentes spent most of his time writing but continued to travel widely as he had in his youth.

The novel *Las buenas conciencias* (1959; *The Good Conscience*) emphasizes the moral compromises that mark the transition from a rural economy to a complex middle-class urban one. *Aura* (1962) is a novella that successfully fuses reality and fantasy. *La muerte de Artemio Cruz* (1962; *The Death of Artemio Cruz*), which presents the agony of the last hours of a wealthy survivor of the Mexican Revolution, was translated into several languages and established Fuentes as a major international novelist.

After *Artemio Cruz* came a succession of novels. *Cambio de piel* (1967; *A Change of Skin*) defines existentially a collective Mexican consciousness by exploring and reinterpreting the country's myths. *Terra nostra* (1975; "Our Land," Eng. trans. *Terra nostra*) explores the cultural substrata of New and Old Worlds as the author, using Jungian archetypal symbolism, seeks to understand his cultural heritage. *Diana; o, la cazadora solitaria* (1994; *Diana the Goddess Who Hunts Alone*) is a fictional version of Fuentes's affair with the American actress Jean Seberg. In 1995 he published *La frontera de cristal: una novela en nueve cuentos* (*The Crystal Frontier: A Novel in Nine Stories*), a tale of nine lives as they are affected by a powerful and unscrupulous man. Among

Fuentes's other works of fiction are *La cabeza de la hidra* (1978; *The Hydra Head*), *Una familia lejana* (1980; *Distant Relations*), *Gringo viejo* (1985; *The Old Gringo*; film 1989), *Cristóbal nonato* (1987; *Christopher Unborn*), *Los años con Laura Díaz* (1999; *The Years with Laura Díaz*), *Instinto de Inez* (2001; *Inez*), and *La voluntad y la fortuna* (2008; *"Will and Fortune"*).

Fuentes also published collections of stories, including *Constancia, y otras novelas para vírgenes* (1989; *Constancia and Other Stories for Virgins*), *El naranjo; o, los círculos del tiempo* (1993; "The Orange Tree; or, The Circles of Time," Eng. trans. *The Orange Tree*), *Inquieta compañía* (2004; "Disturbing Company"), and *Todas las familias felices* (2006; Happy Families: Stories).

Fuentes wrote several plays, including the important *Todos los gatos son pardos* (1970; "All Cats Are Gray"), a drama about the Spanish conquest of Mexico with the pivotal character La Malinche, the quasi-legendary woman agent of Hernán Cortés who is said to have served as a mediator between the Spanish and Mexican civilizations. A revised version of *Todos los gatos* was released in 1991 as Ceremonias del alba ("Ceremonies of the Dawn").

Among Fuentes's works of nonfiction are *La nueva novela hispanoamericana* (1969; "The New Hispano-American Novel"), which is his chief work of literary criticism; *Cervantes; o, la crítica de la lectura* (1976; "Cervantes; or, The Critique of Reading," Eng. trans. *Don Quixote; or, The Critique of Reading*), an homage to the great Spanish writer; and his book-length essay on Hispanic cultures, *El espejo enterrado* (1992; *Buried Mirror*), which was published simultaneously in Spanish and English.

Fuentes was undoubtedly one of the foremost Mexican writers of the 20th century. His broad range of literary accomplishments and his articulate humanism made him highly influential in the world's literary communities, particularly in that of Latin America. Several of his novels effect a cosmopolitan dialogue between Mexican culture and that of other countries and study the effect of foreign cultures, especially the Spanish and the North American, on Mexican identity. He pronounced his most ambitious work, *Terra nostra*, an attempt to synthesize the voices of James Joyce in *Ulysses* and Alexandre Dumas in *The Count of Monte Cristo*. Fuentes exhibits a postmodern sensibility in his use of plural voices to explore a subject. In 1987 he was awarded the Cervantes Prize, the most prestigious Spanish-language literary award.

GABRIEL GARCÍA MÁRQUEZ

(b. March 6, 1928, Aracataca, Colom.)

Gabriel García Márquez, a Colombian novelist and one of the greatest writers of the 20th century, was awarded the Nobel Prize for Literature in 1982, mostly for his master-piece *Cien años de soledad* (1967; *One Hundred Years of Solitude*). He was the fourth Latin American to be so honoured.

With Jorge Luis Borges, García Márquez is the best-known Latin American writer in history. In addition to his masterly approach to the novel, he is a superb crafter of short stories and an accomplished journalist. In both his shorter and longer fictions, García Márquez achieves the rare feat of being accessible to the common reader while satisfying the most demanding of sophisticated critics.

LIFE

Born in the sleepy provincial town of Aracataca, Colombia, García Márquez and his parents spent the first eight years of his life with his maternal grandparents, Colonel Nicolás Márquez and Tranquilina Iguarán de Márquez. After the

Colombian writer Gabriel García Márquez in 1982, after winning the Nobel Prize for Literature. García Márquez is one of the best-known and most successful Latin American writers in the world. Hulton Archive/Getty Images

Colonel's death, they moved to Sucre, a river port. He received a better than average education, but claimed as an adult that his most important literary sources were the stories about Aracataca and his family that his grandfather Nicolás told him.

Although he studied law, García Márquez became a journalist, the trade at which he earned his living before attaining literary fame. As a correspondent in Paris during the 1950s he expanded his education, reading a great deal of American literature, some of it in French translation. In the late 1950s he worked in Caracas and then in New York for Prensa Latina, the news service created by the Castro regime. Later he moved to Mexico City, where he wrote the novel that brought him fame and wealth. From 1967 to 1975, he lived in Spain. Subsequently he kept a house in Mexico City and an apartment in Paris, but he also spent much time in Havana, where Fidel Castro (whom García Márquez supported) provided him with a mansion.

WORKS

Before 1967 García Márquez had published two novels, *La hojarasca* (1955; *The Leaf Storm*) and *La mala hora* (1962; *In Evil Hour*); a novella, *El coronel no tiene quien le escriba* (1961; *No One Writes to the Colonel*); and a few short stories. Then came *One Hundred Years of Solitude*, in which García Márquez tells the story of Macondo, an isolated town whose history is like the history of Latin America on a reduced scale. While the setting is realistic, there are fantastic episodes, a combination that has come to be known as magic realism, wrongly thought to be the peculiar feature of all Latin American literature. Mixing historical facts and stories with instances of the fantastic is a practice that García Márquez derived from Cuban master Alejo Carpentier, considered to be one of the founders of magic realism. The inhabitants of Macondo are driven by elemental passions—lust, greed, thirst for power—which are thwarted by crude societal, political, or natural forces, as in Greek tragedy and myth.

Continuing his magisterial output, García Márquez issued *El otoño del patriarca* (1975; *The Autumn of the Patriarch*), *Crónica de una muerte anunciada* (1981; *Chronicle of a Death Foretold*), *El amor en los tiempos del cólera* (1985; *Love in the Time of Cholera*; filmed 2007), *El general en su laberinto* (1989; *The General in His Labyrinth*), and *Del amor y otros demonios* (1994; *Of Love and Other Demons*). The best among these books are *El amor en los tiempos del cólera*, a touching love affair that takes decades to be consummated, and *The General in His Labyrinth*, a chronicle of Simón Bolívar's last days.

In 1996 García Márquez published a journalistic chronicle of drug-related kidnappings in his native Colombia, *Noticia de un secuestro* (*News of a Kidnapping*).

After being diagnosed with cancer in 1999, García Márquez wrote the memoir *Vivir para contarla* (2002; *Living to Tell the Tale*), which focuses on his first 30 years. He returned to fiction with *Memoria de mis putas tristes* (2004; *Memories of My Melancholy Whores*), a novel about a lonely man who finally discovers the meaning of love when he hires a virginal prostitute to celebrate his 90th birthday.

ASSESSMENT

García Márquez is known for his capacity to create vast, minutely woven plots and brief, tightly knit narratives in the fashion of his two North American models, William Faulkner and Ernest Hemingway. The easy flow of even the most intricate of his stories has been compared to that of Miguel de Cervantes, as have his irony and overall humour. García Márquez's novelistic world is mostly that of provincial Colombia, where medieval and modern practices and beliefs clash both comically and tragically.

NICOLÁS GUILLÉN

(b. July 10, 1902, Camagüey, Cuba—d. July 16, 1989, Havana)

Nicolás Guillén Batista was a Cuban poet of social protest and a leader of the Afro-Cuban movement in the late 1920s and 1930s. His commitment to social justice and membership in the Communist Party made him the national poet of revolutionary Cuba.

Guillén read widely during his youth and abandoned law studies at the University of Havana in 1921 to concentrate on writing poetry. Of mixed African and Spanish descent, he combined a knowledge of traditional literary form with firsthand experience of the speech, legends, songs, and *sones* (popular dances) of the Afro-Cubans in his first volume of poetry, *Motivos de son* (1930; "Motifs of Son"), which was soon hailed as a masterpiece and widely imitated.

During the following years Guillén became more outspoken politically. No longer satisfied with mere picturesque portrayal of the daily life of the poor, he began to decry their oppression in the volumes *Sóngoro cosongo* (1931) and *West Indies Ltd.* (1934). The poems of *Cantos para soldados y sones para turistas* (1937; "Songs for Soldiers and Sones for Tourists") reflect his growing commitment; that year Guillén went to Spain to fight with the Republicans in the Spanish Civil War. From this experience came the poems collected in *España* (1937; "Spain").

Guillén returned to Cuba after the defeat of the Spanish Republic, joined the Communist Party, and continued to speak out for social and political reform. He became recognized by many critics as the most influential of those Latin

American poets who dealt with African themes and re-created African song and dance rhythms in literary form. He was arrested several times and was exiled from Cuba during the regime of Fulgencio Batista in the 1950s, and he was an ardent supporter of Fidel Castro's revolution in 1959. Guillén subsequently served as the longtime director of Cuba's Union of Writers and Artists and was a member of the Central Committee of the Cuban Communist Party. He continued to treat themes of revolution and social protest in such later volumes of poetry as *La paloma de vuelo popular: Elegías* (1958; "The Dove of Popular Flight: Elegies") and *Tengo* (1964; "I Have").

A bilingual edition of his selected poems, *Man-making Words: Selected Poems of Nicolas Guillén*, was published in 1975. In 1994 another bilingual edition appeared: *Nueva poesia de amor: En algun sitio de la primavera*, or *New Love Poetry: In Some Springtime Place*.

JUANA DE IBARBOUROU

(b. March 8, 1895, Melo, Uru.—d. July 1979, Montevideo)

Juana de Ibarbourou, a Uruguayan poet, remains one of the most famous Latin American women poets. She was venerated for her lyrical celebration of love and nature.

Born Juanita Fernández Morales, she spent her childhood in a small village surrounded by country things. She was largely self-educated. In 1914 she married and later she bore a son. After a somewhat peripatetic existence, the family moved to Montevideo in 1918.

Ibarbourou's poetry, rich in sensual images and expressed in simple language, deals with the themes of love and nature. *Las lenguas de diamante* (1919; "Tongues of Diamond") is strikingly sensual, erotic, and pantheistic. These qualities, along with a youthful narcissism, are also present in *Raíz salvaje* (1922; "Savage Root"). The urgency and abundance in these early works gave way later, in *La rosa de los vientos* (1930; "Compass Rose"), to a sense of declining beauty and vitality and, finally, in *Perdida* (1950; "Lost"), to an expression of despair. She was deeply affected by her own illness and the deaths of her parents and husband.

Although Ibarbourou's later poetry lacked the passion and feeling of her earlier work, she remained one of the most popular poets of South America. She was elected president of the Sociedad Uruguaya de Escritores (Society of Uruguayan Writers) in 1950.

JORGE ICAZA
(b. July 10, 1906, Quito, Ecua.—d. May 26, 1978, Quito)

The brutally realistic portrayals of the exploitation of his country's Indians brought Ecuadorean novelist and playwright Jorge Icaza Coronel international recognition as a spokesman for the oppressed.

Icaza started writing for the theatre, but when he was censured for a 1933 dramatic script, *El dictador,* he turned his attention, and his indignation, to the novel. He gained immediate fame and generated much controversy with his first novel, *Huasipungo* (1934; rev. ed., 1951; *Huasipungo: The Villagers,* or *The Villagers*). The title is an Indian term for the small plot of land given to the Indian worker by a landowner in return for the worker's labour on the estate. The book depicts the manner in which the Indians are deprived of their *huasipungo* and then slaughtered when they rebel against their oppressors. It was greeted with outrage by the upper classes in Ecuador and quickly became a left-wing propaganda implement. Some critics have called the work mere propaganda, and others fault its construction. But its powerful language has led many critics to acclaim it as a masterpiece of realism.

Icaza continued to dramatize the struggles of the poor in novels, and he never stopped writing for the theatre. His further writings include *En las calles* (1934; "In the Streets"), *Media vida deslumbrados* (1942; "Half a Life Amazed"), *Huairapamushcas* (1948), *Seis veces la muerte* (1954; "Death Six Times"), and *El chulla Romero y Flores* (1958; "The Loner Romero y Flores"). Over the same period Icaza also wrote numerous plays. His *Obras escogidas* ("Selected Works") was published in Mexico in 1961.

After 1973 Icaza served as his country's ambassador to Peru and the Soviet Union. His themes as well as his realistic style influenced a generation of writers in Ecuador and throughout Latin America.

JOSÉ LEZAMA LIMA

(b. Dec. 19, 1910, Havana, Cuba—d. Aug. 9, 1976, Havana)

The writing of the poet, novelist, and essayist José Lezama Lima profoundly influenced other Cuban writers.

After studying law in Havana, Lezama became one of the founders and supporters of *Verbum* (1937) and other literary reviews, and he was leader of the literary group associated with *Orígenes* (1944–56). They published the work of a number of excellent young poets who revolutionized Cuban letters.

His solid foundation in the Spanish classics of the Golden Age and his knowledge of the French Symbolists greatly influenced his early work. *Muerte de Narciso* (1937; "Death of Narcissus"), Lezama's first book of poems, reveals his vast cultural background. *Enemigo rumor* (1941; "Enemy Rumor"), in addition to aesthetic preoccupations about the essence of poetry, reveals the poet's belief that the act of creation is laden with religious and metaphysical possibilities. In *Aventuras sigilosas* (1945; "Silent Adventures"), he re-creates incidents of his youth and treats his mother's powerful influence on his artistic and cultural growth after his father's death in 1919. His novel *Paradiso* (1966) has a similar tone and content. It is considered to be his masterpiece and reaffirms faith in his art and in himself.

The poems in *La fijeza* (1949; "Stability") are an attempt to recapture his past experiences. *Analecta del reloj* (1953; "Selected Work of the Clock"), a collection of essays, is notable for "Las imágenes posibles" ("Possible Images"), which gives his poetic credo. *La expresión americana* (1957) includes essays that attempt to decipher the essence of Latin-American reality. His *Tratados en la Habana* ("Treatises on Havana") was published in 1958, and in 1959 Fidel Castro named him director of the Department of Literature and Publications of the National Council of Culture.

LEOPOLDO LUGONES

(b. June 13, 1874, Villa María del Río Seco, Arg.—d. Feb. 19, 1938, Buenos Aires)

Leopoldo Lugones was an Argentine poet, literary and social critic, and cultural ambassador considered by many to be the outstanding figure of his age in the cultural life of Argentina. He was a strong influence on the younger generation of writers that included the prominent short-story writer and novelist Jorge Luis Borges. His influence in public life set the pace for national development in the arts and education.

Lugones began as a socialist journalist, settling in Buenos Aires, where in 1897 he helped found *La montaña* ("The Mountain"), a socialist journal, and became an active member of the group of Modernist experimental poets led by the Nicaraguan Rubén Darío. Lugones's first important collection of poems, *Las montañas del oro* (1897; "Mountains of Gold"), reveals his affinity with the goals of Modernism in its use of free verse and exotic imagery, devices that he continued in *Los crepúsculos del jardín* (1905; "Twilights in the Garden") and *Lunario sentimental* (1909; "Sentimental Lunar Almanac").

Between 1911 and 1914 Lugones lived in Paris, editing the *Revue Sudaméricaine* ("South American Review"), but he returned to Argentina at the outbreak of World War I. A change in his political outlook from the radical socialism of his youth to an intense conservative nationalism was paralleled in his art by a rejection of Modernism in favour of a treatment of national themes in a realistic style. This change, already foreshadowed in the prose sketches of *La guerra gaucha* (1905; "The Gaucho War"), was fully revealed in the poems of *El libro de los paisajes* (1917; "The Book of Landscapes"), which extolled the beauty of the Argentine countryside. Lugones continued to develop native themes in such prose works as *Cuentos fatales* (1924; "Tales of Fate"), a collection of short stories, and the novel *El ángel de la sombra* (1926; "The Angel of the Shadow").

Lugones was director of the National Council of Education (1914–38), and he represented Argentina in the Committee on Intellectual Cooperation of the League of Nations (1924). He was also noted for several volumes of Argentine history, for studies of Classical Greek literature and culture, and for his Spanish translations of the *Iliad* and the *Odyssey*.

An introverted man who thought of himself primarily as a poet, Lugones was genuinely uneasy about the prominence that he had achieved and the public responsibilities that it entailed. He became a fascist in 1929. Under great emotional strain in later years, he committed suicide.

JOSÉ JULIÁN MARTÍ

(b. Jan. 28, 1853, Havana, Cuba—d. May 19, 1895, Dos Ríos)

The poet and essayist, patriot and martyr José Julián Martí y Pérez became the symbol of Cuba's struggle for independence from Spain. His dedication to the goal of Cuban freedom made his name a synonym for liberty

Cuban poet and essayist José Julián Martí, c. 1890. Martí's work, which is politically charged and highly personal in nature, helped bring about several innovations in Spanish-language prose. Hulton Archive/Getty Images

throughout Latin America. As a patriot, Martí organized and unified the movement for Cuban independence and died on the battlefield fighting for it. As a writer, he was distinguished for his personal prose and deceptively simple, sincere verse on themes of a free and united America.

Educated first in Havana, Martí had published several poems by the age of 15, and at age 16 he founded a newspaper, *La Patria Libre* ("The Free Fatherland"). During a revolutionary uprising that broke out in Cuba in 1868, he sympathized with the patriots, for which he was sentenced to six months of hard labour and, in 1871, deported to Spain. There he continued his education and his writing, receiving both an M.A. and a degree in law from the University of Zaragoza in 1874 and publishing political essays. He spent the next few years in France, in Mexico, and in Guatemala, writing and teaching, and returned to Cuba in 1878.

Because of his continued political activities, however, Martí was again exiled from Cuba to Spain in 1879. From there he went to France, to New York City, and, in 1881, to Venezuela, where he founded the *Revista Venezolana* ("Venezuelan Review"). The politics of his journal, however, provoked Venezuela's dictator, Antonio Guzmán Blanco, and Martí returned that year to New York City, where he remained, except for occasional travels, until the year of his death.

Martí continued to write and publish newspaper articles, poetry, and essays. His regular column in *La Nación of Buenos Aires* made him famous throughout Latin America. His poetry, such as the collection *Versos libres* (1913; "Free Verses"), written between 1878 and 1882 on the theme of freedom, reveals a deep sensitivity and an original poetic vision. Martí's essays, which are considered by most critics his greatest contribution to Spanish American letters, helped to bring about innovations in Spanish prose and to promote better understanding among the American nations. In essays such as *Emerson* (1882), *Whitman* (1887), *Nuestra América* (1881; "Our America"), and *Bolívar* (1893), Martí expressed his original thoughts about Latin America and the United States in an intensely personal style that is still considered a model of Spanish prose. His writings reflect his exemplary life, his kindness, his love of liberty and justice, and his deep understanding of human nature. Collections of English translations of Martí's writings are *Inside the Monster: Writings on the United States and American Imperialism* (1975), *Our America: Writings on Latin America and the Cuban Struggle for Independence* (1978), and *On Education* (1979)—all edited by Philip Foner.

In 1892 Martí was elected *delegado* ("delegate"; he refused to be called president) of the Partido Revolucionario Cubano ("Cuban Revolutionary Party") that he had helped to form. Making New York City the centre of operations, he began to draw up plans for an invasion of Cuba. He left New York for Santo Domingo on Jan. 31, 1895, accompanied by the Cuban revolutionary leader Máximo Gómez and other compatriots. They arrived in Cuba to begin the invasion on April 11. Martí's death a month later in battle on the plains of Dos Ríos, Oriente province, came only seven years before his life-long goal of Cuban independence was achieved.

PEDRO MIR

(b. June 3, 1913, San Pedro de Macorís, Dom. Rep.—d. July 11, 2000, Santo Domingo)

The poems of the Dominican poet Pedro Mir celebrate the working class and examine aspects of his country's painful past, including colonialism, slavery, and dictatorship.

By his mid-30s Mir had developed a prominent literary reputation. His social commentary, however, angered Dominican dictator Rafael Trujillo, and Mir was forced into exile in 1947. He spent the next 15 years in Cuba (where he published what is perhaps his best-known poetry collection, *Hay un país en el mundo* ["There Is a Country in the World"], in 1949), Mexico, and the Soviet Union. Mir returned to the Dominican Republic in 1962, a few months after Trujillo's assassination, and continued his prolific writing career, publishing essays and novels as well as poems.

Mir was awarded the Dominican Republic's National Prize for History in 1975 and its National Prize for Literature for lifetime achievement in 1993. He was also appointed national poet in 1982, a post he held until his death. A selection of his poems in English translation appears in *Countersong to Walt Whitman, and Other Poems* (1993).

ÁLVARO MUTIS

(b. Aug. 25, 1923, Bogotá, Colom.)

The versatile Colombian writer and poet Álvaro Mutis is best known for his novels featuring his alter ego, a character named Maqroll el Gaviero ("Maqroll the Lookout").

The son of a diplomat, Mutis attended schools in Brussels, Belgium. He returned to Colombia to live on his family's coffee plantation in the department of Tolima while continuing his studies in Bogotá under the tutelage of the Colombian poet Eduardo Carranza. He entered the literary world in Bogotá as a poet, a member of the young and diverse Cántico (Canticle) group that emerged in the 1940s. In 1948 Mutis and Carlos Patino published a chapbook of poems called *La balanza*. After 1956 he lived in Mexico, gaining renown there as the result of Octavio Paz's positive reviews of his work.

After his first few volumes of verse had been published, Mutis began to write prose in addition to poetry, producing a number of collections of short stories and novellas. In *Diario do Lecumberri* (1960; "Lecumberri Diary"), Mutis wrote about his experience in a Mexican jail. His novella *La mansión de Araucaíma* (1973; "Araucaíma Mansion," Eng. trans. *The Mansion*) was subtitled "A Gothic Tale from the Hot Lands."

Mutis introduced Maqroll el Gaviero, his recurring character, in his early poetry and published his first collection of Maqroll poems in 1973. Like his creator, Maqroll is a solitary traveler who brings a stranger's detachment to his encounters and his loves; he searches for meaning in a time of violence and inhumanity. In a series of novels, Maqroll engages in a variety of adventures that together form a single, sweeping life story. These novels include *La nieve del almirante* (1986; *Snow of the Admiral*), Maqroll's diary of a journey on a vast tropical river; *Ilono llega con la lluvia* (1987; *Ilona Comes with the Rain*), which finds Maqroll managing a brothel in Panama; and *Un bel morir* (1989; Eng. trans. *Un Bel Morir*), set in a guerrilla war in South America.

In 1997 Mutis published a collection of Maqroll poems as *Summa de Maqroll el Gaviero: Poesía 1948–1997*. His novellas *La última escala del tramp steamer* (1988; *The Tramp Steamer's Last Port of Call*), *Amirbar* (1990; Eng. trans. *Amirbar*), *Abdul Bashur, soñador de navíos* (1991; *Abdul Bashur, Dreamer of Ships*), and Tríptico de mar y tierra (1993; *Triptych on Sea and Land*) were translated into English and collected in *The Adventures of Maqroll: Four Novellas* (1995). In 2002 Mutis won the Neustadt International Prize for

Literature, awarded by the University of Oklahoma and *World Literature Today*.

PABLO NERUDA

(b. July 12, 1904, Parral, Chile—d. Sept. 23, 1973, Santiago)

The Chilean poet, diplomat, and politician Pablo Neruda was awarded the Nobel Prize for Literature in 1971. He was perhaps the most important Latin American poet of the 20th century.

EARLY LIFE AND LOVE POETRY

Born Neftalí Ricardo Reyes Basoalto, Neruda was the son of José del Carmen Reyes, a railway worker, and Rosa Basoalto. His mother died within a month of Neruda's birth, and two years later the family moved to Temuco, a small town farther south in Chile, where his father remarried. Neruda was a precocious boy who began to write poetry at age 10. His father tried to discourage him from writing and never cared for his poems, which was probably why the young poet began to publish under the pseudonym Pablo Neruda, which he was legally to adopt in 1946. He entered the Temuco Boys' School in 1910 and finished his secondary schooling there in 1920. Tall, shy, and lonely, Neruda read voraciously and was encouraged by the principal of the Temuco Girls' School, Gabriela Mistral, a gifted poet who would herself later become a Nobel laureate.

Neruda first published his poems in the local newspapers and later in magazines published in the Chilean capital, Santiago. In 1921 he moved to Santiago to continue his studies and become a French teacher. There he experienced loneliness and hunger and took up a bohemian lifestyle. His first book of poems, *Crepusculario*, was published in 1923. The poems, subtle and elegant, were in the tradition of Symbolist poetry, or rather its Hispanic version, Modernismo. His second book, *Veinte poemas de amor y una canción desesperada* (1924; *"Twenty Love Poems and a Song of Despair"*), was inspired by an unhappy love affair. It became an instant success and is still one of Neruda's most popular books. The verse in *Twenty Love Poems* is vigorous, poignant, and direct, yet subtle and very original in its imagery and metaphors. The poems express young, passionate, unhappy love perhaps better than any book of poetry in the long Romantic tradition.

The Experimental Poet as Diplomat

At age 20, with two books published, Neruda had already become one of the best-known Chilean poets. He abandoned his French studies and began to devote himself entirely to poetry. Three more books appeared in quick succession: *Tentativa del hombre infinito* (1926; "Attempt of the Infinite Man"); *Anillos* (1926; "Rings"), in collaboration with Tomás Lago; and *El hondero entusiasta* (1933; "The Enthusiastic Slingshooter"). Yet his poetry was not a steady source of income, so he translated hastily from several languages and published magazine and newspaper articles. Neruda's future looked uncertain without a steady job, so he managed to get himself appointed honorary consul to Rangoon in Burma (now Yangôn, Myanmar). For the next five years he represented his country in Asia. He continued to live in abject poverty, however, since as honorary consul he received no salary, and he was tormented by loneliness.

From Rangoon, Neruda moved to Colombo in Ceylon (now Sri Lanka). He increasingly came to identify with the South Asian masses, who were heirs to ancient cultures

but were downtrodden by poverty, colonial rule, and political oppression. It was during these years in Asia that he
wrote *Residencia en la tierra*, 1925–1931 (1933; *Residence on
Earth*). In this book Neruda moves beyond the lucid, conventional lyricism of *Twenty Love Poems*, abandoning
normal syntax, rhyme, and stanzaic organization to create
a highly personalized poetic technique. His personal and
collective anguish gives rise to nightmarish visions of disintegration, chaos, decay, and death that he recorded in a
cryptic, difficult style inspired by Surrealism. These puz-
zling and mysterious poems both attract and repel the
reader with the powerful and awe-inspiring vision they
present of a modern descent into hell.

In 1930 Neruda was named consul in Batavia (modern
Jakarta), which was then the capital of the Dutch East
Indies (now Indonesia). There he fell in love with a Dutch
woman, Maria Antonieta Hagenaar, and married her. In
1932 Neruda returned to Chile, but he still could not earn
a living from his poetry. In 1933 he was appointed Chilean
consul in Buenos Aires, Argentina. There he met the
Spanish poet Federico García Lorca, who at that time was
traveling in Argentina and who was to become a close
friend and an enthusiastic defender of Neruda's poetry.

Communism and Poetry

In 1934 Neruda took up an appointment as consul in
Barcelona, Spain, and soon he was transferred to the con-
sulate in Madrid. His success there was instantaneous after
García Lorca introduced him. Neruda's new friends, especially Rafael Alberti and Miguel Hernández, were involved
in radical politics and the Communist Party. Neruda shared
their political beliefs and moved ever closer to communism. In the meantime, his marriage was foundering. He

and his wife separated in 1936, and Neruda met a young Argentine woman, Delia del Carril, who would be his second wife until their divorce in the early 1950s.

A second, enlarged edition of the *Residencia* poems entitled *Residencia en la tierra*, 1925–35 was published in two volumes in 1935. In this edition, Neruda begins to move away from the highly personal, often hermetic poetry of the first *Residencia* volume, adopting a more extroverted outlook and a clearer, more accessible style in order to better communicate his new social concerns to the reader. This line of poetic development was interrupted suddenly by the outbreak of the Spanish Civil War in 1936, however. While García Lorca was executed by the Nationalists, and Alberti and Hernández fought at the front, Neruda traveled in and out of Spain to gather money and mobilize support for the Republicans. He wrote *España en el corazón* (1937; *"Spain in My Heart"*) to express his feelings of solidarity with them. The book was printed by Republican troops working with improvised presses near the front lines.

In 1937 Neruda returned to Chile and entered his country's political life, giving lectures and poetry readings while also defending Republican Spain and Chile's new centre-left government. In 1939 he was appointed special consul in Paris, where he supervised the migration to Chile of many defeated Spanish Republicans who had escaped to France. In 1940 he took up a post as Chile's consul general in Mexico. He also began work on a long poem, *Canto general* (1950; "General Song," Eng. trans. *Canto general*), resonant with historical and epic overtones, that would become one of his key works. In 1943, during a trip to Peru, Neruda climbed to the ancient Inca city of Machu Picchu. The strong emotions aroused by the sight of this spectacular ruin inspired one of his finest poems, *Alturas de Macchu Picchu* (1943; *Heights of Macchu Picchu*). This powerful celebration of pre-Columbian civilization would become the centrepiece of *Canto general*.

In the meantime, Neruda suffered a stunning reversal in his native country. He had returned to Chile in 1943, was elected a senator in 1945, and also joined the Communist Party. He campaigned for the leftist candidate Gabriel González Videla in the elections of 1946, only to see President Videla turn to the right two years later. Feeling betrayed, Neruda published an open letter critical of Videla; as a consequence, he was expelled from the Senate and went into hiding to avoid arrest. In February 1948 he left Chile, crossing the Andes Mountains on horseback by night with the manuscript of *Canto general* in his saddlebag.

In exile Neruda visited the Soviet Union, Poland, Hungary, and Mexico. In Mexico he again met Matilde Urrutia, a Chilean woman whom he had first encountered in 1946. Their marriage would last until the end of his life, and she would inspire some of the most passionate Spanish love poems of the 20th century. The third volume of Neruda's *Residencia* cycle, *Tercera residencia*, 1935–45 (1947; "Third Residence"), completed his rejection of egocentric angst and his open espousal of left-wing ideological concerns. His communist political beliefs receive their culminating expression in *Canto general*. This epic poem celebrates Latin America—its flora, its fauna, and its history, particularly the wars of liberation from Spanish rule and the continuing struggle of its peoples to obtain freedom and social justice. It also, however, celebrates Joseph Stalin, the bloody Soviet dictator in power at the time.

LATER YEARS

In 1952 the political situation in Chile once again became favourable, and Neruda was able to return home. By that time his works had been translated into many languages. Rich and famous, he built a house on Isla Negra, facing the Pacific Ocean, and also maintained houses in Santiago and Valparaíso. While traveling in Europe, Cuba, and China, Neruda embarked upon a period of incessant writing and feverish creation. One of his major works, *Odas elementales* (*"Elemental Odes"*), was published in 1954. Its verse was written in a new poetic style—simple, direct, precise, and humorous—and it contained descriptions of everyday objects, situations, and beings (e.g., "Ode to the Onion" and "Ode to the Cat"). Many of the poems in *Odas elementales* have been widely anthologized. Neruda's poetic output during these years was stimulated by his international fame and personal happiness; 20 books of his appeared between 1958 and his death in 1973, and eight more were published posthumously. In his memoirs, *Confieso que he vivido* (1974; *"Memoirs"*), Neruda summed up his life through reminiscences, comments, and anecdotes.

In 1969 Neruda campaigned for the leftist candidate Salvador Allende, who appointed him ambassador to France after being elected president of Chile. While already ill with cancer in France, Neruda in 1971 learned that he had been awarded the Nobel Prize for Literature. After traveling to Stockholm to receive his prize, he returned to Chile bedridden and terminally ill. He was survived by only a few days his friend Allende, who died in a right-wing military coup.

Assessment

Neruda's body of poetry is so rich and varied that it defies classification or easy summary. It developed along four main directions, however. His love poetry, such as the youthful *Twenty Love Poems* and the mature *Los versos del Capitán* (1952; "The Captain's Verses"), is tender, melancholy, sensuous, and passionate. In "material" poetry, such as *Residencia en la tierra*, loneliness and depression immerse the author in a subterranean world of dark, demonic forces. His epic poetry is best represented by *Canto general*, which is a Whitmanesque attempt at reinterpreting the past and present of Latin America and the struggle of its oppressed and downtrodden masses toward freedom. And finally there is Neruda's poetry of common, everyday objects, animals, and plants, as in *Odas elementales*.

These four trends correspond to four aspects of Neruda's personality: his passionate love life; the nightmares and depression he experienced while serving as a consul in Asia; his commitment to a political cause; and his ever-present attention to details of daily life, his love of things made or grown by human hands. Many of his other books, such as *Libro de las preguntas* (1974; *The Book of Questions*), reflect philosophical and whimsical questions about the present and future of humanity. Neruda was one of the most original and prolific poets to write in Spanish in the 20th century, but despite the variety of his output as a whole, each of his books has unity of style and purpose.

Neruda's work is collected in *Obras completas* (1973; 4th ed. expanded, 3 vol.). Most of his work is available in various English translations. Four essential works are *Twenty Love Poems and a Song of Despair*, trans. by W.S. Merwin (1969, reissued 1993); *Residence on Earth, and Other Poems*, trans. by Angel Flores (1946, reprinted 1976); *Canto general*, trans. by Jack Schmitt (1991); and *Elementary Odes of Pablo Neruda*, trans. by Carlos Lozano (1961).

HEBERTO PADILLA

(b. Jan. 20, 1932, Puerta de Golpe, Pinar del Río, Cuba — d. Sept. 25, 2000, Auburn, Ala., U.S.)

The controversial poet Heberto Padilla came to international attention for a political scandal in revolutionary Cuba that is known as the "Padilla affair."

After elementary and secondary education in his native province of Pinar del Río, Padilla studied law at the University of Havana but did not finish a degree. From 1949 to 1952 and 1956 to 1959, he lived in the United States. After the 1959 revolution, Padilla returned to Cuba, where he published a book of poems, *El justo tiempo humano* ("The Fair Human Time"). He traveled through Europe representing Cuba's Ministry of Commerce and as a correspondent for Cuban publications. In 1968 his book of poems *Fuera del juego* ("Out of the Game") was awarded the yearly poetry prize offered by the Writers' Union, but the book appeared with an afterword denouncing it as counterrevolutionary. Selections from *El justo tiempo humano* and *Fuera del juego* were published in English translation as *Sent Off the Field: A Selection from the Poetry of Heberto Padilla* (1972).

Under attack by the authorities, Padilla was imprisoned on vague charges in 1971, which brought about vigorous protests by individuals, organizations, and governments. Many of those condemning the Cuban regime had been its supporters, and the controversy divided Latin American intellectuals and artists along party lines. Padilla was made to read a public confession accusing himself and others of vaguely defined attitudes and activities contrary to Fidel Castro's regime, which increased the protests abroad. In 1980 Padilla was allowed to leave the country for the United States, where he taught at a number of colleges and universities and published an autobiographical novel about his life in revolutionary Cuba, *En mi jardín pastan los héroes* (1981; *Heroes Are Grazing in My Garden*).

In 1981 he also published a volume of selected poems, *El hombre junto al mar*, which later appeared in a bilingual edition (*Legacies: Selected Poems* [1982]), with English translations by Alastair Reid and Andrew Hurley. In 1989 he published a memoir, *La mala memoria* (translated as *Self-Portrait of the Other*). A Spanish/English edition of poetry titled *A Fountain, a House of Stone* appeared in 1991, with English translations by Alastair Reid and Alexander Coleman.

Padilla's verse is deceptively simple and incorporates events of current history in its discourse. It is a poetry in which the poet appears committed to daily life and fearful of the encroachment of politics, which he, at the same time, knows he cannot escape.

OCTAVIO PAZ

(b. March 31, 1914, Mexico City, Mex.—d. April 19, 1998, Mexico City)

Octavio Paz, a Mexican poet, writer, and diplomat, is recognized as one of the major Latin American writers of the 20th century. He received the Nobel Prize for Literature in 1990.

Paz's family was ruined financially by the Mexican Civil War, and he grew up in straitened circumstances. Nonetheless, he had access to the excellent library that had been stocked by his grandfather, a politically active liberal intellectual who had himself been a writer. Paz was educated at a Roman Catholic school and at the University of Mexico. He published his first book of poetry, *Luna silvestre* ("Forest Moon"), in 1933 at age 19. In 1937 the young poet visited Spain, where he identified strongly with the Republican cause in the Spanish Civil War. His

Mexican writer, diplomat, and Nobel laureate Octavio Paz at a 1984 American Academy of Arts and Letters reception. Fred R. Conrad/Hulton Archive/Getty Images

reflection on that experience, *Bajo tu clara sombra y otros poemas* ("Beneath Your Clear Shadow and Other Poems"), was published in Spain in 1937 and revealed him as a writer of real promise. Before returning home Paz visited Paris, where Surrealism and its adherents exerted a profound influence on him.

Back in Mexico, Paz founded and edited several important literary reviews, including *Taller* ("Workshop") from 1938 to 1941 and *El hijo pródigo* ("The Prodigal Son"), which he cofounded in 1943. His major poetic publications included *No pasaran!* (1937; "They Shall Not Pass!"), *Libertad bajo palabra* (1949; "Freedom Under Parole"), *¿Águila o sol?* (1951; "*Eagle or Sun?*"), and *Piedra de sol* (1957; *The Sun Stone*). In the same period, he produced prose volumes of essays and literary criticism, including *El laberinto de la soledad* (1950; *The Labyrinth of Solitude*), an influential essay in which he analyzes the character, history, and culture of Mexico; and *El arco y la lira* (1956; *The Bow and the Lyre*) and *Las peras del olmo* (1957; "The Pears of the Elm"), which are studies of contemporary Spanish American poetry.

Paz entered Mexico's diplomatic corps in 1945, after having lived for two years in San Francisco and New York, and served in a variety of assignments, including one as Mexico's ambassador to India from 1962 to 1968; in the latter year he resigned in protest over Mexico's brutal treatment of student radicals that year. In the 1970s he edited *Plural*, a review of literature and politics.

His poetry after 1962 includes *Blanco* (1967; Eng. trans. *Blanco*), influenced by Stéphane Mallarmé's poetry and John Cage's theories on music; *Ladera este* (1971; "East Slope"), which is suffused with Paz's understanding of East Indian myths; *Hijos del aire* (1979; "*Airborn*"), sonnet sequences created by Paz and the poet Charles Tomlinson building on each other's lines; and *Árbol adentro* (1987; "*A*

Tree Within"), in which many of the poems are based on works by artists such as Marcel Duchamp and Robert Rauschenberg. An English-language selection, *The Collected Poems of Octavio Paz, 1957–1987*, was published in 1987.

His later prose works, some originally in English, include *Conjunciones y disyunciones* (1969; *Conjunctions and Disjunctions*), a discussion of the world's cultural attitudes; *El mono gramático* (1974; *The Monkey Grammarian*), a meditation on language; and *Tiempo nublado* (1983; "Cloudy Weather," translated as *One Earth, Four or Five Worlds: Reflections on Contemporary History*), a study of international politics with emphasis on the relationship between the United States and Latin America.

Paz was influenced in turn by Marxism, Surrealism, existentialism, Buddhism, and Hinduism. In the poetry of his maturity, he used a rich flow of surrealistic imagery in dealing with metaphysical questions. As one critic said, he explored the zones of modern culture outside the marketplace, and his most prominent theme was the human ability to overcome existential solitude through erotic love and artistic creativity. In addition to the Nobel Prize, Paz received numerous other awards, including the Cervantes Prize, the most prestigious Spanish-language accolade. His *Obra completas* ("Complete Works") were published in 1994.

CRISTINA PERI ROSSI
(b. Nov. 12, 1941, Montevideo, Uru.)

The short-story writer, novelist, and poet Cristina Peri Rossi is considered one of the leading Latin American writers to have published in the period after the "boom of the Latin American novel" in the 1960s. She is also one of a group of Latin American women writers—such as Nélida Piñón, Isabel Allende, Rosario Ferré, and Elena Poniatowska—who gained fame at the end of the 20th century. Although Peri Rossi's fiction is often about women, gender issues do not limit her work, which is broadly ironic, witty, and metaphysical.

Peri Rossi's great-grandparents on both sides were Italian immigrants, but when she left Uruguay in 1972 to escape political repression by the military government, she went to Spain, where she worked as a journalist in Barcelona, publishing in *Diario 16, El Periódico*, and *Agencia Efe*.

Peri Rossi's first book, *Viviendo* ("Living"), was published in 1963, but it had been written much earlier. It is a collection of narratives with female protagonists. She won several literary prizes early in her career for her poetry and short stories. Her award-winning *Los museos abandonados* (1969; "Abandoned Museums") is a series of short stories, but some consider it to be a brief novel. (One of the features of her work is disregard for genre boundaries and conventions.) Peri Rossi's *Diáspora* (1976; "Diaspora") is a book of poetry.

In *Descripción de un naufragio* (1975; "Description of a Shipwreck") and *Una pasión prohibida* (1986; "*A Forbidden Passion*"), Peri Rossi explores the theme of exile. *La tarde del dinosaurio* (1976; "The Afternoon of the Dinosaur") is a volume of stories with a prologue by Julio Cortázar. Witty *El museo de los esfuerzos inútiles* (1983; *The Museum of Useless Efforts*) is yet another book of stories about estrangement. Other works are *La nave de los locos* (1984; "*The Ship of Fools*") and *La última noche de Dostoievski* (1992; "*Dostoevsky's Last Night*").

Solitario de amor (1988; *Solitaire of Love*) explores an obsessive sexual relationship; *Fantasías eróticas* (1991;

"Erotic Fantasies") also brings to the fore the theme of obsessive sex. In one story of *Los museos abandonados*, a couple abandon themselves to erotic play in the midst of a museum in ruins. Peri Rossi's occasional vaguely pornographic story has a touch of the allegorical; love against death and destruction.

MANUEL PUIG

(b. Dec. 28, 1932, General Villegas, Arg.—d. July 22, 1990, Cuernavaca, Mex.)

The Argentine novelist and motion-picture scriptwriter Manuel Puig achieved international acclaim with his novel *El beso de la mujer araña* (1976; *Kiss of the Spider Woman*, filmed 1985).

Puig spent his childhood in a small village on the pampas, but moved at age 13 to Buenos Aires, where he pursued his high school and university studies. He had hoped that Buenos Aires would prove to be like life in the movies, but the city's reality, with its repression and violence, disappointed his expectations. Puig learned English as a child by seeing every American film he could. He went to Rome in 1957 to study film directing and resided for a time in Stockholm and London. When he returned to Buenos Aires his film scripts were not well received, and he decided that the cinema was not to be his only career.

Puig's first novel, *La traición de Rita Hayworth* (1968; *"Betrayed by Rita Hayworth"*), is a semiautobiographical account of a boy who escapes the boredom of living on the pampas by fantasizing about the lives of the stars he has seen in motion pictures. The book was later described by Puig as a vehicle for dealing with the oppression of women and the development of a latent-homosexual child. Puig used shifting points of view, flashbacks, and interior monologue to portray the frustration and alienation of his characters, whose only escape is offered by the vacuous world of films and pop art.

The style of his second novel, *Boquitas pintadas* (1969; "Painted Little Mouths"; Eng. trans. *Heartbreak Tango*), parodied the serialized novels that are popular in Argentina. *The Buenos Aires Affair* (1973) is a detective novel describing the psychopathic behaviour of characters who are sexually repressed. *Kiss of the Spider Woman* is a novel told in dialogues between a middle-aged homosexual and a younger revolutionary who are detained in the same jail cell. The book's denunciation of sexual and political repression, treated poetically and with an uncommon degree of tenderness, contributed to its success. Puig's later books include *Pubis angelical* (1979; Eng. trans. *Pubis angelical*) and *Maldición eterna a quien lea estas páginas* (1980; "*Eternal Curse on the Reader of These Pages*"). The major novels were translated into more than a dozen languages, and several of his film scripts won awards.

In the mid-1970s, unhappy with the Peróns' regime in Argentina and perhaps still seeking a life that would resemble the movies, Puig left his native country. He lived in Mexico, New York, and Brazil, and then again in Mexico, where he died.

HORACIO QUIROGA

(b. Dec. 31, 1878, Salto, Uru. — d. Feb. 19, 1937, Buenos Aires, Arg.)

The Uruguayan-born short-story writer Horacio Quiroga, whose imaginative portrayal of the struggle of man and animal to survive in the tropical jungle earned him recognition as a master of the short story, also excelled in depicting mental illness and hallucinatory states.

After travels in Europe during his youth, Quiroga spent most of his life in Argentina, living in Buenos Aires and taking frequent trips to San Ignacio in the jungle province of Misiones, which provided the material for most of his stories. He was a journalist for the greater part of his life, briefly a teacher and a justice of the peace. Such early works as the collection of prose and verse *Los arrecifes de coral* (1901; "The Coral Reefs") show Quiroga's imitation of then-fashionable literary devices. Soon, however, he found his own direction in the short story. He was influenced at first by 19th-century writers; from the United States, the macabre visions of Edgar Allan Poe, and from England, the jungle settings of stories by Rudyard Kipling.

Exploring his view of life as an endless struggle for survival, Quiroga depicted the primitive and the savage with exotic imagery in such collections as Cuentos de la selva (1918; *Stories of the Jungle*) and *La gallina degollada y otras cuentos* (1925; *The Decapitated Chicken and Other Stories*). The work generally recognized as his masterpiece, *Anaconda* (1921), portrays on several levels—realistic, philosophical, and symbolic—the battles of the snakes in the tropical jungle, the nonpoisonous anaconda and the poisonous viper.

Quiroga's preoccupation with the short story as genre led him to publish the influential "Decalogo del perfecto cuentista" ("Decalogue of the Perfect Short-Story Writer"). Though perhaps tongue-in-cheek, his "commandments" preached what his own short stories exemplified—a model of perfection for Latin American writers.

Quiroga began to suffer from illness and chronic depression. His later writings reflect the overwhelming sense of futility that eventually led to his suicide in a charity hospital.

JOSÉ ENRIQUE RODÓ

(b. July 15, 1872, Montevideo, Uru.—d. May 1, 1917, Palermo, Italy)

The Uruguayan philosopher, educator, and essayist José Enrique Rodó, whose vision of a unified Spanish America inspired the region, is considered by many to have been Spanish America's greatest philosopher. His credo, *reformarse es vivir* ("to reform oneself is to live"), and his devotion to the people of the Americas pervaded all his writings. Rodó spent most of his life in Montevideo, devoting himself to writing, voracious reading, teaching, and political activity. In 1895 he helped found the *Revista nacional de literatura y ciencias sociales* ("National Review of Literature and Social Sciences"), and from 1898 he was professor of literature at the national university (University of the Republic) in Montevideo. He also served as director of the National Library of Uruguay. Twice, in 1902 and 1908, he was a member of the Chamber of Deputies.

In the essay generally considered to be his masterpiece, *Ariel* (1900), Rodó set forth his moral credo. Concerned with patterns of human life and with both personal and political conduct, Rodó maintained that individual self-scrutiny is the basis for enlightened action for the good of all. Próspero, the venerable teacher in *Ariel*, cautions his young listeners not to be impressed by material triumph but to use their own spiritual, moral, and intellectual resources to strive for a well-rounded life. Warning against what he saw as North American materialism, Rodó called for idealism from young Spanish Americans to bring forth the best features of democracy. This essay, which brought Rodó international recognition and is today considered one of the most influential works of philosophy written in Spanish America, has been called by one critic "the ethical gospel of the Spanish-speaking new world."

Rodó's other writings include *Motivos de Proteo* (1908; *The Motives of Proteus*) and *El mirador de Próspero* (1913; "The Gallery of Próspero"), a series of essays on some of the outstanding figures of Spanish America. In 1916 Rodó left Montevideo to travel in Europe, where he died.

ERNESTO SÁBATO
(b. June 24, 1911, Rojas, Arg.)

The Argentine novelist, journalist, and essayist Ernesto Sábato wrote novels notable for their concern with philosophical and psychological issues and political and social studies that were highly influential in Argentina in the latter half of the 20th century.

Educated as a physicist and mathematician, Sábato attended the National University of La Plata (1929–36), where he received a doctorate in physics in 1937. He did post-doctoral work at the Curie Laboratory in Paris in 1938 and Massachusetts Institute of Technology in 1939, and returned to Argentina in 1940. From 1940 to 1945 he taught theoretical physics at the National University of La Plata and at a teachers' college in Buenos Aires. He began to contribute articles to the literary section of *La Nación*, one of Argentina's leading newspapers, and as a result he was removed from his teaching post in 1945 for his stated opposition to the Juan Perón government.

Uno y el universo (1945; "One and the Universe"), a series of aphorisms, statements, and personal observations by Sábato on diverse philosophical, social, and political matters, was his first literary success. The novel *El túnel* (1948; "The Tunnel"; Eng. trans. *The Outsider*) won Sábato national and international notice. The protagonist of the novel is a typical existential antihero who is unable to communicate with anyone. Faced with the absurdity of the human condition, he withdraws from society.

After the fall of Perón in 1955, Sábato published *El otro rostro del peronismo* (1956; "The Other Face of Peronism"), which is an attempt to study the historical and political causes of the violence and unrest of Perón's rule. The essay *El caso Sábato* (1956; "The Sábato Case") is a plea for reconciliation of Peronist and anti-Peronist forces.

His second novel, *Sobre héroes y tumbas* (1961; *On Heroes and Tombs*), is a penetrating psychological study of man, interwoven with philosophical ideas and observations previously treated in his essays. *Tres aproximaciones a la literatura de nuestro tiempo* (1968; "Three Approximations to the Literature of Our Times") are critical literary essays that deal specifically with the works of Alain Robbe-Grillet, Jorge Luis Borges, and Jean-Paul Sartre. The novel *Abaddón el exterminador* (1974, corrected and revised, 1978; "Abaddón the Exterminator"; Eng. trans. *The Angel of Darkness*) contains the ironic statements on literature, art, philosophy, and the excesses of rationalism that characterize his work.

In 1984 Sábato received the Cervantes Prize, Hispanic literature's most prestigious award. The award followed the publication in Spain of the "Sábato Report" (*Nunca más* ["Never Again"]; an investigation of human-rights violations in Argentina), of which Sábato was the principal author. Subsequently he published nonfiction works such as *Hombres y engranajes* (1991; "Men and Machines"), examining the myth of progress and the use of machine technology as a model for social structures, and *Heterodoxia* (1991; "Heterodoxy"), on the problems of modern civilization and what Sábato sees as an attendant loss of earlier moral and metaphysical foundations. In 2000, in his 89th year, he released a new work, a reflection on Western culture titled *La Resistencia* ("The Resistance"), on the Internet prior to its print publication.

SEVERO SARDUY

(b. Feb. 25, 1937, Camagüey, Cuba—d. June 8, 1993, Paris, France)

The novelist, poet, critic, and essayist Severo Sarduy was one of the most daring and brilliant writers of the 20th century.

Born in a working-class family of Spanish, African, and Chinese heritage, Sarduy was the top student in his high school. He went to Havana in the mid-1950s to study medicine. Though he did not finish his studies, he retained a lifelong interest in science. While living in the capital he pursued his vocation for poetry and painting, and came into contact with older writers such as José Rodríguez Feo and José Lezama Lima. He published his first poems in the journal *Ciclón*, directed by the former.

With the advent of the revolution in 1959, Sarduy became one of a group of young writers given the task of renewing Cuban literature. Sent to Paris by the government in 1960 to study art at the École du Louvre, Sarduy decided not to return to Cuba when his scholarship ran out a year later. Disaffected with Castro's regime and fearful of its persecution of homosexuals and the censorship imposed on writers, Sarduy never went home. In Paris he became close to the group of critics and theoreticians who published the journal *Tel Quel*, which promoted structuralism and experimental writing. He was also involved with *Mundo Nuevo*, a Spanish-language journal directed by Uruguayan critic Emir Rodríguez Monegal. Through these journals and his considerable production, Sarduy acquired a good deal of fame, even though he was systematically ignored by the Cuban cultural bureaucracy, who never mentioned him in their publications and left him out of all reference works.

Sarduy's first novel, *Gestos* (1963; "Gestures"), is about a young woman involved in terrorist activities against the

Batista regime in the Cuba of the 1950s. It was well received. His most important book, however, was the highly experimental novel *De donde son los cantantes* (1967; *From Cuba with a Song*). The book includes three narratives that encompass the entire history of Cuba and aspire to give a global view of its culture. An even more experimental novel followed, *Cobra* (1972; Eng. trans. *Cobra*), where the setting is a transvestite theatre and some episodes occur in India and China. His novel *Maitreya* (1978; Eng. trans. *Maitreya*) opens in Tibet, but the characters, in search of a messiah, travel to Cuba and the United States, then end up in Iran. *Colibrí* (1982; "Hummingbird") is a book about the South American jungle, and *El Cristo de la rue Jacob* (1987; *Christ on the Rue Jacob*) is a series of impressionistic sketches, some of them autobiographical.

Sarduy's posthumous *Pájaros de la playa* (1993; "Beach Fowl") is about a sanatorium for sufferers of AIDS, the disease that killed the author. He is also known for his theories about the Baroque, which he expounded in his essay *Barroco* (1974; Eng. trans. *Barroco*).

DOMINGO FAUSTINO SARMIENTO

(b. Feb. 14, 1811, San Juan, Viceroyalty of the Río de la Plata [now in Argentina] — d. Sept. 11, 1888, Asunción, Para.)

The educator, statesman, and writer Domingo Faustino Sarmiento rose from a position as a rural schoolmaster to become president of Argentina (1868–74). As president, he laid the foundation for later national progress by fostering public education, stimulating the growth of commerce and agriculture, and encouraging the development of rapid transportation and communication. As a writer, he is best remembered for his sociological-biographical study *Civilización y barbarie: vida de Juan*

Facundo Quiroga, y aspecto físico, costumbres, y hábitos de la República Argentina (1845; *Life in the Argentine Republic in the Days of the Tyrants; or, Civilization and Barbarism*), which is a plea for industrialization and urbanization as opposed to the culture of the gauchos of the Argentine pampas. But it is largely his loving depiction of the gaucho and the pampas that has made this book a classic of Latin American literature.

Largely self-taught, Sarmiento began his career as a rural schoolteacher at age 15 and soon entered public life as a provincial legislator. His political activities and his outspokenness provoked the rage of the military dictator Juan Manuel de Rosas, who exiled him to Chile in 1840. There Sarmiento was active in politics and became an important figure in journalism through his articles in the Valparaíso newspaper *El Mercurio*. In 1842 he was appointed founding director of the first teachers' college in South America and began to give effect to a lifelong conviction that the primary means to national development was through a system of public education.

During that period in Chile, Sarmiento wrote Facundo, an impassioned denunciation of Rosas's dictatorship in the form of a biography of Juan Facundo Quiroga, Rosas's tyrannical gaucho lieutenant. The book has been criticized for its erratic style and oversimplifications, but it has also been called the single most important book produced in Spanish America.

In 1845 the Chilean government sent Sarmiento abroad to study educational methods in Europe and the United States. After three years he returned, convinced that the United States provided the model for Latin America to follow in its development. Sarmiento returned to Argentina to help overthrow Rosas in 1852; he continued his writing and educational activities and reentered Argentine politics.

Sarmiento was elected president of Argentina in 1868 and immediately began to apply his liberal ideals—his belief in democratic principles and civil liberties and his opposition to dictatorial regimes in any form—to the building of a new Argentina. He ended the war with Paraguay inherited by his administration and concentrated on domestic achievements. To a largely illiterate country he brought primary and secondary schools, teachers' colleges, schools for professional and technical training, and libraries and museums.

When his term ended in 1874, Sarmiento continued to be active in public life. Most of the 52 volumes of his published work are devoted to educational themes.

CÉSAR VALLEJO

(b. March 16, 1892, Santiago de Chuco, Peru—d. April 15, 1938, Paris, France)

The Peruvian poet César Abraham Vallejo became, while in exile, a major voice of social change in Spanish American literature.

Born the 11th child to parents who were both of mixed Spanish and Quechua Indian origins, Vallejo as a child witnessed firsthand hunger and poverty, and the injustices done to the Indians of the region. He attended the University of Trujillo (1913–17), where he studied both law and literature, writing a thesis entitled *El romanticismo en la poesía castellana* ("Romanticism in Castilian Poetry"; published 1954).

Vallejo's first book of poems, *Los heraldos negros* (1918; "The Black Heralds [or Messengers]"), showed him still under the stylistic influence of Parnassianism and Modernism in his exploration of what were to be his major themes: his loss of security when his mother and an older brother died; his resulting sense of the futility and inherent limitations of life; and the inability of human beings to achieve their potential because of social oppression and injustice.

In 1920 Vallejo's involvement in political matters concerning Indians led to his imprisonment for nearly three months. This experience heightened his feeling of loss at the death of his mother and contributed to a state of depression that was to torment him the rest of his life. *Escalas melografiadas* (1922; "Musical Scales"), a collection of short stories, and many of the more complex poems of *Trilce* (1922; Eng. trans. *Trilce*) were conceived during his imprisonment. In his major work *Trilce*, Vallejo signaled his complete break with tradition by incorporating neologisms, colloquialisms, typographic innovations, and startling imagery, with which he sought to express the disparity that he felt existed between human aspirations and the limitations imposed on people by biological existence and social organization.

After publishing *Fabula salvaje* (1923; "Savage Story"), a short psychological novel about the decline of a mentally disturbed Indian, Vallejo left for Paris and never returned to his native land. Life in Paris was difficult for him; he barely made a living from translations, language tutoring, and political writing. But while he felt like an outsider because of his Indian heritage, he succeeded in establishing contacts with leading avant-garde artists. He kept in touch with Peru by publishing articles in *Amauta*, the journal founded by his friend José Carlos Mariátegui, founder of the Peruvian Communist Party.

Vallejo came to believe that the language of poetry should be devoid of all traditional devices in its description of the human condition, and that literature should also serve the cause of the masses. Marxism seemed to him to be the only way of rectifying the abuses and injustices he saw in society, and two visits to Russia in 1928 and

1929 served to reinforce his political commitment. He joined the Communist Party in 1931.

Vallejo was expelled from Paris in 1930 as a political militant and went to Madrid. There he wrote the proletarian novel *El tungsteno* (1931; *Tungsten*), showing the brutal exploitation and degradation of Indian workers at a Peruvian tungsten mine. He returned to Paris in 1932, and he then spent two years in Spain during that nation's civil war (1936–39). The Spanish Civil War inspired most of his last important volume of poetry, *Poemas humanos* (1939; *Human Poems*), which presents an apocalyptic vision of an industrial society in crisis and unable to advance beyond a state of mass evil, alienation, and despair.

Most of the poems of the 1930s were published only after Vallejo's death. His fiction is collected in *Novelas y cuentos completos* (1970; "Complete Novels and Stories") and his poetry in *Obra poética completa* (1974; "Complete Poetical Works"). *The Complete Posthumous Poetry* (1978) is an English translation by Clayton Eshleman and José Rubia Barcia.

MARIO VARGAS LLOSA

(b. March 28, 1936, Arequipa, Peru)

The Peruvian writer Jorge Mario Pedro Vargas Llosa's novels, plays, and essays show his commitment to social change. In 1990 he was an unsuccessful candidate for president of Peru.

Vargas Llosa received his early education in Cochabamba, Bolivia, where his grandfather was the Peruvian consul. He later attended a series of schools in Peru before entering a military school, Leoncio Prado, in Lima in 1950. His first published work was *La huida del Inca* (1952; "The Escape of the Inca"), a three-act play. Thereafter his stories began to appear in Peruvian literary reviews, and he coedited *Cuadernos de composición* (1956–57; "Composition Book") and *Literatura* (1958–59). He worked as a journalist and broadcaster and attended the University of Madrid. In 1959 he moved to Paris, where he lived until 1966.

Vargas Llosa's first novel, *La ciudad y los perros* (1963; "The City and the Dogs"; Eng. trans. *The Time of the Hero*), was widely acclaimed. Translated into more than a dozen languages, this novel, set in the Leoncio Prado Military School, describes adolescents striving for survival in a hostile and violent environment. The corruption of the military school reflects the larger malaise afflicting Peru. The book was filmed twice, in Spanish (1985) and in Russian (1986), the second time as *Yaguar.*

The novel *La casa verde* (1966; *The Green House*), set in the Peruvian jungle, combines mythical, popular, and heroic elements to capture the sordid, tragic, and fragmented reality of its characters. *Los cachorros* (1967; *The Cubs, and Other Stories*, filmed 1973) is a psychoanalytical portrayal of an adolescent who has been accidentally castrated. *Conversación en la catedral* (1969; *Conversation in the Cathedral*) deals with Manuel Odría's regime (1948–56). The novel *Pantaleón y las visitadoras* (1973; "Pantaleón and the Visitors"; Eng. trans. *Captain Pantoja and the Special Service*, filmed 2000) is a satire of the Peruvian military and religious fanaticism. His semiautobiographical novel *La tía Julia y el escribidor* (1977; *Aunt Julia and the Scriptwriter*, filmed 1990 as *Tune in Tomorrow*) combines two distinct narrative points of view to provide a contrapuntal effect.

Vargas Llosa also wrote a critical study of the fiction of Gabriel García Márquez in *García Márquez: Historia de un deicidio* (1971; "García Márquez: Story of a God-Killer"), a study of Gustave Flaubert in *La orgía perpetua: Flaubert y "Madame Bovary"* (1975; *The Perpetual Orgy: Flaubert and*

Madame Bovary), and a study of the works of Jean-Paul Sartre and Albert Camus in *Entre Sartre y Camus* (1981; "Between Sartre and Camus").

After living three years in London, he was a writer-in-residence at Washington State University in 1969. In 1970 he settled in Barcelona. He returned to Lima in 1974 and lectured and taught widely throughout the world. A collection of his critical essays in English translation was published in 1978. *La guerra del fin del mundo* (1981; *The War of the End of the World*), an account of the 19th-century political conflicts in Brazil, became a best seller in Spanish-speaking countries. Three of his plays—*La señorita de Tacna* (1981; *The Young Lady of Tacna*), *Kathie y el hipopotamo* (1983; *Kathie and the Hippopotamus*), and *La chunga* (1986; "The Jest"; Eng. trans. *La chunga*)—were published in *Three Plays* (1990).

In 1990 Vargas Llosa lost his bid for the presidency of Peru in a runoff against Alberto Fujimori, an agricultural engineer and the son of Japanese immigrants. Vargas Llosa wrote about this experience in *El pez en el agua: memorias* (1993; "A Fish in the Water: A Memoir"). He became a citizen of Spain in 1993 and was awarded the Cervantes Prize in 1994. Despite his new nationality, he continued to write about Peru in such novels as *Los cuadernos de don Rigoberto* (1997; *The Notebooks of Don Rigoberto*). His later works include the novels *La fiesta del chivo* (2000; *The Feast of the Goat*) and *El paraíso en la otra esquina* (2003; *The Way to Paradise*), as well as the nonfiction *Cartas a un joven novelista* (1997; *Letters to a Young Novelist*) and *El lenguaje de la pasión* (2001; *The Language of Passion*).

NEW DIRECTIONS

During the 1980s and 1990s, new fictional paradigms emerged in Spain as exiles who left the country during Franco's reign returned; new subgenres flourished at the turn of the 21st century, including detective fiction, the neo-Gothic novel, science fiction, adventure novels, and the thriller.

Despite this proliferation of modes, however, many novelists continued producing what might be considered "traditional" narrative. In Latin America after the turn of the 21st century, the playful element of modern literature prevailed and produced a move toward lightness. This has meant a moving away from the thematics of cultural identity that dominated modern literature and going back to the Romantics.

Fiction in particular was dispersed, disseminated among characters of shifting sexuality who did not make up conventional family groups. In the plots of these novels serendipity seems to rule. The multiplication of forms and perspectives found in fiction extended to poetry and the theatre as well, with the end result being the vibrancy common today to the literature of both Spain and Latin America.

bucolic Relating to or typical of rural life.

conceptismo A concise, aphoristic, and epigrammatic style of Spanish literature belonging primarily to prose, especially satire, during the 17th century.

converso A Jew who publicly recanted his or her faith and adopted Christianity under the Spanish Inquisition.

culteranismo An ornate, roundabout, high-flown style of Spanish literature.

didactic Designed or intended to teach.

gaucho A cowboy of the South American pampas.

hermetic Completely sealed; impervious to outside influence or interference.

heteroglossia A term, meaning "multiple voices," used to refer to a text that consists of many varying perspectives and beliefs.

leitmotiv A dominant recurring theme.

Modernismo Literary movement that rejected 19th-century bourgeois materialism and instead sought specifically aesthetic values.

octava real A difficult eight-line unit of 11-syllable verses that are linked by a tight rhyme scheme; common to many Renaissance Castilian epics.

panegyric A eulogistic oration or writing; formal praise.

pastoral Of or relating to the countryside; pleasingly peaceful and innocent.

picaresque novel A genre of literature native to Spain featuring as its protagonist a *pícaro* ("rogue"), essentially an antihero, living by his or her wits and concerned only with staying alive.

prolix Unduly prolonged and drawn out; using an excess of words.

quixotic Foolishly impractical, especially in the pursuit of ideals; derived from the name of the hero of Cervantes's novel *Don Quixote*.

romance A medieval ballad, typically on heroic themes, that uses an octosyllabic form in which alternate lines have a single assonance throughout.

salon A fashionable assemblage of notable artists and writers.

strophe A rhythmic system composed of two or more lines repeated as a unit.

vanguardism The ideas or tendencies of those who take up the foremost or leading position in a trend or movement.

vernacular The language or dialect native to a region or country; typically spoken language rather than literary language.

viceroyalty The powers and duties of a person who is the governor of a province or colony who rules on behalf of a county's sovereign.

zarzuela A musical play with alternating spoken and sung dialogue.

BIBLOGRAPHY

SPANISH LITERATURE

CASTILIAN LITERATURE

Works that provide a broad overview of Spanish literature are Gerald Brenan, *The Literature of the Spanish People: From Roman Times to the Present*, 2nd ed. (1953, reprinted 1976); Richard E. Chandler and Kessel Schwartz, *A New History of Spanish Literature*, rev. ed. (1991); R.O. Jones (ed.), *A Literary History of Spain*, 8 vol. (1971–73); Janet Pérez and Maureen Ihrie (eds.), *The Feminist Encyclopedia of Spanish Literature*, 2 vol. (2002); Germán Bleiberg, Maureen Ihrie, and Janet Pérez (eds.), *Dictionary of the Literature of the Iberian Peninsula*, 2 vol. (1993); Philip Ward (ed.), *The Oxford Companion to Spanish Literature* (1978); Harriet Turner and Adelaida López de Martínez (eds.), *The Cambridge Companion to the Spanish Novel* (2003); and David Gies (ed.), *The Cambridge History of Spanish Literature* (2004).

Works that focus on specific periods or trends in Spanish literary history include Otis H. Green, *The Literary Mind of Medieval and Renaissance Spain* (1970), a collection of essays by an eminent scholar; A.D. Deyermond, *The Middle Ages* (1971), a very good introduction, with bibliography; Otis H. Green, *Spain and the Western Tradition: The Castilian Mind in Literature from El Cid to Calderón*, 4 vol. (1963–66), readable and authoritative; Margaret D. Jacobson, *The Origins of Spanish Romanticism: A Selective Annotated Bibliography* (1985); R.O. Jones, *The Golden Age: Prose and Poetry: The Sixteenth and*

Seventeenth Centuries (1971), an excellent introduction; Edward M. Wilson and Duncan Moir, *The Golden Age: Drama* (1971); John A. Cook, *Neo-Classic Drama in Spain: Theory and Practice* (1959, reprinted 1974); Nigel Glendinning, *The Eighteenth Century* (1972); R. Merritt Cox, *Eighteenth-Century Spanish Literature* (1979); Donald L. Shaw, *The Nineteenth Century* (1972); E. Allison Peers, *A History of the Romantic Movement in Spain*, 2 vol. (1940, reprinted 1976), a comprehensive account; L.B. Walton, *Pérez Galdós and the Spanish Novel of the Nineteenth Century* (1927, reprinted 1970), dated but still useful; Lou Charnon-Deutsch and Jo Labanyi (eds.), *Culture and Gender in Nineteenth-Century Spain* (1995); Catherine Davies, *Spanish Women's Writing, 1849–1996* (1998); Carl W. Cobb, *Contemporary Spanish Poetry (1898–1963)* (1976); Ricardo Landeira, *The Modern Spanish Novel, 1898–1936* (1985); Margaret E.W. Jones, *The Contemporary Spanish Novel, 1939–1975* (1985); Paul Ilie, *The Surrealist Mode in Spanish Literature: An Interpretation of Basic Trends from Post-Romanticism to the Spanish Vanguard* (1968), the first examination of Spanish Surrealism, and *Literature and Inner Exile: Authoritarian Spain, 1939–1975* (1980); Santiago Daydí-Tolson, *The Post-Civil War Spanish Social Poets* (1983); Marion P. Holt, *The Contemporary Spanish Theater (1949–1972)* (1975); G.G. Brown, *A Literary History of Spain, vol. 6: The Twentieth Century* (1972), one of the most thorough surveys in English; Janet Pérez, *Contemporary Women Writers of Spain* (1988), and *Modern and Contemporary Spanish Women Poets* (1996).

Catalan and Galician Literature

Arthur Terry, *Catalan Literature* (1972), and *A Companion to Catalan Literature* (2003), provide the best overall view in

English of Catalan literary history. Josep Miquel Sobrer (ed. and trans.), *Catalonia: A Self-Portrait* (1992), offers an analysis of modern Catalan culture alongside translations of many Catalan authors. Critical studies include David J. Viera, *Medieval Catalan Literature: Prose and Drama* (1988); Patricia J. Boehne, *The Renaissance Catalan Novel* (1989); and Kathryn A. Everly, *Catalan Women Writers and Artists* (2003). Very few works on Galician literature are available in English. Two anthologies are Frede Jensen (ed. and trans.), *Medieval Galician-Portuguese Poetry* (1992); and Kathleen March (ed. and trans.), *An Anthology of Galician Short Stories* (1991).

LATIN AMERICAN LITERATURE

GENERAL HISTORIES AND REFERENCE WORKS

A translation of the standard reliable history, with somewhat dated value judgments, is Enrique Anderson-Imbert, *Spanish-American Literature: A History*, 2nd ed., rev., updated, and trans. by Elaine Malley, 2 vol., (1969; originally published in Spanish, 6th ed., 1967). Paula H. Covington (ed.), *Latin America and the Caribbean: A Critical Guide to Research Sources* (1992), is an excellent introduction to the field with valuable bibliographies. Roberto González Echevarría and Enrique Pupo-Walker (eds.), *The Cambridge History of Latin American Literature*, 3 vol. (1996), covers the sweep of Latin American literature from pre-Columbian times to the present, including Brazil (vol. 3), and gives ample general and specialized bibliographies. William Luis (ed.), *Modern Latin-American Fiction Writers: First Series* (1992); vol. 113 of the *Dictionary of Literary Biography* has well-written life-and-works essays, with reliable bibliographies, on major and minor authors. Carlos

A. Solé and Maria Isabel Abreu (eds.), *Latin American Writers*, 3 vol. (1989), is well-edited, with generally good essays on authors from colonial times to the present.

ANTHOLOGIES

Roberto González Echevarría (ed.), *The Oxford Book of Latin American Short Stories*, trans. from Spanish (1997, reissued 1999), has stories from pre-Columbian times to the present, includes Brazil, and has a general introduction, headnotes on each author, and a bibliography. Lively introductions are included in Emir Rodríguez Monegal and Thomas Colchie (eds.), *The Borzoi Anthology of Latin American Literature*, 2 vol. (1977), and its coverage of the 20th century (vol. 2) is particularly good. Stephen Tapscott (ed.), *Twentieth-Century Latin American Poetry: A Bilingual Anthology* (1996), is a superb collection covering the late 19th to the late 20th century, including both Spanish and Brazilian Portuguese poetry, and it has excellent bibliographies, introductions, and indexes.

THE COLONIAL PERIOD

Rolena Adorno, *Guaman Poma: Writing and Resistance in Colonial Peru*, 2nd ed. (2000), is incisive on Guamán Poma with observations applicable to other colonial historians. Electa Arenal and Stacey Schlau, *Untold Sisters: Hispanic Nuns in Their Own Works* (1989), is well-researched and nicely introduces writing by colonial nuns. Roberto González Echevarría, *Myth and Archive: A Theory of Latin American Narrative* (1990, reissued 1998), has a chapter on legal rhetoric and chronicles of the discovery and conquest, and *Celestina's Brood: Continuities of the Baroque in Spanish and Latin American Literatures* (1993) has chapters on the colonial Baroque. An overview of writing by women in the colonial period appears in Julie Greer Johnson, *Women in Colonial Spanish American Literature: Literary Images* (1983). Irving A. Leonard, *Books of the Brave: Being an Account of Books and of Men in the Spanish Conquest and Settlement of the Sixteenth-Century New World* (1949, reissued 1992), is a classic on what was read in colonial Latin America, and *Baroque Times in Old Mexico: Seventeenth-Century Persons, Places, and Practices* (1959, reprinted 1981) is still the best introduction to the colonial Baroque.

THE 18TH CENTURY

A good primary source is José Joaquín Fernández de Lizardi, *The Itching Parrot*, trans. by Eugene Pressly and ed. by Katherine Anne Porter (1942; originally published in Spanish, 1816).

Wide-ranging but dated treatments of the Spanish American Enlightenment are Arthur P. Whitaker (ed.), *Latin America and the Enlightenment*, 2nd ed. (1961, reissued 1969); and A. Owen Aldridge (ed.), *The Ibero-American Enlightenment* (1971). An introduction to the dissemination of Enlightenment thought by seminaries and universities in 18th-century Spanish America is provided by John Tate Lanning, *The Eighteenth-Century Enlightenment in the University of San Carlos de Guatemala* (1956).

A brief analysis of Vela's *Apostolado en las Indias* in the context of Spanish theatre is Bernardita Llanos, "Images of America in Eighteenth-Century Spanish Comedy," in René Jara and Nicholas Spadaccini (eds.), *Amerindian Images and the Legacy of Columbus* (1992), pp. 565–583. Important insights into the works and ideologies of Espejo and Carrió are in Julie Greer Johnson, *Satire in Colonial*

Spanish America: Turning the New World Upside Down (1993). A study with an up-to-date bibliography on Eguiara and Landívar and original insights into their works is Antony Higgins, *Constructing the Criollo Archive: Subjects of Knowledge in the Bibliotheca Mexicana and the Rusticatio Mexicana* (2000). Other books of interest are Ruth Hill, *Sceptres and Sciences in the Spains: Four Humanists and the New Philosophy (ca. 1680–1740)* (2000); and Francisco Javier Cevallos-Candau et al. (eds.), *Coded Encounters: Writing, Gender, and Ethnicity in Colonial Latin America* (1994).

ROMANTICISM TO MODERNISMO

Antonio Cussen, *Bello and Bolívar: Poetry and Politics in the Spanish American Revolution* (1992), is authoritative on Bello's classicism and Bolívar's thought. Aníbal González, *Journalism and the Development of Spanish American Narrative* (1993), is brilliant on the development of 19th-century narrative in relation to journalism and also covers the 20th century. Roberto González Echevarría, *Myth and Archive: A Theory of Latin American Narrative* (1990, reissued 1998), has a chapter on travel literature and 19th-century narrative, particularly Sarmiento's. Tulio Halperín Donghi et al., *Sarmiento, Author of a Nation* (1994), is a collection of essays of uneven value on most aspects of Sarmiento's writings. Cathy Login Jrade, *Modernismo, Modernity, and the Development of Spanish American Literature* (1998), is an excellent study of Modernismo and its legacy. Vera M. Kutzinski, *Sugar's Secrets: Race and the Erotics of Cuban Nationalism* (1993), is an insightful exploration of the representation in 19th-century Cuban literature of sexual relations among members of different races and classes.

William Luis, *Literary Bondage: Slavery in Cuban Narrative* (1990), has important chapters on 19th-century antislavery narratives. Another incisive treatment of

19th-century Cuban literature is Doris Sommer, *Foundational Fictions: The National Romances of Latin America* (1991, reprinted 1993), which discusses the link between narrative and family structure in early Latin American narratives.

Poetry from the *Vanguardias* to the Present

A volume that is good on the transition from Modernismo to the *vanguardias* is Gwen Kirkpatrick, *The Dissonant Legacy of Modernismo: Lugones, Herrera y Reissig, and the Voices of Modern Spanish American Poetry* (1989). Vicky Unruh, *Latin American Vanguards: The Art of Contentious Encounters* (1994), is comprehensive and authoritative on the various avant-garde movements and their manifestos.

The Modern Novel

The best study of regionalist fiction is Carlos J. Alonso, *The Spanish American Regional Novel: Modernity and Autochthony* (1990). Salvador Bacarisse (ed.), *Contemporary Latin American Fiction: Carpentier, Sabato, Onetti, Roa, Donoso, Fuentes, García Márquez* (1980), has some good essays on major figures. Harold Bloom (ed.), *Modern Latin American Fiction* (1990), is an excellent collection of essays by reputable critics. A good reference work is John S. Brushwood, *The Spanish American Novel: A Twentieth-Century Survey* (1975). Roberto González Echevarría, *Alejo Carpentier: The Pilgrim at Home* (1977, reissued 1990), covers Carpentier's entire oeuvre and discusses other writers, the Afro-Cuban movement, and magic realism; *The Voice of the Masters: Writing and Authority in Modern Latin American Literature* (1985, reissued 1988) has chapters on Gallegos, Cortázar, Carpentier, Fuentes, and Cabrera Infante; and *Myth and Archive: A Theory of Latin American*

Narrative (1990, reissued 1998) has a chapter on anthropology and modern Latin American fiction. An influential collection of interviews with major writers exists in Luis Harss and Barbara Dohmann, *Into the Mainstream: Conversations with Latin-American Writers* (1967, reissued 1969). William Luis (ed.), *Voices from Under: Black Narrative in Latin America and the Caribbean* (1984), is a good discussion of blacks in literature and of literature by blacks. Useful essays on late 20th-century fiction appear in Raymond Leslie Williams (ed.), *The Novel in the Americas* (1992). Raymond Leslie Williams, *The Postmodern Novel in Latin America: Politics, Culture, and the Crisis of Truth* (1995, reissued 1997), has discussion by regions (Andean, Southern Cone, Caribbean), including late 20th-century novels.

The Modern Essay

An authoritative and well-written work on the early modern essay is William Rex Crawford, *A Century of Latin American Thought*, rev. ed. (1961, reissued 1967). Harold Eugene Davis, *Latin American Thought: A Historical Introduction* (1972, reissued 1974), is a good overview by a historian. Roberto González Echevarría, *The Voice of the Masters: Writing and Authority in Modern Latin American Literature* (1985, reprinted 1988), has a long essay on *Ariel* and the modern essayistic tradition. The standard work on the modern essay up to the mid-20th century is Martin S. Stabb, *In Quest of Identity: Patterns in the Spanish American Essay of Ideas, 1890–1960* (1967).

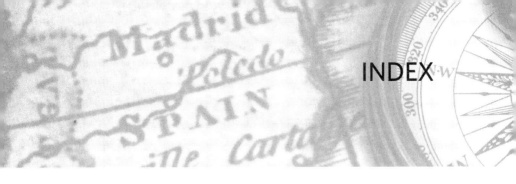

INDEX

ACKNOWLEDGMENTS

Encyclopædia Britannica and Rosen Educational Publishing gratefully acknowledge permission to reprint the following previously published material:

"Ballad of the Spanish Civil Guard," excerpt, reprinted by permission of Farrar, Straus and Giroux, LLC, from *Collected Poems by Federico García Lorca*. Translated by Will Kirkland. Translation copyright © 1991 by Will Kirkland. Introduction and notes copyright © 1991 by Christopher Maurer. Spanish texts copyright © 1991 by Herederos de Federico García Lorca.

"Ode to Walt Whitman," excerpt, reprinted by permission of Farrar, Straus and Giroux, LLC, from *Poet in New York* by Federico García Lorca. Translation copyright © 1988 by the Estate of Federico García Lorca, and Greg Simon and Steven F. White. Introduction, notes, and translation of letters copyright © 1988 by Christopher Maurer.